Henry George

A perplexed philosopher

Being an examination of Mr. Herbert Spencer's various utterances on the land question

Henry George

A perplexed philosopher

Being an examination of Mr. Herbert Spencer's various utterances on the land question

ISBN/EAN: 9783337233273

Printed in Europe, USA, Canada, Australia, Japan

Cover: Foto ©Andreas Hilbeck / pixelio.de

More available books at **www.hansebooks.com**

A PERPLEXED PHILOSOPHER

WORKS BY HENRY GEORGE.

A Perplexed Philosopher.
12mo, cloth, $1.00; paper, 50 cents.

Progress and Poverty.
12mo, cloth, $1.00; paper, 50 cents.

Social Problems.
12mo, cloth, $1.00; paper, 50 cents.

Protection or Free Trade?
12mo, cloth, $1.00; paper, 50 cents.

The Land Question.
Paper, 20 cents.

Property in Land. A Controversy with the Duke of Argyll.
Paper, 20 cents.

The Condition of Labor. An Open Letter to Pope Leo XIII.
12mo, cloth, 75 cents; paper, 30 cents.

For sale by all booksellers, or sent postpaid on receipt of price.

A PERPLEXED PHILOSOPHER

BEING

AN EXAMINATION OF MR. HERBERT SPENCER'S VARIOUS UTTERANCES ON THE LAND QUESTION, WITH SOME INCIDENTAL REFERENCE TO HIS SYNTHETIC PHILOSOPHY

BY

HENRY GEORGE

Just for a handful of silver he left us,
  Just for a ribbon to stick in his coat—
Found the one gift of which fortune bereft us,
  Lost all the others she lets us devote.

* * * * * * * * * * *

Blot out his name, then, record one lost soul more,
  One task more declined, one more footpath untrod,
One more triumph for devils, and sorrow for angels,
  One wrong more to man, one more insult to God!

Robert Browning.

NEW YORK
CHARLES L. WEBSTER & COMPANY
1892

Copyright, 1892,
By HENRY GEORGE.
(*All rights reserved.*)

CONTENTS.

INTRODUCTION.

THE REASON FOR THIS EXAMINATION.

No consecrated absurdity would have stood its ground in this world if the man had not silenced the objection of the child.— *Michelet.*

INTRODUCTION.

THE REASON FOR THIS EXAMINATION.

ALTHOUGH he stands for much that is yet in dispute, there can be no question that at the present time — 1892 — Herbert Spencer, of all his contemporaries, holds the foremost place in the intellectual world, and through a wider circle than any man now living, and perhaps than any man of our century, is regarded as a profound, original and authoritative thinker — by many indeed as the greatest thinker the world has ever yet seen.

So large is the field over which Mr. Spencer's writings have ranged, so many are the special branches of knowledge he has laid under contribution, so difficult to the ordinary mind are the abstractions in which he has dealt and the terminology in which they are couched, that this great reputation is with the large majority of the intelligent men who accept it more a matter of faith than of reason. But this rather adds to than detracts from the popular estimate; for what to us is vague often seems on that account the greater, and what we have no means of measuring, all the more profound. Nor does Mr. Spencer's standing as one of the greatest, to many the very greatest, of philosophers, lack substantial basis in the opinions of those deemed competent to gauge intellectual power.

John Stuart Mill styled him "one of the acutest metaphysicians of recent times, one of the most vigorous as well as the boldest thinker that English speculation has yet produced." Professor Ray Lancaster spoke of him as "an acute observer and experimentalist versed in physics and chemistry, but above all, thoroughly instructed in scientific methods." Richard A. Proctor characterized him as the "clearest of thinkers." G. H. Lewes said "it is questionable whether any thinker of finer calibre has appeared in our century," and that "he alone of all British thinkers has organized a philosophy." Professor David Masson deemed him "the one of all our thinkers who has founded for himself the largest new scheme of a systematic philosophy." Dr. McCosh, who fundamentally differed from him, said "his bold generalizations are always instructive, and some of them may in the end be established as the profoundest laws of the knowable universe." St. George Mivart, who as a Catholic is also at variance in important matters, says "we cannot deny the title of philosopher to such a thinker as Mr. Spencer, who does genuinely bind together different and hitherto alien subjects, and that by a clear and wide though neither an all-comprehensive nor a spiritual hypothesis, the principle of evolution." Professor Tyndall calls him "the apostle of the understanding." His "profound and vigorous writings" have been likened by Professor Huxley to "the embodiment of the spirit of Descartes in the knowledge of our own day." Darwin spoke of him as "our great philosopher," greeted him as "the great expounder of the principle of evolution," and wrote to him that "every one with eyes to see and ears to hear ought to bow their knee to you." Professor Stanley Jevons ranked his work with the "Principia" of Newton. John Fiske, representing unquestionably the opinion of large numbers of intelligent and influential men, declares it to be of the calibre of that of Aristotle and Newton, but "as far surpassing their work in its vastness of performance as the railway surpasses the sedan-chair or as the telegraph surpasses the carrier pigeon." President Barnard in the same strain said, "his philosophy is the only philosophy that satisfies an earnestly inquiring mind," adding that "we have in Herbert Spencer not only the profoundest thinker of our time, but the most capacious and powerful intellect of all time. Aristotle and his master were not more beyond the pygmies who preceded them than he is beyond Aristotle. Kant, Hegel, Fichte and Schelling are gropers in the dark by the side of him."

Such estimates are not unquestioned, and opinions of a different kind might be cited from men of high standing. But the current of general thought, swelled by the wonderful scientific achievements of our time, has run powerfully, almost irresistibly, in favor of ideas with which Mr. Spencer is identified, absorbing, intimidating and driving back opposition even where it seemed most firmly intrenched, until to question them has come largely to be looked upon as evidence not merely of unscientific beliefs, but of ignorance and superstition. Whatever may be the verdict of the future, the man who is regarded as the great philosopher of evolution has within his own time won an acceptance and renown such as no preceding philosopher ever personally enjoyed. Thus, these estimates represent the view that has had the largest currency and produced the greatest effect, and that gives the weight of high authority to any declaration of Mr. Spencer's on a subject that has engaged his attention. Such a declaration, made with the utmost deliberation, in his latest, and as he and his admirers deem, his ripest and most important work, I propose in what follows to examine.

I do not propose to discuss Mr. Spencer's philosophy or review his writings, except as embraced in or related to his teachings on one subject. That, while a subject of the first practical importance, is one where no special knowledge, no familiarity with metaphysical terminology, no wrestling with abstractions, is needed, and one where the validity of the reasoning may be judged for himself by any one of ordinary powers and acquirements.

My primary object is to defend and advance a principle in which I see the only possible relief from much that enthralls and degrades and distorts, turning light to darkness and good to evil, rather than to gauge a philosopher or weigh a philosophy. Yet the examination I propose must lead to a decisive judgment upon both. As Mr. Spencer's treatment of this principle began with his first book and ends with his last, we have in it a cross section of his teachings, traversing the open plain of obvious facts and common perceptions, in which we who have no more than ordinary knowledge and powers may test for ourselves his intellectual ability, and, what is even more important, his intellectual honesty. For to whatever extent we may elsewhere separate ability and honesty, respecting the talent while distrusting the man, such separation cannot be made in the field of philosophy. Since philosophy is the search for truth, the philosopher who in his teachings is swerved by favor or by fear forfeits all esteem as a philosopher.

Nor is the connection between the practical problems that are forcing themselves on our civilization and the deepest questions with which speculative philosophy deals, merely personal or accidental. It belongs to the nature of the human mind, to our relations to the universe in which we awake to consciousness. And just as in "Progress and Poverty" the connection that developed as I went along carried me from an inquiry into economic phenomena to considerations that traversed Mr. Spencer's theory of social evolution and raised such supreme questions as the existence of God and the immortality of man, so now I find a similar connection asserting itself between Mr. Spencer's utterances on the most important of social questions and the views on wider and deeper subjects that have given him such a great reputation.

It is this — that a question of the utmost practical importance thus leads to questions beside which in our deeper moments the practical sinks into insignificance; that the philosopher whose authority is now invoked to deny to the masses any right to the physical basis of life in this world is also the philosopher whose authority darkens to many all hope of life hereafter — that has made it seem to me worth while to enter into an examination which in its form must be personal, and that will lead me to treat at greater length than I would otherwise be inclined to those utterances of Mr. Spencer which I propose to discuss.

I shall not ask the reader to accept anything from me. All I ask of him is to judge for himself Mr. Spencer's own public declarations. The respect for authority, the presumption in favor of those who have won intellectual reputation, is within reasonable limits, both prudent and becoming. But it should not be carried too far, and there are some things especially as to which it behooves us all to use our own judgment and to maintain free minds. For not only does the history of the world show that undue deference to authority has been the potent agency through which errors have been enthroned and superstitions perpetuated, but there are regions of thought in which the largest powers and the greatest acquirements cannot guard against aberrations or assure deeper insight. One may stand on a box and look over the heads of his fellows, but he no better sees the stars. The telescope and the microscope reveal depths which to the unassisted vision are closed. Yet not merely do they bring us no nearer to the cause of suns and animalcula, but in looking through them the observer must shut his eyes to what lies about him. That intension is at the expense of extension is seen in the mental as in the physical sphere. A man of special learning may be a fool as to common relations. And that he who passes for an intellectual prince may be a moral pauper there are examples enough to show.

As we must go to the shoemaker if we would be well shod and to the tailor if we would be well clad, so as to special branches of knowledge must we rely on those who have studied them. But while yielding to reputation the presumption in its favor, and to authority the respect that is its due, let us not too much underrate our own powers in what is concerned with common facts and general relations. While we may not be scientists or philosophers, we too are men. Let us remember that there is no religious superstition that has not been taught by professed teachers of religious truth; that there is no vulgar economic fallacy that may not be found in the writings of professors; no social vagary current among "the ignorant" whose roots may not be discovered among "the educated and cultured." The power to reason correctly on general subjects is not to be learned in schools, nor does it come with special knowledge. It results from care in separating, from caution in combining, from the habit of asking ourselves the meaning of the words we use and making sure of one step before building another on it — and above all, from loyalty to truth.

Giving to Mr. Spencer, therefore, the presumption that is due to his great reputation, but at the same time using his own reason, let the reader consider the matter I shall lay before him.

Herbert Spencer's last volume, "Justice," contains his latest word on the land question — the question in which, as I believe, lies the only solution of all the vexed and threatening social and political problems of our time. Accompanied, as it has been, by the withdrawal of earlier utterances, it places him definitely on the side of those who contend that the treatment of land as private property cannot equitably be interfered with, a position the reverse of that he once ably asserted.

While the opinions of a man of such wide reputation and large influence, on a question already passing into the domain of practical politics and soon to become the burning question of the time, are most worthy of attention, they derive additional importance from the fact of this change. For a change from a clearly reasoned opinion to its opposite carries the implication of fair and full consideration. And if the reasons for such a change be sufficient and there be no suspicion of ulterior motive, the fact that a man now condemns opinions he once held adds to the admiration that previously we may have entertained for him the additional admiration we must feel for one who has shown that he would rather be right than be consistent.

What gives additional interest to the matter is that Mr. Spencer makes no change in his premises, but only in his conclusion, and now, in sustaining private property in land, asserts the same principle of equal liberty from which he originally deduced its condemnation. How he has been led to this change becomes, therefore, a most interesting inquiry, not merely from the great importance of the subject itself, but from the light it must throw on the logical processes of so eminent a philosopher.

Since no one else has attempted it, it seems incumbent on me to examine this change and its grounds. For not only do I hold the opinions which Mr. Spencer now controverts, but I have been directly and indirectly instrumental in giving to his earlier conclusions a much greater circulation than his own books would have given them. It is due, therefore, that I should make his rejection of these conclusions as widely known as I can, and thus correct the mistake of those who couple us together as holding views he now opposes.

To fairly weigh Mr. Spencer's present opinion on the land question, and to comprehend his reasons for the change, it is necessary to understand his previous position. Beginning, therefore, with his first declaration, I propose to trace his public expressions on this subject to the present time, and, that no injustice may be done him, to print them in full. In what follows the reader will find what Mr. Spencer has published on the land question from 1850 to 1892, and, by the difference in type, may readily distinguish his utterances from my comments.

PART I.

DECLARATION.

Our social edifice may be constructed with all possible labor and ingenuity, and be strongly cramped together with cunningly-devised enactments, but if there be no *rectitude* in its component parts, if it is not built on *upright* principles, it will assuredly tumble to pieces. . . . Not as adventitious, therefore, will the wise man regard the faith that is in him, not as something which may be slighted, and made subordinate to calculations of policy; but as the supreme authority to which all his actions should bend. The highest truth conceivable by him he will fearlessly utter; and will endeavor to get embodied in fact his purest idealisms: knowing that, let what may come of it, he is thus playing his appointed part in the world — knowing that, if he can get done the thing he aims at — well: if not — well also; though not so well. —*Herbert Spencer, 1850.*

CHAPTER I.

"SOCIAL STATICS" — THE RIGHT TO LAND.

In his first book, "Social Statics," published in 1850, Mr. Spencer essayed to discover some fixed principle that might serve as a starting-point in political ethics and afford a surer guide than shifting notions of expediency or the vague formula of the greatest good to the greatest number. He found it in the principle that "every man may claim the fullest liberty to exercise his faculties compatible with the possession of like liberty by every other man." Or, as he otherwise puts it, that "every man has freedom to do all that he wills, provided he infringes not the equal freedom of any other man."

The first deduction he makes from this "first principle" is the equal right to life and personal liberty, and the second, the equal right to the use of the earth.

This first deduction he treats briefly in Chapter VIII., "The Rights of Life and Personal Liberty," saying, "These are such evident corollaries from our first principle as scarcely to need a separate statement."

The second deduction, only next in importance to the rights to life and personal liberty, and indeed involved in them, he treats at length in a chapter which I give in full:

CHAPTER IX.—THE RIGHT TO THE USE OF THE EARTH.

§ 1. Given a race of beings having like claims to pursue the objects of their desires—given a world adapted to the gratification of those desires—a world into which such beings are similarly born, and it unavoidably follows that they have equal rights to the use of this world. For if each of them "has freedom to do all that he wills provided he infringes not the equal freedom of any other," then each of them is free to use the earth for the satisfaction of his wants, provided he allows all others the same liberty. And conversely, it is manifest that no one, or part of them, may use the earth in such a way as to prevent the rest from similarly using it; seeing that to do this is to assume greater freedom than the rest, and consequently to break the law.

§ 2. Equity, therefore, does not permit property in land. For if *one* portion of the earth's surface may justly become the possession of an individual, and may be held by him for his sole use and benefit, as a thing to which he has an exclusive right, then *other* portions of the earth's surface may be so held; and eventually the *whole* of the earth's surface may be so held; and our planet may thus lapse altogether into private hands. Observe now the dilemma to which this leads. Supposing the entire habitable globe to be so enclosed, it follows that if the land-owners have a valid right to its surface, all who are not land-owners have no right at all to its surface. Hence, such can exist on the earth by sufferance only. They are all trespassers. Save by the permission of the lords of the soil, they can have no room for the soles of their feet. Nay, should the others think fit to deny them a resting-place, these landless men might equitably be expelled from the earth altogether. If, then, the assumption that land can be held as property, involves that the whole globe may become the private domain of a part of its inhabitants; and if, by consequence, the rest of its inhabitants can then exercise their faculties—can then exist even—only by consent of the land-owners; it is manifest, that an exclusive possession of the soil necessitates an infringement of the law of equal freedom. For, men who cannot "live and move and have their being" without the leave of others, cannot be equally free with those others.

§ 3. Passing from the consideration of the possible to that of the actual, we find yet further reason to deny the rectitude of property in land. It can never be pretended that the existing titles to such property are legitimate. Should any one think so, let him look in the chronicles. Violence, fraud, the prerogative of force, the claims of superior cunning—these are the sources to which those titles may be traced. The original deeds were written with the sword, rather than with the pen: not lawyers, but soldiers, were the conveyancers: blows were the current coin given in payment; and for seals, blood was used in preference to wax. Could valid claims be thus constituted? Hardly. And if not, what becomes of the pretensions of all subsequent holders of estates so obtained? Does sale or bequest generate a right where it did not previously exist? Would the original claimants be nonsuited at the bar of reason, because the thing stolen from them had changed hands? Certainly not. And if one act of transfer can give no title, can many? No: though *nothing* be multiplied forever, it will not produce *one*. Even the law recognizes this principle. An existing holder must, if called upon, substantiate the claims of those from whom he purchased or inherited his property; and any flaw in the original parchment, even though the property should have had a score intermediate owners, quashes his right.

"But Time," say some, "is a great legalizer. Immemorial possession must be taken to constitute a legitimate claim. That which has been held from age to age as private property, and has been bought and sold as such, must now be considered as irrevocably belonging to individuals." To which proposition a willing assent shall be given when its propounders can assign it a definite meaning. To do this, however, they must find satisfactory answers to such questions as, How long does it take for what was originally a *wrong* to grow into a *right?* At what rate per annum do invalid claims become valid? If a title gets perfect in a thousand years, how much more than perfect will it be in two thousand years? — and so forth. For the solution of which they will require a new calculus.

Whether it may be expedient to admit claims of a certain standing, is not the point. We have here nothing to do with considerations of conventional privilege or legislative convenience. We have simply to inquire what is the verdict given by pure equity in the matter. And this verdict enjoins a protest against every existing pretension to the individual possession of the soil; and dictates the assertion, that the right of mankind at large to the earth's surface is still valid; all deeds, customs, and laws notwithstanding.

§ 4. Not only have present land-tenures an indefensible origin, but it is impossible to discover any mode in which land *can* become private property. Cultivation is commonly considered to give a legitimate title. He who has reclaimed a tract of ground from its primitive wildness, is supposed to have thereby made it his own. But if his right is disputed, by what system of logic can he vindicate it? Let us listen a moment to his pleadings.

"Hallo, you Sir," cries the cosmopolite to some backwoodsman, smoking at the door of his shanty, "by what authority do you take possession of these acres that you have cleared; round which you have put up a snake-fence, and on which you have built this log house?"

"By what authority? I squatted here because there was no one to say nay — because I was as much at liberty to do so as any other man. Besides, now that I have cut down the wood, and ploughed and cropped the ground, this farm is more mine than yours, or anybody's; and I mean to keep it."

"Ay, so you all say. But I do not yet see how you have substantiated your claim. When you came here you found the land producing trees — sugar-maples, perhaps; or may be it was covered with prairie-grass and wild strawberries. Well, instead of these you made it yield wheat, or maize, or tobacco. Now I want to understand how, by exterminating one set of plants, and making the soil bear another set in their place, you have constituted yourself lord of this soil for all succeeding time."

"Oh, those natural products which I destroyed were of little or no use; whereas I caused the earth to bring forth things good for food—things that help to give life and happiness."

"Still you have not shown why such a process makes the portion of earth you have so modified yours. What is it that you have done? You have turned over the soil to a few inches in depth with a spade or a plough; you have scattered over this prepared surface a few seeds; and you have gathered the fruits which the sun, rain, and air, helped the soil to produce. Just tell me, if you please, by what magic have these acts made you sole owner of that vast mass of matter, having for its base the surface of your estate, and for its apex the centre of the globe? all of which it appears you would monopolize to yourself and your descendants forever."

"Well, if it isn't mine, whose is it? I have dispossessed nobody. When I crossed the Mississippi yonder, I found nothing but the silent woods. If some one else had settled here, and made this clearing, he would have had as good a right to the location as I have. I have done nothing but what any other person was at liberty to do had he come before me. Whilst they were unreclaimed, these lands belonged to all men—as much to one as to another—and they are now mine simply because I was the first to discover and improve them."

"You say truly, when you say that 'whilst they were unreclaimed these lands belonged to all men.' And it is my duty to tell you that they belong to all men still; and that your 'improvements' as you call them, cannot vitiate the claim of all men. You may plough and harrow, and sow and reap; you may turn over the soil as often as you like; but all your manipulations will fail to make that soil yours, which was not yours to begin with. Let me put a case. Suppose now that in the course of your wanderings you come upon an empty house, which in spite of its dilapidated state takes your fancy; suppose that with the intention of making it your abode you expend much time and trouble in repairing it—that you paint and paper, and whitewash, and at considerable cost bring it into a habitable state. Suppose further, that on some fatal day a stranger is announced, who turns out to be the heir to whom this house has been bequeathed; and that this professed heir is prepared with all the necessary proofs of his identity; what becomes of your improvements? Do they give you a valid title to the house? Do they quash the title of the original claimant?"

"No."

"Neither then do your pioneering operations give you a valid title to this land. Neither do they quash the title of its original claimants — the human race. The world is God's bequest to mankind. All men are joint heirs to it; you amongst the number. And because you have taken up your residence on a certain part of it, and have subdued, cultivated, beautified that part — improved it as you say, you are not therefore warranted in appropriating it as entirely private property. At least if you do so, you may at any moment be justly expelled by the lawful owner — Society."

"Well, but surely you would not eject me without making some recompense for the great additional value I have given to this tract, by reducing what was a wilderness into fertile fields. You would not turn me adrift and deprive me of all the benefit of those years of toil it has cost me to bring this spot into its present state."

"Of course not: just as in the case of the house, you would have an equitable title to compensation from the proprietor for repairs and new fittings, so the community cannot justly take possession of this estate, without paying for all that you have done to it. This extra worth which your labor has imparted to it is fairly yours; and although you have, without leave, busied yourself in bettering what belongs to the community, yet no doubt the community will duly discharge your claim. But admitting this, is quite a different thing from recognizing your right to the land itself. It may be true that you are entitled to compensation for the improvements this enclosure has received at your hands; and at the same time it may be equally true that no act, form, proceeding, or ceremony, can make this enclosure your private property."

§ 5. It does indeed at first sight seem possible for the earth to become the exclusive possession of individuals by some process of equitable distribution. "Why," it may be asked, "should not men agree to a fair subdivision? If all are co-heirs, why may not the estate be equally apportioned, and each be afterwards perfect master of his own share?"

To this question it may in the first place be replied, that such a division is vetoed by the difficulty of fixing the values of respective tracts of land. Variations in productiveness, different degrees of accessibility, advantages of climate, proximity to the centres of civilization — these, and other such considerations, remove the problem out of the sphere of mere mensuration into the region of impossibility.

But, waiving this, let us inquire who are to be the allottees. Shall adult males, and all who have reached twenty-one on a specified day, be the fortunate individuals? If so, what is to be done with those who come of age on the morrow? Is it proposed that each man, woman, and child, shall have a section? If so, what becomes of all who are to be born next year? And what will be the fate of those whose fathers sell their estates and squander the proceeds? These portionless ones must constitute a class already described as having no right to a resting-place on earth — as living by the sufferance of their fellow-men — as being practically serfs. And the existence of such a class is wholly at variance with the law of equal freedom.

Until, therefore, we can produce a valid commission authorizing us to make this distribution — until it can be proved that God has given one charter of privileges to one generation, and another to the next — until we can demonstrate that men born after a certain date are doomed to slavery, we must consider that no such allotment is permissible.

§ 6. Probably some will regard the difficulties inseparable from individual ownership of the soil, as caused by pushing to excess a doctrine applicable only within rational limits. This is a very favorite style of thinking with some. There are people who hate anything in the shape of exact conclusions; and these are of them. According to such, the right is never in either extreme, but always half way between the extremes. They are continually trying to reconcile *Yes* and *No*. Ifs and buts, and excepts, are their delight. They have so great a faith in "the judicious mean" that they would scarcely believe an oracle, if it uttered a full-length principle. Were you to inquire of them whether the earth turns on its axis from East to West, or from West to East, you might almost expect the reply — "A little of both," or "Not exactly either." It is doubtful whether they would assent to the axiom that the whole is greater than its part, without making some qualification. They have a passion for compromises. To meet their taste, Truth must always be spiced with a little Error. They cannot conceive of a pure, definite, entire, and unlimited law. And hence, in discussions like the present, they are constantly petitioning for limitations — always wishing to abate, and modify, and moderate — ever protesting against doctrines being pursued to their ultimate consequences.

But it behooves such to recollect, that ethical truth is as exact and as peremptory as physical truth; and that in this matter of land-tenure, the verdict of morality must be distinctly *yea* or *nay*. Either men *have* a right to make the soil private property, or they *have not.* There is no medium. We must choose one of the two positions. There can be no half-and-half opinion. In the nature of things the fact must be either one way or the other.

If men *have not* such a right, we are at once delivered from the several predicaments already pointed out. If they *have* such a right, then is that right absolute, sacred, not on any pretence to be violated. If they *have* such a right, then is his Grace of Leeds justified in warning-off tourists from Ben Mac Dhui, the Duke of Atholl in closing Glen Tilt, the Duke of Buccleuch in denying sites to the Free Church, and the Duke of Sutherland in banishing the Highlanders to make room for sheep-walks. If they *have* such a right, then it would be proper for the sole proprietor of any kingdom — a Jersey or Guernsey, for example — to impose just what regulations he might choose on its inhabitants — to tell them that they should not live on his property, unless they professed a certain religion, spoke a particular language, paid him a specified reverence, adopted an authorized dress, and conformed to all other conditions he might see fit to make. If they *have* such a right, then is there truth in that tenet of the ultra-Tory school, that the land-owners are the only legitimate rulers of a country — that the people at large remain in it only by the land-owners' permission, and ought consequently to submit to the land-owners' rule, and respect whatever institutions the land-owners set up. There is no escape from these inferences. They are necessary corollaries to the theory that the earth can become individual property. And they can only be repudiated by denying that theory.

§ 7. After all, nobody does implicity believe in landlordism. We hear of estates being held under the king, that is, the state; or of their being kept in trust for the public benefit; and not that they are the inalienable possessions of their nominal owners. Moreover, we daily deny landlordism by our legislation. Is a canal, a railway, or a turnpike road to be made? we do not scruple to seize just as many acres as may be requisite; allowing the holders compensation for the capital invested. We do not wait for consent. An Act of Parliament supersedes the authority of title deeds, and serves proprietors with notices to quit, whether they will or not. Either this is equitable, or it is not. Either the public are free to resume as much of the earth's surface as they think fit, or the titles of the land-owners must be considered absolute, and all national works must be postponed until lords and squires please to part with the requisite slices of their estates. If we decide that the claims of individual ownership must give way, then we imply that the right of the nation at large to the soil is supreme — that the right of private possession only exists by general consent — that general consent being withdrawn it ceases — or, in other words, that it is no right at all.

§ 8. "But to what does this doctrine, that men are equally entitled to the use of the earth, lead? Must we return to the times of unenclosed wilds, and subsist on roots, berries, and game? Or are we to be left to the management of Messrs. Fourier, Owen, Louis Blanc, and Co.?"

Neither. Such a doctrine is consistent with the highest state of civilization; may be carried out without involving a community of goods; and need cause no very serious revolution in existing arrangements. The change required would simply be a change of landlords. Separate ownerships would merge into the joint-stock ownership of the public. Instead of being in the possession of individuals, the country would be held by the great corporate body — Society. Instead of leasing his acres from an isolated proprietor, the farmer would lease them from the nation. Instead of paying his rent to the agent of Sir John or his Grace, he would pay it to an agent or deputy-agent of the community. Stewards would be public officials instead of private ones; and tenancy the only land-tenure.

A state of things so ordered would be in perfect harmony with the moral law. Under it all men would be equally landlords; all men would be alike free to become tenants. A, B, C, and the rest, might compete for a vacant farm as now, and one of them might take that farm, without in any way violating the principles of pure equity. All would be equally free to bid; all would be equally free to refrain. And when the farm had been let to A, B, or C, all parties would have done that which they willed — the one in choosing to pay a given sum to his fellow-men for the use of certain lands — the others in refusing to pay that sum. Clearly, therefore, on such a system, the earth might be enclosed, occupied, and cultivated, in entire subordination to the law of equal freedom.

§ 9. No doubt great difficulties must attend the resumption, by mankind at large, of their rights to the soil. The question of compensation to existing proprietors is a complicated one — one that perhaps cannot be settled in a strictly equitable manner. Had we to deal with the parties who originally robbed the human race of its heritage, we might make short work of the matter. But, unfortunately, most of our present land-owners are men who have, either mediately or immediately — either by their own acts, or by the acts of their ancestors — given for their estates, equivalents of honestly-earned wealth, believing that they were investing their savings in a legitimate manner. To justly estimate and liquidate the claims of such, is one of the most intricate problems society will one day have to solve. But with this perplexity and our extrication from it, abstract morality has no concern. Men having got themselves into the dilemma by disobedience to the law, must get out of it as well as they can; and with as little injury to the landed class as may be.

Meanwhile, we shall do well to recollect, that there are others besides the landed class to be considered. In our tender regard for the vested interests of the few, let us not forget that the rights of the many are in abeyance; and must remain so, as long as the earth is monopolized by individuals. Let us remember, too, that the injustice thus inflicted on the mass of mankind, is an injustice of the gravest nature. The fact that it is not so regarded, proves nothing. In early phases of civilization even homicide is thought lightly of. The suttees of India, together with the practice elsewhere followed of sacrificing a hecatomb of human victims at the burial of a chief, shows this; and probably cannibals consider the slaughter of those whom "the fortune of war" has made their prisoners, perfectly justifiable. It was once also universally supposed that slavery was a natural and quite legitimate institution—a condition into which some were born, and to which they ought to submit as to a Divine ordination; nay, indeed, a great proportion of mankind hold this opinion still. A higher social development, however, has generated in us a better faith, and we now to a considerable extent recognize the claims of humanity. But our civilization is only partial. It may by-and-by be perceived, that Equity utters dictates to which we have not yet listened; and men may then learn, that to deprive others of their rights to the use of the earth, is to commit a crime inferior only in wickedness to the crime of taking away their lives or personal liberties.

§ 10. Briefly reviewing the argument, we see that the right of each man to the use of the earth, limited only by the like rights of his fellow-men, is immediately deducible from the law of equal freedom. We see that the maintenance of this right necessarily forbids private property in land. On examination all existing titles to such property turn out to be invalid; those founded on reclamation inclusive. It appears that not even an equal apportionment of the earth amongst its inhabitants could generate a legitimate proprietorship. We find that if pushed to its ultimate consequences, a claim to exclusive possession of the soil involves a land-owning despotism. We further find that such a claim is constantly denied by the enactments of our legislature. And we find lastly, that the theory of the co-heirship of all men to the soil, is consistent with the highest civilization; and that, however difficult it may be to embody that theory in fact, Equity sternly commands it to be done.

Briefly stated, the argument of this chapter is —

1. The equal right of all men to the use of land springs from the fact of their existence in a world adapted to their needs, and into which they are similarly born.

2. Equity, therefore, does not permit private property in land, since that would involve the right of some to deny to others the use of land.

3. Private property in land, as at present existing, can show no original title valid in justice, and such validity cannot be gained either by sale or bequest, or by peaceable possession during any length of time.

4. Nor is there any mode by which land *can* justly become private property. Cultivation and improvement can give title only to their results, not to the land itself.

5. Nor could an equitable division of land with the consent of all, even if it were not impossible that such a division could be made, give valid title to private property in land. For the equal right to the use of land would attach to all those thereafter born,

irrespective of any agreement made by their predecessors.

6. There can be no modification of this dictate of equity. Either all men have equal rights to the use of the land, or some men have the just right to enslave others and deprive them of life.

7. As a matter of fact, nobody does really believe in private property in land. An Act of Parliament, even now, supersedes title-deeds. That is to say, the right of private ownership in land only exists by general consent; that being withdrawn, it ceases.

8. But the doctrine that all men are equally entitled to the use of land does not involve communism or socialism, and need cause no serious change in existing arrangements. It is not necessary that the state should manage land: it is only necessary that rent, instead of going, as now, to individuals, should be taken by society for common purposes.

9. There may be difficulty in justly liquidating the claims of existing land-owners, but men having got themselves into a dilemma must get out of it as well as they can. The landed class are not alone to be considered. So long as the treatment of land as private property continues, the masses suffer from an injustice only inferior in wickedness to depriving them of life or personal liberty.

10. However difficult it may be to embody in fact the theory of the co-heirship of all men to the soil, equity sternly demands it to be done.

CHAPTER II.

THE INCONGRUOUS PASSAGE.

ALTHOUGH this chapter shows that Mr. Spencer had not fully thought out the question, and saw no way to secure equality in the use of land, save the clumsy one of having the state formally resume land and let it out in lots to suit, the argument is clear and logical, except in one place. This one weak and confusing spot is the beginning of Section 9:

> No doubt great difficulty must attend the resumption by mankind at large, of their rights to the soil. The question of compensation to existing proprietors is a complicated one — one that perhaps cannot be settled in a strictly equitable manner. Had we to deal with the parties who originally robbed the human race of its heritage, we might make short work of the matter. But, unfortunately, most of our present land-owners are men who have either mediately or immediately — either by their own acts, or by the acts of their ancestors — given for their estates equivalents of honestly earned wealth, believing that they were investing their savings in a legitimate manner. To justly estimate and liquidate the claims of such is one of the most intricate problems society will one day have to solve.

Taken by itself, this passage seems to admit that existing land-owners should be compensated for the land they hold whenever society shall resume land for the benefit of all. Though this is diametrically opposed to all that has gone before and all that follows after, it is the sense in which it has been generally understood. It is the sense in which I understood it when, in quoting from "Social Statics" in "Progress and Poverty," I spoke of it as a careless concession, which Mr. Spencer on reflection would undoubtedly reconsider. For after even such a man as John Stuart Mill could say, "The land of every country belongs to the people of that country; the individuals called land-owners have no right in morality and justice to anything but the rent, or compensation for its salable value," the English writers had seemed to me afflicted with a sort of color-blindness on the subject of compensation. And that this affliction had suddenly befallen Mr. Spencer also was the only explanation of this passage that then occurred to me. Nor, if it means compensation for land, is there any other explanation; for all along Mr. Spencer has been insisting on the natural, inalienable and equal right of all men to the use of land. He has not only denied the validity of all existing claims to the private ownership of land, but has declared that there is no possible way in which land *can* become private property. He has mercilessly and scornfully exposed the fallacy on which the notion of compensation to land-owners is based — the idea that change of hands and lapse of time can turn wrong into right, make valid claims originally invalid, and deprive the human race of what in the nature of things is, not at any one time, but at all times, their inalienable heritage. Nothing but moral color-blindness can explain how a writer who has just asserted all this can in the same breath propose to compensate landlords.

But a more careful reading of this chapter leads me now to think that the apparent inconsistency of these sentences may arise from careless statement, and that what Mr. Spencer was really thinking of was the compensation of land-owners, not for their land, but for their improvements.

In the context Mr. Spencer has scouted the idea of force, or acquiescence, or voluntary partition, or unopposed appropriation, or cultivation, or improvement, or sale or bequest, or lapse of time, giving any title to private property in land. But he realizes, as we all do (see especially the last two paragraphs of Section 4), that should the community resume for all the inalienable right to the use of land, there would remain to holders of improvements made in good faith an equitable claim for those improvements.

It is evident throughout "Social Statics" that no idea of the possibility of securing equal rights to land in any other way than that of the state taking possession of the land and renting it out had dawned on Mr. Spencer. And since in all settled countries the land thus taken possession of by the state would be land to which in large part improvements of various kinds had in good faith been inseparably attached, the matter of determining what equitable compensation should be paid to owners on account of these improvements naturally seemed to him a delicate and difficult task — one, in fact, incapable of more than an approximation to justice.

Keeping this in mind, it is clear that a few interpolations, justified by the context, and indeed made necessary by it, will remove all difficulty. Let me print these sentences again with such interpolations, which I will distinguish by italics:

> The question of compensation to existing proprietors *for their improvements* is a complicated one — one that perhaps cannot be settled in a strictly equitable manner. Had we to deal with the parties who originally robbed the human race of its heritage, we might make short work of the matter, *for their improvements we should be under no obligation to regard.* But, unfortunately, most of our present land-holders are men who have, either mediately or immediately — either by their own acts or the acts of their ancestors — given for their estates, *which include many inseparable improvements,* equivalents of honestly earned wealth, believing that they were investing their savings in a legitimate manner. To justly estimate and liquidate the claims of such *for these improvements* is one of the most intricate problems society will one day have to solve.

Thus understood, these sentences become coherent with their context. And that this was what Mr. Spencer had in mind is supported by his more recent utterances; for while he has allowed these sentences to be understood as meaning compensation to land-owners for their land, yet in the only places where he has stated in terms what the compensation he has proposed is to be for, he has, as will hereafter be seen, spoken of it as "compensation for the artificial value given by cultivation," or by some similar phrase showed that what was in his mind was merely compensation for improvements. I therefore gladly make what honorable amend I can for having so misunderstood him as to imagine that in "Social Statics" he intended to give any countenance to the idea that it was incumbent on men, when taking possession of their heritage, to pay any compensation to existing land-owners for the value of that heritage.

CHAPTER III.

"SOCIAL STATICS" — THE RIGHT OF PROPERTY.

THE chapter of "Social Statics" on "The Right to the Use of the Earth" is followed by a chapter on "The Right of Property." For the reason that Mr. Spencer has since referred to this chapter as to be taken in connection with what was said in the preceding one, it is also worth while to reprint it in full:

CHAPTER X. — THE RIGHT OF PROPERTY.

§ 1. The moral law, being the law of the social state, is obliged wholly to ignore the ante-social state. Constituting, as the principles of pure morality do, a code of conduct for the perfect man, they cannot be made to adapt themselves to the actions of the uncivilized man, even under the most ingenious hypothetical conditions — cannot be made even to recognize those actions so as to pass any definite sentence upon them. Overlooking this fact, thinkers, in their attempts to prove some of the first theorems of ethics, have commonly fallen into the error of referring back to an imaginary state of savage wildness, instead of referring forward to an ideal civilization, as they should have done; and have, in consequence, entangled themselves in difficulties arising out of the discordance between ethical principles and the assumed premises. To this circumstance is attributable that vagueness by which the arguments used to establish the right of property in a logical manner, are characterized. Whilst possessed of a certain plausibility, they yet cannot be considered conclusive; inasmuch as they suggest questions and objections that admit of no satisfactory answers. Let us take a sample of these arguments, and examine its defects.

"Though the earth and all inferior creatures," says Locke, "be common to all men, yet every man has a property in his own person: this nobody has a right to but himself. The labor of his body, and the work of his hands, we may say are properly his. Whatever then he removes out of the state that nature hath provided and left it in, he hath mixed his labor with, and joined to it something that is his own, and thereby makes it his property. It being by him removed from the common state nature hath placed it in, it hath by this labor something annexed to it that excludes the common right of other men. For this labor being the unquestionable property of the laborer, no man but he can have a right to what that is once joined to, at least when there is enough and as good left in common for others."

If inclined to cavil, one might in reply to this observe, that as, according to the premises, "the earth and all inferior creatures" — all things, in fact, that the earth produces — are "common to all men," the consent of all men must be obtained before any article can be equitably "removed from the common state nature hath placed it in." It might be argued that the real question is overlooked, when it is said, that, by gathering any natural product, a man "hath mixed his labor with it, and joined to it something that is his own, and thereby made it his property;" for that the point to be debated is, whether he had any right to gather, or mix his labor with that, which, by the hypothesis, previously belonged to mankind at large. The reasoning used in the last chapter to prove that no amount of labor, bestowed by an individual upon a part of the earth's surface, can nullify the title of society to that part, might be similarly employed to show that no one can, by the mere act of appropriating to himself any wild unclaimed animal or fruit, supersede the joint claims of other men to it. It may be quite true that the labor a man expends in catching or gathering, gives him a better right to the thing caught or gathered, than any *one* other man; but the question at issue is, whether by labor so expended, he has made his right to the thing caught or gathered, greater than the pre-existing rights of *all* other men put together. And unless he can prove that he has done this, his title to possession cannot be admitted as a matter of *right,* but can be conceded only on the ground of convenience.

Further difficulties are suggested by the qualification, that the claim to any article of property thus obtained, is valid only "when there is enough and as good left in common for others." A condition like this gives birth to such a host of queries, doubts, and limitations, as practically to neutralize the general proposition entirely. It may be asked, for example — How is it to be known that enough is "left in common for others"? Who can determine whether what remains is "as good" as what is taken? How if the remnant is less accessible? If there is not enough "left in common for others," how must the right of appropriation be exercised? Why, in such case, does the mixing of labor with the acquired object, cease to "exclude the common right of other men"? Supposing *enough* to be attainable, but not all equally *good,* by what rule must each man choose? Out of which inquisition it seems impossible to liberate the alleged right, without such mutilations as to render it, in an ethical point of view, entirely valueless.

Thus, as already hinted, we find, that the circumstances of savage life, render the principles of abstract morality inapplicable; for it is impossible, under ante-social conditions, to determine the rightness or wrongness of certain actions by an exact measurement of the amount of freedom assumed by the parties concerned. We must not expect, therefore, that the right of property can be satisfactorily based upon the premises afforded by such a state of existence.

§ 2. But, under the system of land-tenure pointed out in the last chapter, as the only one that is consistent with the equal claims of all men to the use of the earth, these difficulties disappear; and the right of property obtains a legitimate foundation. We have seen that, without any infraction of the law of equal freedom, an individual may lease from society a given surface of soil, by agreeing to pay in return a stated amount of the produce he obtains from that soil. We found that, in doing this, he does no more than what every other man is equally free with himself to do — that each has the same power with himself to become the tenant — and that the rent he pays accrues alike to all. Having thus hired a tract of land from his fellow-men, for a given period, for understood purposes, and on specified terms — having thus obtained, for a time, the exclusive use of that land by a definite agreement with its owners, it is manifest that an individual may, without any infringement of the rights of others, appropriate to himself that portion of produce which remains after he has paid to mankind the promised rent. He has now, to use Locke's expression, "mixed his labor with" certain products of the earth; and his claim to them is in this case valid, because he obtained the *consent* of society before so expending his labor; and having fulfilled the condition which society imposed in giving that consent — the payment of rent — society, to fulfil its part of the agreement, must acknowledge his title to that surplus which remains after the rent has been paid. "Provided you deliver to us a stated share of the produce which by cultivation you can obtain from this piece of land, we give you the exclusive use of the remainder of that produce:" these are the words of the contract; and in virtue of this contract, the tenant may equitably claim the supplementary share as his private property: may so claim it without any disobedience to the law of equal freedom; and has therefore a *right* so to claim it.

Any doubt that may be felt as to the fact that this is a logical deduction from our first principle, that every man has freedom to do all that he wills provided he infringes not the equal freedom of any other man, may be readily cleared up by comparing the respective degrees of freedom assumed in such a case by the occupier and the members of society with whom he bargains. As was shown in the preceding chapter, if the public altogether deprive any individual of the use of the earth, they allow him *less* liberty than they themselves claim; and by so breaking the law of equal freedom, commit a wrong. If, conversely, an individual usurps a given portion of the earth, to which, as we have seen, all other men have as good a title as himself, *he* breaks the law by assuming *more* liberty than the rest. But when an individual holds land as a tenant of society, a balance is maintained between these extremes, and the claims of both parties are respected. A price is paid by the one, for a certain privilege granted by the other. By the fact of the agreement being made, it is shown that such price and privilege are considered to be equivalents. The lessor and the lessee have both, within the prescribed limits, done that which they *willed:* the one in letting a certain holding for a specified sum; the other in agreeing to give that sum. And so long as this contract remains intact, the law of equal freedom is duly observed. If, however, any of the prescribed conditions be not fulfilled, the law is necessarily broken, and the parties are involved in one of the predicaments above named. If the tenant refuses to pay the rent, then he tacitly lays claim to the exclusive use and benefit of the land he occupies — practically asserts that he is the sole owner of its produce; and consequently violates the law, by assuming a greater share of freedom than the rest of mankind. If, on the other hand, society take from the tenant that portion of the fruits obtained by the culture of his farm which remains with him after the payment of rent, they virtually deny him the use of the earth entirely (for by the use of the earth we mean the use of its products), and in so doing, claim for themselves a greater share of liberty than they allow him. Clearly, therefore, this surplus produce equitably remains with the tenant: society *cannot* take it without trespassing upon his freedom; he *can* take it without trespassing on the freedom of society. And as, according to the law, he is free to do all that he wills, provided he infringes not the equal freedom of any other, he is free to take possession of such surplus as his property.

§ 3. The doctrine that all men have equal rights to the use of the earth, does indeed, at first sight, seem to countenance a species of social organization at variance with that from which the right of property has just been deduced; an organization, namely, in which the public, instead of letting out the land to individual members of their body, shall retain it in their own hands; cultivate it by joint-stock agency; and share the produce: in fact, what is usually termed Socialism or Communism.

Plausible though it may be, such a scheme is not capable of realization in strict conformity with the moral law. Of the two forms under which it may be presented, the one is ethically imperfect; and the other, although correct in theory, is impracticable.

Thus, if an equal portion of the earth's produce is awarded to every man, irrespective of the amount or quality of the labor he has contributed toward the obtainment of that produce, a breach of equity is committed. Our first principle requires, not that all shall have like shares of the things which minister to the gratification of the faculties, but that all shall have like freedom to pursue those things — shall have like scope. It is one thing to give to each an opportunity of acquiring the objects he desires; it is another, and quite a different thing, to give the objects themselves, no matter whether due endeavor has or has not been made to obtain them. The one we have seen to be the primary law of the Divine scheme; the other, by interfering with the ordained connection between desire and gratification, shows its disagreement with that scheme. Nay more, it necessitates an absolute violation of the principle of equal freedom. For when we assert the entire liberty of each, bounded only by the like liberty of all, we assert that each is free to do whatever his desires dictate, within the prescribed limits — that each is free, therefore, to claim for himself all those gratifications, and sources of gratification, attainable by him within those limits — all those gratifications, and sources of gratification, which he can procure without trespassing upon the spheres of action of his neighbors. If, therefore, out of many starting with like fields of activity, one obtains, by his greater strength, greater ingenuity, or greater application, more gratification and sources of gratification than the rest, and does this without in any way trenching upon the equal freedom of the rest, the moral law assigns him an exclusive right to all those extra gratifications and sources of gratification; nor can the rest take from him without claiming for themselves greater liberty of action than he claims, and thereby violating that law. Whence it follows, that an equal apportionment of the fruits of the earth amongst all, is not consistent with pure justice.

If, on the other hand, each is to have allotted to him a share of produce proportionate to the degree in which he has aided production, the proposal, whilst it is abstractedly just, is no longer practicable. Were all men cultivators of the soil, it would perhaps be possible to form an approximate estimate of their several claims. But to ascertain the respective amounts of help given by different kinds of mental and bodily laborers, toward procuring the general stock of the necessaries of life, is an utter impossibility. We have no means of making such a division save that afforded by the law of supply and demand, and this means the hypothesis excludes.[1]

§ 4. An argument fatal to the communist theory, is suggested by the fact, that a desire for property is one of the elements of our nature. Repeated allusion has been made to the admitted truth, that acquisitiveness is an unreasoning impulse quite distinct from the desires whose gratifications property secures — an impulse that is often obeyed at the expense of those desires. And if a propensity to personal acquisition be really a component of man's constitution, then that cannot be a right form of society which affords it no scope. Socialists do indeed allege that private appropriation is an abuse of this propensity, whose normal function, they say, is to impel us to accumulate for the benefit of the public at large. But in thus attempting to escape from one difficulty, they do but entangle themselves in another. Such an explanation overlooks the fact that the *use* and *abuse* of a faculty (whatever the etymology of the words may imply) differ only in *degree;* whereas their assumption is, that they differ in *kind.* Gluttony is an abuse of the desire for food; timidity, an abuse of the feeling which in moderation produces prudence; servility, an abuse of the sentiment that generates respect; obstinacy, of that from which firmness springs: in all of which cases we find that the legitimate manifestations differ from the illegitimate ones, merely in quantity, and not in quality. So also with the instinct of accumulation. It may be quite true that its dictates have been, and still are, followed to an absurd excess; but it is also true that no

[1] These inferences do not at all militate against joint-stock systems of production and living, which are in all probability what Socialism prophesies.

change in the state of society will alter its nature and its office. To whatever extent moderated, it must still be a desire for personal acquisition. Whence it follows that a system affording opportunity for its exercise must ever be retained; which means, that the system of private property must be retained; and this presupposes a *right* of private property, for by right we mean that which harmonizes with the human constitution as divinely ordained.

§ 5. There is, however, a still more awkward dilemma into which M. Proudhon and his party betray themselves. For if, as they assert, "all property is robbery"—if no one can equitably become the exclusive possessor of any article—or as we say, obtain a right to it, then, amongst other consequences, it follows, that a man can have no right to the things he consumes for food. And if these are not his before eating them, how can they become his at all? As Locke asks, "when do they begin to be his? when he digests? or when he eats? or when he boils? or when he brings them home?" If no previous acts can make them his property, neither can any process of assimilation do it; not even their absorption into the tissues. Wherefore, pursuing the idea, we arrive at the curious conclusion, that as the whole of his bones, muscles, skin, etc., have been thus built up from nutriment not belonging to him, a man has no property in his own flesh and blood—can have no valid title to himself—has no more claim to his own limbs than he has to the limbs of another—and has as good a right to his neighbor's body as to his own! Did we exist after the same fashion as those compound polyps, in which a number of individuals are based upon a living trunk common to them all, such a theory would be rational enough. But until Communism can be carried to that extent, it will be best to stand by the old doctrine.

§ 6. Further argument appears to be unnecessary. We have seen that the right of property is deducible from the law of equal freedom—that it is presupposed by the human constitution—and that its denial involves absurdities.

Were it not that we shall frequently have to refer to

the fact hereafter, it would be scarcely needful to show that the taking away another's property is an infringement of the law of equal freedom, and is therefore wrong. If A appropriates to himself something belonging to B, one of two things must take place: either B does the like to A, or he does not. If A has no property, or if his property is inaccessible to B, B has evidently no opportunity of exercising equal freedom with A, by claiming from him something of like value; and A has therefore assumed a greater share of freedom than he allows B, and has broken the law. If again, A's property is open to B, and A permits B to use like freedom with himself by taking an equivalent, there is no violation of the law; and the affair practically becomes one of barter. But such a transaction will never take place save in theory; for A has no motive to appropriate B's property with the intention of letting B take an equivalent: seeing that if he really means to let B have what B thinks an equivalent, he will prefer to make the exchange by consent in the ordinary way. The only case simulating this, is one in which A takes from B a thing that B does not wish to part with; that is, a thing for which A can give B nothing that B thinks an equivalent; and as the amount of gratification which B has in the possession of this thing, is the measure of its value to him, it follows that if A cannot give B a thing which affords B equal gratification, or in other words what he thinks an equivalent, then A has taken from B what affords A satisfaction, but does not return to B what affords B satisfaction; and has therefore broken the law by assuming the greater share of freedom. Wherefore we find it to be a logical deduction from the law of equal freedom, that no man can rightfully take property from another against his will.

There is in this, it will be observed, no modification whatever of the strenuous assertion in Chapter IX. of the equal, natural and inalienable right of all men to the use of land. On the contrary, so strongly, so uncompromisingly, does Mr. Spencer insist on the ethical invalidity of private property in land that he makes the formal consent of the community and the payment of rent to it a condition precedent to the individual right of property in things produced by labor. And, since no formal consent of this kind can be given until society has been well organized, he even goes to the length of denying that there can be any full right of property, or, indeed, any application of the principles of abstract morality, in any social condition lower than the civilized.

In brief, the argument of this chapter is —

1. That the right of the individual to his labor does not give individual property in the product of labor, because labor can produce only by using land, which does not belong to any individual, but to all.

2. But under the system of land-tenure previously set forth as the only just one, in which the organized society assigns the use of a portion of land to an individual and collects rent from him for it, the conditions of the equal liberty of all are complied with, and the individual acquires a right of property in what remains of the product of his labor after paying rent.

3. This system, under which the social organization would let land to individuals and collect rent from them, does not countenance the system under which it would carry on production and divide the product among its members, since, the powers and application of men being different, this would give to some more than they are entitled to, and to others less.

4. This communistic or socialistic system is also condemned by the natural desire to acquire individual property.

5. The denial of individual property may be brought into the awkward dilemma of a denial of the right of the individual to himself.

6. The right of property having thus been established, the appropriation by one of property belonging to another is a denial of the law of equal freedom.

CHAPTER IV.

MR. SPENCER'S CONFUSION AS TO RIGHTS.

My purpose in quoting Chapter X. is to show what were the views on the land question expressed by Mr. Spencer in "Social Statics." It may, however, be worth while, in passing, to clear up the confusion in which he here entangles the right to the products of labor with the right to land. This confusion he has not yet escaped from, as it is still to be seen in his latest book, "Justice," where, though evidently anxious to minimize the land question, he still assumes that to justify the right of property in things produced from nature the consent of all men must be obtained or inferred.

Nor is it the right of property alone that is thus confused. Mr. Spencer really puts himself in the same dilemma that, in Section 5, he proposes to Proudhon; for if, as in this chapter he asserts, no one can equitably become the exclusive possessor of any natural substance or product until the joint rights of all the rest of mankind have been made over to him by some species of quit claim —

> Then amongst other consequences, it follows that a man can have no right to the things he consumes for food. And if these are not his before eating them, how

can they become his at all? As Locke asks, "when do they begin to be his? when he digests? or when he eats? or when he boils? or when he brings them home?" If no previous acts can make them his property, neither can any process of assimilation do it; not even in their absorption into the tissues. Wherefore, pursuing the idea, we arrive at the curious conclusion, that, as the whole of his bones, muscles, skin, etc., have thus been built up from nutriment not belonging to him, a man has no property in himself — has no more claim to his own limbs than he has to the limbs of another — and has as good a right to his neighbor's body as to his own.

The fact is, that without noticing the change, Mr. Spencer has dropped the idea of equal rights to land, and taken up in its stead a different idea — that of joint rights to land. That there is a difference may be seen at once. For joint rights may be and often are unequal rights.

The matter is an important one, as it is the source of a great deal of popular confusion. Let me, therefore, explain it fully.

When men have equal rights to a thing, as for instance, to the rooms and appurtenances of a club of which they are members, each has a right to use all or any part of the thing that no other one of them is using. It is only where there is use or some indication of use by one of the others that even politeness dictates such a phrase as "Allow me!" or "If you please!"

But where men have joint rights to a thing, as for instance, to a sum of money held to their joint credit, then the consent of all the others is required for the use of the thing or of any part of it, by any one of them.

Now, the rights of men to the use of land are not joint rights: they are equal rights.

Were there only one man on earth, he would have a right to the use of the whole earth or any part of the earth.

When there is more than one man on earth, the right to the use of land that any one of them would have, were he alone, is not abrogated: it is only limited. The right of each to the use of land is still a direct, original right, which he holds of himself, and not by the gift or consent of the others; but it has become limited by the similar rights of the others, and is therefore an equal right. His right to use the earth still continues; but it has become, by reason of this limitation, not an absolute right to use any part of the earth, but (1) an absolute right to use any part of the earth as to which his use does not conflict with the equal rights of others (*i. e.*, which no one else wants to use at the same time), and (2) a co-equal right to the use of any part of the earth which he and others may want to use at the same time.

It is, thus, only where two or more men want to use the same land at the same time that equal rights to the use of land come in conflict, and the adjustment of society becomes necessary.

If we keep this idea of equal rights in mind — the idea, namely, that the rights are the first thing, and the equality merely their limitation — we shall have no difficulty. It is through forgetting this that Mr. Spencer has been led into confusion.

In Chapter IX., "The Right to the Use of the Earth," he correctly apprehends and states the right to the use of land as an equal right. He says:

> Each of them is free to use the earth for the satisfaction of his wants,
> Provided he allows all others the same liberty.

Here, in the first clause, is the primary right; in the second clause, the proviso or limitation.

But in the next chapter, "The Right of Property," he has, seemingly without noticing it himself, substituted for the idea of equal rights to land the idea of joint rights to land. He says (Section 1):

> No amount of labor bestowed by an individual upon a part of the earth's surface can nullify the title of society to that part, . . . no one can, by the mere act of appropriating to himself any wild, unclaimed animal or fruit, supersede the joint claims of other men to it. It may be quite true that the labor a man expends in catching or gathering, gives him a better right to the thing caught or gathered, than any *one* other man; but the question at issue is, whether by labor so expended he has made his right to the thing caught or gathered, greater than the pre-existing rights of all other men put together. And unless he can prove that he has done this, his title to possession cannot be admitted as a matter of *right*, but can be conceded only on the ground of convenience.

Here the primary right—the right by which "each of them is free to use the earth for the satisfaction of his wants"—has been dropped out of sight, and the mere proviso has been swelled into the importance of the primary right, and has taken its place.

What Mr. Spencer here asserts, without noticing his change of position, is not that the rights of men to the use of land are equal rights, but that they are joint rights. And, from this careless shifting of ground, he is led, not only into hypercritical questioning of Locke's derivation of the right of property, but into the assumption that a man can have no *right* to the wild berries he has gathered on an untrodden prairie, unless he can prove the consent of all other men to his taking them. This *reductio ad absurdum* is a deduction from the idea of joint rights to land, whereas the deduction from the equality of rights to land would be that under such circumstances a man would have a right to take all the berries he wanted, and that *all* other men together would have no right to forbid him. Indeed, so great is Mr. Spencer's confusion, and so utterly unable does he become to assume a clear and indisputable right of property, that he has to cut the knot into which he has tangled the subject, and finds no escape but in the preposterous declaration that the dictates of ethics have no application to, and do not exist in, any social state except that of the highest civilization.

Locke was not in error. The right of property in things produced by labor — and this is the only true right of property — springs directly from the right of the individual to himself, or as Locke expresses it, from his "property in his own person." It is as clear and has as fully the sanction of equity in any savage state as in the most elaborate civilization. Labor can, of course, produce nothing without land; but the right to the use of land is a primary individual right, not springing from society, or depending on the consent of society, either expressed or implied, but inhering in the individual, and resulting from his presence in the world. Men must have rights before they can have equal rights. Each man has a right to use the world because he is here and wants to use the world. The equality of this right is merely a limitation arising from the presence of others with like rights. Society, in other words, does not grant, and cannot equitably withhold from any individual, the right to the use of land. That right exists before society and independently of society, belonging at birth to each individual, and ceasing only with his death. Society itself has no original right to the use of land. What right it has with regard to the use of land is simply that which is derived from and is necessary to the determination of the rights of the individuals who compose it. That is to say, the function of society with regard to the use of land only begins where individual rights clash, and is to secure equality between these clashing rights of individuals.

What Locke meant, or at least the expression that will give full and practical form to his idea, is simply this: That the equal right to life involves the equal right to the use of natural materials; that, consequently, any one has a right to the use of such natural opportunities as may not be wanted by any one else; and that the result of his labor, so expended, does of right become his individual property against all the world. For, where one man wants to use a natural opportunity that no one else wants to use, he has a *right* to do so, which springs from and is attested by the fact of his existence. This is an absolute, unlimited right, so long and in so far as no one else wants to use the same natural opportunity. Then, but not till then, it becomes limited by the similar rights of others. Thus no question of the right of any one to use any natural opportunity can arise until more than one man wants to use the same natural opportunity. It is only then that any question of this right, any need for the action of society in the adjustment of equal rights to land, can come up.

Thus, instead of there being no right of property until society has so far developed that all land has been properly appraised and rented for terms of years, an absolute right of property in the things produced by labor exists from the beginning — is coeval with the existence of man.

In the right of each man to himself, and his right to use the world, lies the sure basis of the right of property. This Locke saw — just as the first man must have seen it. But Mr. Spencer, confused by a careless substitution of terms, has lost his grasp on the right of property and has never since recovered it.

Getting rid of the idea of joint rights we see that the task of securing, in an advanced and complex civilization, the equal rights of all to the use of land is much simpler and easier than Mr. Spencer and the land nationalizationists suppose; that it is not necessary for society to take land and rent it out. For so long as only one man wants to use a natural opportunity it has no value; but as soon as two or more want to use the same natural opportunity, a value arises. Hence, any question as to the adjustment of equal rights to the use of land occurs only as to valuable land; that is to say, land that has a value irrespective of the value of any improvements in or on it. As to land that has no value, or to use the economic phrase, bears no rent, whoever may choose to use it has not only an equitable title to all that his labor may produce from it, but society cannot justly call on him for any payment for the use of it. As to land that has a value, or, to use the economic phrase in the economic meaning, bears rent, the principle of equal freedom requires only that this value, or economic rent, be turned over to the community. Hence the formal appropriation and renting out of land by the community is not necessary: it is only necessary that the holder of valuable land should pay to the community an equivalent of the ground value, or economic rent; and this can be assured by the simple means of collecting an assessment in the form of a tax on the value of land, irrespective of improvements in or on it.

In this way all members of the community are placed on equal terms with regard to natural opportunities that offer greater advantages than those any one member of the community is free to use, and are consequently sought by more than one of those having equal rights to use the land. And, since the value of land arises from competition and is constantly fixed by competition, the question of who shall use this superior land desired by more than one is virtually decided by competition, which settles clashing individual desires by determining at once both who shall be accorded the use of the superior land, and who will make the most productive use of it. In this way all, including the user of the superior natural opportunity, obtain their equal shares of the superiority, by the taking of its value for their common uses; while all the difficulties of state rental of land and of determining and settling for the value of improvements are avoided. This is the single tax system.

CHAPTER V.

MR. SPENCER'S CONFUSION AS TO VALUE.

It seems strange that a man who has touched on so many branches of knowledge, and written so largely on sociology, should even to this time have neglected the primary principles of political economy. But the failure to distinguish between equal rights and joint rights, which has so confused Mr. Spencer, is allied with a failure to comprehend the nature of rent. In "Social Statics" he assumes that all land ought to pay rent to the state, and on this assumption, joined with and perhaps giving rise to his transmutation of equal rights into joint rights, he bases important conclusions as to the right of property. In his latest book, "Justice," he is not only no clearer in this but shows plainly — what in "Social Statics" is only to be surmised — his failure to appreciate the nature of the fundamental economic concept — value.

Thus, in the chapter in "Justice" entitled "The Right of Property," he speaks (Section 55) of weapons, instruments, dress and decorations as "things in which the value given by labor bears a specially large relation to the value of the raw material," and thus continues:

When with such articles we join huts, which, however, being commonly made by the help of fellow men who receive reciprocal aid, are thus less distinctly products of an individual's labor, we have named about all the things in which, at first, the worth given by effort is great in comparison with the inherent worth; for the inherent worth of the wild food gathered or caught is more obvious than the worth of the effort spent in obtaining it. And this is doubtless the reason why, in the rudest societies, the right of property is more definite in respect of personal belongings than in respect of other things.

Passing the queer notion that things made by two or more men are *less distinctly* products of an individual's labor than things made by one man, we have here the idea that there is an inherent value in the materials and spontaneous products of nature — *i.e.*, land in the economic category — a value underived from labor and independent of it. The slightest acquaintance with economic literature, the slightest attempt to analyze the meaning of the term, would have shown Mr. Spencer the preposterousness of this idea.

The word "value" in English speech has two meanings. One is that of usefulness or utility, as when we speak of the value of the ocean to man, the value of fresh air, the value of the compass in navigation, the value of the stethescope in the diagnosis of disease, the value of the antiseptic treatment in surgery; or, when having in mind the intrinsic merits of the mental production itself, its quality of usefulness to the reader or to the public, we speak of the value of a book. In this sense of utility there *is* inherent worth or intrinsic value — a quality or qualities belonging to the thing itself, which give it usefulness to man.

The other sense of the word "value" — the sense

in which Mr. Spencer uses it when he says that the value given by labor bears a specially large ratio to the value of the raw materials, or when, later on, he substitutes the word "worth" as synonymous in such use for "value" — is that of exchangeability. In this sense value or worth means not utility, not any quality inhering in the thing itself, but a quality which gives to the possession of a thing the power of obtaining other things in return for it or for its use. Thus we speak of the value of gold as greater than that of iron; of a book bound in cloth as being more valuable than a book bound in paper; of the value of a copyright or a patent; of the lessening in the value of steel by the Bessemer process, or in that of aluminium by the improvements in extraction now going on.

Value in this sense — the usual sense — is purely relative. It exists from and is measured by the power of obtaining things for things by exchanging them. It is therefore absurd to speak in this sense of inherent worth or intrinsic value. Air has the intrinsic quality of utility, or value in use, to the very highest degree; for without an abundant supply of it we could not live a minute. But air has no value whatever in the sense of value in exchange. We speak of a man of worth, or a worthy man, when we mean a man whose inherent qualities entitle him to esteem; but, when we speak of a man who is worth so and so much, or of a wealthy man, we speak of him in certain external relations, purely relative, which give him the power of obtaining things by exchange. A worthy man may retain his worthiness through all changes of external conditions; but a wealthy man is in this the creature of external conditions: the same man, in nothing changed, may through external circumstances be wealthy to-day and poverty-stricken to-morrow.

Now, what gives to anything the quality of exchangeability for other things — the quality of worth in exchange, or value? — for, having explained the other sense of the word "value," I will in subsequent use confine it to its common and proper sense, that of value in exchange.

That a thing has value, and may be exchanged for other things, is not because of its weight, or color, or divisibility, or any other quality inherent in the thing itself. Nor yet is it because of its utility to man. Utility is necessary to value, for nothing can be valuable unless it has the quality of gratifying some physical or mental desire of man, though it be but a fancy or whim. But utility of itself does not give value. Air, which has the highest utility, has no value, while diamonds, which have very little utility, have great value.

If we ask ourselves the reason of such variations in the quality of value; if we inquire what is the attribute or condition concurring with the presence, absence, or degree of value attaching to anything — we see that things having some form of utility or desirability, are valuable or not valuable, as they are hard or easy to get. And, if we ask further, we may see that with most of the things that have value this difficulty or ease of getting them, which determines value, depends on the amount of labor which must be expended in producing them; *i.e.*, bringing them into the place, form and condition in which they are desired. Thus air, which is of the highest utility, since it is at every instant necessary to our existence, can be had without labor. It is the substance of that ocean, enveloping the surface of the globe, in which we are constantly immersed. So far from requiring labor to get it, it forces itself upon us, requiring labor, when we are so disposed, to keep it away. Hence air, in spite of its high utility, has no value. Large and pure diamonds, on the contrary, since they are found only in few places and require much search and toil to get, can be had only with great labor. Hence, although they have very low utility, since they gratify only the sense of beauty and the desire for ostentation, they have very high value. Thus gold, weight for weight, is more valuable than silver, and much more valuable than iron, simply because it requires on the average more labor to get a given quantity of gold than to get the same quantity of silver, and much more than to get the same quantity of iron.

That as to such things as these the quality of value is derived from the labor required to produce them; and that, consequently, as to them at least, there is no such thing as inherent value — becomes clearer still when we consider how their value is affected by the increase or decrease of the requirement for labor.

Iron as compared to gold used to be much more valuable than it is now. Why? Because improved processes in smelting have lessened the labor of producing it. A few years since aluminium was more valuable than gold, because it took more labor to get it. Labor-saving improvements have already lowered the value of aluminium to less than that of silver, and little more than that of copper; and it is altogether likely that continued improvement will ere long bring it to that of iron. So the value of steel has been greatly lessened by the introduction of the Bessemer and other processes. So the value of beaver skins, of whalebone, of ivory, etc., has been increased by the growing scarcity of the animals from which they are derived, and the greater labor needed to obtain them. So, too, the improvement in transportation has lessened the value of things where it was a considerable item in the labor required for their production. And so, too, customs duties and other indirect taxes add to the value of things on which they fall, because their effect is to increase the amount of labor required to get such things.

It is thus seen, with regard at least to the greater number of valuable things, that there cannot be inherent or intrinsic value; and that value is simply an expression of the labor required for the production of such a thing. But there are some things as to which this is not so clear. Land is not produced by labor; yet land, irrespective of any improvements that labor has made on it, often has value. And so value frequently attaches to the forms of the economic term "land" that we commonly speak of as natural products, such as trees in their natural state, ore in the vein, stone or marble in the quarry, or sand or gravel in the bed.

Yet a little examination will show that such facts are but exemplifications of the general principle, just as the rise of a balloon and the fall of a stone both exemplify the universal law of gravitation.

To illustrate: Let us suppose a man accidentally to stumble on a diamond. Without the expenditure of labor, for his effort has been merely that of stooping down to pick it up, an action in itself a gratification of curiosity, he has here a great value. But what causes this value? Clearly, it springs from the fact that, as a rule, to get such a diamond will require much expenditure of labor. If any one could pick up diamonds as easily as in this case, diamonds would have no value.

Or, here is a grove of natural trees, which, as they stand, and before the touch of labor, have a considerable value, so that a lumberman will gladly pay for the privilege of cutting them. But has not this value the same cause as in the case of the diamond — the fact that to get such lumber ordinarily (or to speak exactly, to get the last amount of such lumber that the existing demand requires) the lumberman must go so far that the cost of transportation will equal what he is willing to pay for these trees?

In the naturally wooded sections of the United States trees had at first not merely no value, but were deemed an incumbrance, to get rid of which the settler had to incur the labor of felling and burning. Then lumber had no value except the cost of working it up after it had been felled; for the work of felling had for object the getting rid of the tree. But soon, as clearing proceeded, the desire to get rid of trees so far slackened, as compared with the desire to get lumber, that trees were felled simply for the purpose of getting the lumber. Then the value of lumber increased, for the labor of felling trees had to be added to it; but trees themselves had as yet no value. As clearing still proceeded and the demand for lumber grew with growing population, it became necessary to go farther and farther to get trees. Then transportation began to be a perceptible element in the labor of getting lumber, and trees that had been left standing began to have a value, since by using them the labor of transportation would be saved. And, as the requirement for lumber has compelled the lumbermen to go farther and farther, the value of the trees remaining has increased. But this value is not inherent in the trees: it is a value having its basis in labor, and representing a saving of labor that must otherwise be incurred. The reason that the tree at such place has a value is, that obtaining it there secures the same result as would the labor of transporting a similar amount of lumber from the greater distance to which resort must be made to satisfy the demand for lumber.

And so with the value which attaches to ore or sand or gravel. Such value is always relative to the labor required to obtain such things from points of greater distance or of less abundant deposits, to which in the existing demand resort is necessary.

We thus see the cause and nature of land values, or, to use the economic term, of rent. No matter how fertile it may be, no matter what other desirable quality it may have, land has no value until, whether by reason of quality or location, the relation between it and the most advantageous land to which labor may have free access gives to its use an advantage equivalent to the saving of labor. Or, to state in another way that accepted theory which is sometimes styled Ricardo's theory of rent, and which John Stuart Mill called the *pons asinorum* of political economy: it is, that the rent of land is determined by the excess of the produce it will yield over that which the same application can obtain from the least productive land in use.

To grasp this principle is to see that land has no inherent value; that value can never attach to all land, but only to some land, and may arise on particular land either by reason of production being extended to inferior land, or by reason of the development of superior productiveness in special localities.

Thus the phenomena of value are at bottom illustrations of one principle. The value of everything produced by labor, from a pound of chalk or a paper of pins to the elaborate structure and appurtenances of a first-class ocean steamer, is resolvable on analysis into an equivalent of the labor required to reproduce such a thing in form and place; while the value of things not produced by labor, but nevertheless susceptible of ownership, is, in the same way, resolvable into an equivalent of the labor which the ownership of such a thing enables the owner to obtain or save.

The reason why in rude societies value attaches mainly or wholly to things produced by labor, and there is little or no value to land — or, to use Mr. Spencer's phrase, "the reason why in the rudest societies the right of property is more definite in respect of personal belongings than in respect of other things" — is not, as he puts it, that weapons, implements, dress, decorations, and huts are "about all the things in which, at first, the worth given by effort is great in comparison with the inherent worth; for the inherent worth of the wild food gathered or caught is more obvious than the worth of the effort spent in obtaining it." It is that labor products always cost effort, and hence have value from the first; while land costs no effort, and in such societies the growth of population and the development of the arts have as yet attached little or no special advantages to the use of particular pieces of land, which at a later stage are equivalent to a saving of effort. Thus, in the absence of the artificial scarcity produced by monopoly, land of practically like quality is easy to obtain and has no value.

For in a sparse population and a rude state of the arts, those differences in productiveness between particular pieces of land, which are so marked in our great cities that land on one side of a street may have twice the value of land on the other side, do not exist. Even differences in the original qualities of land, that with us give rise to enormous differences in value, would, with the hunter or herdsman, or even with the agriculturist, be of no moment. Who, until production had passed even the agricultural stage, could have imagined that in the soil of Western Pennsylvania lurked differences that would some time give to one spot a value hundreds of thousand times greater than that of seemingly the same kind of land around it; or that a narrow strip in Nevada might be worth millions, while the land about it was worth nothing at all?

It is this confusion of Mr. Spencer as to rent and value that has led him into confusion as to the right of property; and that, at first at least, prevented him from seeing that to secure the equal rights of men to land, it is not necessary that society should take formal possession of land and let it out, and, consequently, that the difficulties he anticipated in taking possession of improved land were imaginary.

CHAPTER VI.

FROM "SOCIAL STATICS" TO "POLITICAL INSTITUTIONS."

BUT the crudities and seeds of error in Mr. Spencer's treatment of the land question in "Social Statics" were of little moment beside its sterling merit. It was a clear, and, if we except or explain the one incongruous passage, an unfaltering assertion of a moral truth of the first importance — a truth at that time ignored. If Mr. Spencer had not mastered all the details of its application, he had at least seen and stated the fundamental principle that all men have natural, equal and inalienable rights to the use of land; that the right of ownership which justly attaches to things produced by labor cannot attach to land; that neither force, nor fraud, nor consent, nor transfer, nor prescription can give validity to private property in land; and that equal rights to land are still valid, "all deeds, customs, and laws notwithstanding," and must remain valid "until it can be demonstrated that God has given one charter of privileges to one generation and another to the next."

He had, moreover, shown that the practical recognition of these equal rights, even in the rude way he proposed, involved no community of goods and nothing like socialism or communism; but that it may be carried out in a way that "need cause no very serious revolution in existing arrangements," and would be "consistent with the highest civilization."

And this was in England, where the whole structure of society — social, political and industrial — was based on and embedded in private ownership of land, and in the year 1850, when, except by a few "dreamers," no one thought of making any distinction between property in land and property in other things, and by the vast majority of men of all classes and conditions private property in land was looked on as something that always had existed, and, in the nature of things, always must exist.

But beyond the warnings that this was no way to success, which he doubtless received from friends, there is no reason to think that this revolutionary utterance of Mr. Spencer in "Social Statics" brought him the slightest unpleasant remonstrance at the time or for years after. If "Sir John and his Grace" — by which phrase Mr. Spencer had personified British landed interests — ever heard of the book, it was to snore, rather than to swear. So long as they feel secure, vested wrongs are tolerant of mere academic questioning; for those who profit by them, being the class of leisure and wealth, are also the class of liberal education and tastes, and often find a pleasing piquancy in radicalism that does not go beyond their own circles. A clever sophist might freely declaim in praise of liberty at the table of a Roman emperor. Voltaire, Rousseau and the encyclopedists were the fashionable fad in the drawing-rooms of the French aristocracy. And at the beginning of this century, and for years afterwards, a theoretical abolitionist, provided he did not talk in the hearing of the servants, might freely express his opinion of slavery among the cultured slaveholders of our Southern states. Thomas Jefferson declared his detestation of slavery, and, despite amendment, "writ large" his condemnation of it in the Declaration of Independence itself. Yet that declaration was signed by slaveholders and read annually by slaveholders, and Jefferson himself never became unpopular with slaveholders. But when the "underground railway" got into operation; when Garrison and his colleagues came with their demand for immediate, unconditional emancipation, then the feeling changed, and the climate of the South began to grow hot for any one even suspected of doubting the justice of the "peculiar institution."

So it was with private property in land for over thirty years after "Social Statics" was written. One of the first to congratulate me on "Progress and Poverty," when only an author's edition of a few hundred copies had been printed, and it seemed unlikely to those who knew the small demand for works on economic questions that there would ever be any more, was a very large landowner. He told me that he had been able freely to enjoy what he was pleased to term the clear logic and graceful style of my book, because he knew that it would only be read by a few philosophers, and could never reach the masses or "do any harm."

For a long time this was the fate of Mr. Spencer's declaration against private property in land. It doubtless did good work, finding here and there a mind where it bore fruit. But the question had not passed beyond, and Mr. Spencer's book did not bring it beyond, the point of extremely limited academic discussion.

Though it brought Mr. Spencer the appreciation of a narrow circle, and thus proved the beginning of his literary career, "Social Statics" had but a small and slow circulation. The first and only English edition, as is usual with books for which no large sale is expected, was printed directly from type, without making stereotype plates. As Mr. Spencer tells us in the preface to his recent "revision and abridgment," it took some ten years to sell that, after which, the sale not being enough to justify republication, which, in the absence of stereotype plates, would have involved the cost of setting up the type again, the book went out of print in England, without having attracted any general attention. This was but in the nature of things; for the class that profits by any wrong which affects the distribution of wealth must be the wealthy class, and consequently the class whose views dominate the existing organs of opinion. And until recently private property in land has been the sacred white elephant of English respectability, not even to be named without a salaam. The conspiracy of silence was therefore all that such a book could expect until it began to make way among the masses, and that neither the style of "Social Statics" nor the price at which it was published was calculated for. A similar fate to that which "Social Statics" met in England befell a very similar book, covering much the same ground — "The Theory of Human Progression," by Patrick Edward Dove, published a little before "Social Statics," but in the same year, and also asserting the equal right to the use of land.

While Dove is not so elaborate as Spencer, he is clearer in distinctly disclaiming the idea of compensation, and in proposing to take ground rent for public purposes by taxation, abolishing all other taxes. His book must have done some good work on the minds it reached, but it passed out of print and was practically forgotten.

"Social Statics," however, had a happier fate in passing over to the United States. Among those early attracted by Mr. Spencer's writings was the late Professor E. L. Youmans, who in 1861–62 sought his acquaintance and entered into correspondence with him. Professor Youmans's tireless energy, backed by the resources of the strong publishing house of D. Appleton & Co. of New York, with which he was connected, was thenceforward devoted to the task of popularizing Mr. Spencer and his teachings in the United States. Through the efforts of Professor Youmans, D. Appleton & Co. arranged with Mr. Spencer for the publication of his books, and in 1864, making stereotype plates, they re-issued "Social Statics," and from that time forward kept it in print; and as may be seen, both from the preface of 1877 in their edition of "Social Statics" and from the preface to the abridgment of 1892, such English demand as existed was supplied by the sending-over of sheets printed by them [1]—a more economical arrangement than that of printing a book of small circulation on

[1] A number of years passed — some ten, I think — before the edition was exhausted; and as the demand seemed not great enough to warrant the setting up of type for a new edition, it was decided to import an edition from America, where the work had been stereotyped. After this had been disposed of a third edition was similarly imported. —*Preface to "Social Statics Abridged and Revised," 1892.*

both sides of the Atlantic. Thus in a larger sphere it continued to circulate, mainly in the United States (where Mr. Spencer's reputation, aided by the active work of Professor Youmans, grew first in popular estimation), and to some small extent at least in Great Britain. But the radical utterances on the land question that it contained gave no evidence of attracting active interest or passing for more than an academic opinion.

Between 1850 and 1882, during the greater part of which time Mr. Spencer was engaged in developing his evolution philosophy, nothing more that I am aware of was heard from him on the land question. But "Social Statics," in the United States at least, increased in circulation as Mr. Spencer's reputation grew, and its declarations continued to stand for his opinions without even a suggestion of change. Several prefaces, or notes, were from time to time added, but none indicating any modification of views with regard to the land question. The last of these was dated January 17, 1877. In this, certain changes in Mr. Spencer's opinions as to teleological implications, the political status of women, the useful effects of war, etc., are noted, but there is no modification of the radical utterances as to the tenure of land. On the contrary, he says:

> To the fundamental ethical principle expressing in its abstract form what we know as justice I still adhere. I adhere also to the derivative principles formulated in what are commonly called personal rights, of this or that special kind.

In "Political Institutions," which, after some magazine publications of chapters, was finally published in book form in the early part of 1882, Mr. Spencer again spoke of the tenure of land, and in a way that would lead any one acquainted with his previous fuller treatment of the subject to understand that he still adhered to all that he had said in "Social Statics."

"Political Institutions," like the other divisions of "The Principles of Sociology" to which it belongs, is "in part a retrospect and in part a prospect." First explaining in accordance with his general theory how social institutions have been evolved, Mr. Spencer proceeds to indicate what he thinks will be the course of their further evolution. In the chapter on "Property," after some pages of examination he says, (Section 539):

> Induction and deduction uniting to show as they do that at first land is common property, there presents itself the question — How did the possession of it become individualized? There can be little doubt of the general nature of the answer. Force, in one form or other, is the sole cause adequate to make the members of a society yield up their joint claim to the area they inhabit. Such force may be that of an external aggressor or that of an internal aggressor: but in either case it implies militant activity.

Having thus repeated in a form adapted to the character of the book the declaration of "Social Statics" that the original deeds to private property in land were written with the sword, he proceeds to develop it, showing by the way a comprehension of the fact that the feudal tenures did not recognize the private property in land which has grown up since, or, as he phrases it, that "the private land-ownership established by militancy is an incomplete one," being qualified by the claims of serfs and other dependants, and by obligations to the crown or state, and saying:

> In our own case the definite ending of these tenures took place in 1660; when for feudal obligations (a burden on landowners) was substituted a beer-excise (a burden on the community).

From this, in a passage which will hereafter appear,[1] he proceeds to consider what is likely to be the future evolution of land tenure. Saying that "ownership established by force does not stand on the same footing as ownership established by contract," he likens individual property in land to property in slaves, and intimates that as the one has disappeared so the other will doubtless disappear, to make place for land-holding "by virtue of agreements between individuals as tenants and the community as land-owner, . . . after making full allowance for *the accumulated value artificially given.*"

This is a re-statement of what was said in Section 9 of "Social Statics," where, speaking of the once universal assumption that slavery was natural and right and the better faith that had been generated, he adds:

> It may by-and-by be perceived that equity utters decrees to which we have not yet listened, and men may then learn that to deprive others of their rights to the use of the earth is to commit a crime inferior only in wickedness to the crime of taking away their lives or personal liberty.

Thus, in so far as was consistent with the very different scope and character of the book, Mr. Spencer

---

[1] See Mr. Spencer's letter to the *Times*, pp. 98–9.

repeated in March, 1882, the views on the land question that he had set forth in 1850. And in this connection the words I have italicized are noteworthy as showing what was really meant in that incongruous passage in "Social Statics" previously discussed.

With this re-assertion in "Political Institutions" of the views on the land question set forth in "Social Statics" we must draw a line in our review.

PART II.

REPUDIATION.

I. LETTER TO THE ST. JAMES'S GAZETTE.
II. "THE MAN *VERSUS* THE STATE."
III. LETTER TO THE TIMES.
IV. THIS APOLOGY EXAMINED.
V. SECOND LETTER TO THE TIMES.
VI. MORE LETTERS.

There are people who hate anything in the shape of exact conclusions; and these are of them. According to such, the right is never in either extreme, but always half way between the extremes. They are continually trying to reconcile *Yes* and *No*. Ifs and buts, and excepts, are their delight. They have so great a faith in "the judicious mean" that they would scarcely believe an oracle, if it uttered a full-length principle. Were you to enquire of them whether the earth turns on its axis from east to west, or from west to east, you might almost expect the reply — "A little of both," or "Not exactly either." It is doubtful whether they would assent to the axiom that the whole is greater than its part, without making some qualification. — *Herbert Spencer, 1850.*

CHAPTER I.

LETTER TO THE ST. JAMES'S GAZETTE.

With the early years of the last decade a marked change in common thought began to show itself; and the doctrine of natural, inalienable and equal rights to land, which Mr. Spencer had avowed as it were in academic groves, began to stir in the hearts and minds of common men, and to make way among the great disinherited. Vaguely and blindly, the land question had come to the front in Ireland, and in this form forced its way into British politics. And "Progress and Poverty," first published in the United States in 1879, had begun, by the close of 1882, to circulate in Great Britain as no economic work had ever circulated before, re-inforcing what Herbert Spencer had said of the ethical injustice of private property in land with the weight of political economy and the proposal of a practical measure for restoring equal rights. Everywhere, in short, that the English language is spoken, the idea of natural rights to the use of land, that in 1850 seemed dead, was beginning to revive with a power and in a form that showed that the struggle for its recognition had at last begun.

Believing in Mr. Spencer's good faith, deeming him not a mere prater about justice, but one who ardently desired to carry it into practice, we who sought to promote what he himself had said that equity sternly commanded naturally looked for some word of sympathy and aid from him, the more so as the years had brought him position and influence, the ability to command attention, and the power to affect a large body of admirers who regard him as their intellectual leader.

But we looked in vain. When the Justice that in the academic cloister he had so boldly invoked came forth into the streets and market-places, to raise her standard and call her lovers, Mr. Spencer, instead of hastening to greet her, did his best to get out of her way, like the young wife in the old story, who charmed the by-standers with her invocations to Death to take her rather than her elderly husband, but who, when Death rapped at the door and asked, "Who calls me?" quickly replied, "The gentleman in the next room!"

In March, 1882, when Mr. Spencer issued "Political Institutions," and even in August of the same year, when he left England for a visit to the United States, there was on the surface of English society nothing to indicate that such views as he had expressed in "Social Statics" were any nearer attracting popular attention and arousing feeling than in 1850, for the Irish land movement was considered what it indeed was in the main, — not an attack on private property in land, but an effort of Irish tenants to become land-owners or to get better terms. But when Mr. Spencer returned, towards the close of November, it was to find that the days of contemptuous tolerance on the part of Sir John and his Grace had gone, and that all that was deemed "respectable" in English society had become roused to the wickedness of those who denied the validity of private property in land.

To explain the change that had taken place in this brief interval I must refer to my own books.

"Progress and Poverty" was received by the English press, as all such books are at first, in silence or with brief derision. Messrs. Kegan Paul, Trench & Co., who first published it in England, in sheets brought from the United States, were on publication able to sell only twenty copies in all the three kingdoms. But ere long it began to make its way, and when, towards the close of August, 1882, a sixpenny edition was issued, it began to sell in tens and scores of thousands, "in the alleys and back streets of England," the *Quarterly Review* said — "audibly welcomed there as a glorious gospel of justice."

Hardly was this cheap edition out and beginning to circulate, when, conjoining with it my pamphlet on "The Irish Land Question,"[1] which had also been published in England in cheap form, the *Times*, on September 11, 1882, gave to "Progress and Poverty" a long and fair review. At once the silence of the press was broken, and from the quarterlies to the comic papers the British journals began to teem with notices and references, most of them naturally of a kind that made the Duke of Argyll seem mild when he called me "such a preacher of unrighteousness as the world has never seen," and spoke of my "immoral doctrines" and "profligate conclusions," the

---

[1] Now published under the name of "The Land Question," since its effort is to show that the Irish Land Question is simply the universal land question.

"unutterable meanness of the gigantic villainy" I advocated, and so on.

And from being regarded in this way in the very society in which as a great philosopher he had come to be an honored member, it was evident that Mr. Spencer could not escape if he adhered to his views. For although "Social Statics" was little known in England, the quotations I had made from it, both in "Progress and Poverty" and in "The Irish Land Question" were bringing those views into sharp prominence.

This was the situation as Mr. Spencer found it on his return from the United States. The burning question — a question beside which that of chattel slavery was almost small — had been raised in England. And he must either stand for the truth he had seen, and endure social ostracism for it, or he must deny it.

"Blessed are ye when men shall revile you, and persecute you, and say all manner of evil against you!" For this to the man who has striven to uproot a great wrong — a wrong that by the fact of its hitherto unquestioned existence has necessarily enlisted on its side all the powerful influences that dominate the organs of opinion and rule society — is the sure sign that the day he has hoped for is at hand.

When, in 1850, Mr. Spencer had said that the rent of land could be collected by an agent or deputy agent of the community, quite as well as by an agent of Sir John or his Grace, he must have known that if ever his proposition attracted the attention of the interests he thus personified he would be denounced in all the established organs of opinion, and in "polite society" regarded as a robber. *Then*, I am inclined to think he would have hailed with joy such indications of the progress of thought. But in 1882, he no sooner found that Sir John and his Grace had been aroused by such a proposition and were likely to hear that he had made it, than he hastened to get the evidence out of their sight, and as far as he could to deny it. At once, it seems from what he tells us in 1892, he "resolved not again to import a supply" of "Social Statics,"[1] and took the first opportunity to write a letter.

The *Edinburgh Review*, for January, 1883, in an article entitled "The Nationalization of the Land," reviewed "Progress and Poverty"—as fairly, it seemed to me, as could be expected, but of course adversely. In doing so it referred to what Mr. Spencer had said on the land question in "Social Statics," giving him credit for proposing to indemnify land-owners, and quoting with that interpretation the incongruous sentences in Section 9. In concluding it said:

> Writers like Mr. George and Mr. Herbert Spencer are at war not only with the first principles of political economy and of law, of social order and domestic life, but with the elements of human nature. . . . To attack the rights of private property in land is to attack property in its most concrete form. If landed property is not secure, no property can be protected by law, and the transmission of wealth, be it large or small, is extinguished. With it expires the perpetuity of family life, and that future which cheers and ennobles the labor of the present with the hopes of the future. These are the doctrines of communism, fatal alike to the welfare of society and to the moral character of man.

---

[1] Ten years ago, after all copies of the third edition had been sold, I resolved not again to import a supply to meet the still continued demand.—*Preface to "Social Statics, Abridged and Revised," 1892.*

This brought out from Mr. Spencer a letter to the *St. James's Gazette* of London, an able Tory journal. Since he was writing on the subject, here was an opportunity for Mr. Spencer to correct the misapprehension (as I now think it to be) that he had in "Social Statics" proposed to compensate land-owners for their land. And, if he wished to defend himself against the charge of attacking property rights and upholding the doctrines of communism, here was an opportunity for him to show, for all of us as well as for himself, that the denial of the justice of private property in land involves no denial of true property rights. Or if he chose to do so, here was a chance for him straightforwardly to recant, to apologize to land-owners, and to plead that he was young and foolish when he asserted, as quoted by the *Edinburgh*, that "equity does not permit property in land, and that the right of mankind to the earth's surface is still valid, all deeds, customs, and laws notwithstanding."

But, instead of manfully defending the truth he had uttered, or straightforwardly recanting it, Mr. Spencer sought to shelter himself behind ifs and buts, perhapses and it-may-bes, and the implication of untruths. Here is his letter:

To the Editor of the St. James's Gazette:

During my absence in America, there appeared in the *St. James's Gazette* (27th of October, 1882) an article entitled "Mr. Herbert Spencer's Political Theories." Though, when it was pointed out to me after my return, I felt prompted to say something in explanation of my views, I should probably have let the matter pass had I not found that elsewhere such serious misapprehensions of them are being diffused that rectification seems imperative.

Before commenting on the statements of your contributor, I must devote a paragraph to certain more recent statements which have far less justification. In old days among the Persians, the subordination of subject to ruler was so extreme that, even when punished, the subject thanked the ruler for taking notice of him. With like humility I suppose that now, when after I have been publishing books for a third of a century "the leading critical organ" has recognized my existence, I ought to feel thankful, even though the recognition draws forth nothing save blame. But such elation as I might otherwise be expected to feel is checked by two facts. One is that the *Edinburgh Review* has not itself discovered me, but has had its attention drawn to me by quotations in the work of Mr. Henry George — a work which I closed after a few minutes on finding how visionary were its ideas. The other is that, though there has been thus made known to the reviewer a book of mine published thirty-two years ago, which I have withdrawn from circulation in England, and of which I have interdicted translations, he is apparently unconscious that I have written other books, sundry of them political; and especially he seems not to know that the last of them, "Political Institutions," contains passages concerning the question he discusses. Writers in critical journals which have reputations to lose usually seek out the latest version of an author's views; and the more conscientious among them take the trouble to ascertain whether the constructions they put on detached passages are warranted or not by other passages. Had the Edinburgh reviewer read even the next chapter to the one from which he quotes, he would have seen that, so far from attacking the right of private property, as he represents, my aim is to put that right upon an unquestionable basis, the basis alleged by Locke being unsatisfactory. He would have further seen that, so far from giving any countenance to communistic doctrines, I have devoted four sections of that chapter to the refutation of them. Had he dipped into the latter part of the work, or had he consulted the more recently published "Study of Sociology" and "Political Institutions," he would not have recklessly coupled me with Mr. George as upholding "the doctrines of communism, fatal alike to the welfare of society and to the moral character of man"; for he would have discovered the fact (familiar to many, though unknown to him) that much current legislation is regarded by me as communistic, and is for this reason condemned as socially injurious and individually degrading.

The writer of the article in the *St. James's Gazette* does not represent the facts correctly when he says that the view concerning ownership of land in "Social Statics" is again expounded in "Political Institutions"—"not so fully, but with as much confidence as ever." In this last work I have said that, "though industrialism has thus far tended to individualize possession of land, while individualizing all other possession, *it may be doubted* whether the final stage is at present reached." Further on I have said that "at a stage still more advanced, *it may be* that private ownership of land will disappear"; and that "*it seems possible* that the primitive ownership of land by the community . . . will be revived." And yet again I have said that "*perhaps* the right of the community to the land, thus tacitly asserted, will, in time to come, be overtly asserted." Now it seems to me that the words I have italicised imply no great "confidence." Contrariwise, I think they show quite clearly that the opinion conveyed is a tentative one. The fact is, that I have here expressed myself in a way much more qualified than is usual with me; because I do not see how certain tendencies, which are apparently conflicting, will eventually work out. The purely ethical view of the matter does not obviously harmonize with the political and the politico-economical views; some of the apparent incongruities being of the kind indicated by your contributor. This is not the place to repeat my reasons for thinking that the present system will not be the ultimate system. Nor do I propose to consider the obstacles, doubtless great, which stand in the way of change. All which I wish here to point out is that my opinion is by no means a positive one; and, further, that I regard the question as one to be dealt with in the future rather than at present. These two things the quotations I have given above prove conclusively. I am, etc.,

HERBERT SPENCER.

Mr. Spencer has had much to say of the unfairness of his critics. But this reply is not merely unfair; it is dishonest, and that in a way that makes flat falsehood seem manly.

From this letter the casual reader would understand that the Edinburgh reviewer, on the strength of detached passages, had charged Mr. Spencer with attacking the right of private property and upholding socialism, in a sense unwarranted by the context and disproved by the next chapter; and that the passage quoted from "Political Institutions" covers the same ground and disproves the constructions put on "Social Statics."

The fact is, that the *Edinburgh Review* had not charged either Mr. Spencer or myself with more than attacking private property in land. This we had both unquestionably done, not only in the passages it had quoted, but in many others. It had made no misconstruction whatever. What it had said of "attacking the right of private property" and "upholding the doctrines of communism" was a mere rhetorical flourish, made as an inference from, and by way of reply to, our denial of the right of private property in land. Mr. Spencer ignores the real charge and assumes the mere inference to be the charge. Thus, changing the issue, he cites the next chapter as if it disproved the *Edinburgh's* charge. This chapter (Chapter X., "The Right of Property") which has been given in full, contains nothing to lessen the force of the attack on private property in land made in the preceding chapter. On the contrary, in this chapter he reiterates his attack on private property in land, and seeks a basis for property by carrying the idea that the community should control land to the length of absurdity.

Nor was the writer in the *St. James's* unjustified in taking the reference to land in "Political Institutions" to be a briefer indorsement of the views more fully set forth in "Social Statics;" for "Political Institutions" refers to private property in land as established by force, says that it does not stand on the same basis as ownership established by contract, likens it to slavery and predicts its abolition—expressions which, in the absence of any modification of the views elaborately asserted in "Social Statics," could be taken in no other way than as indorsing them. The passages Mr. Spencer quotes no more modify the view of land ownership set forth in "Social Statics" than Lord Lytton's "Coming Race" controverts Adam Smith's "Wealth of Nations." In "Social Statics" Mr. Spencer declares what *ought* to be done; in the passage he quotes from "Political Institutions" he is prognosticating as to what it is likely *will* be done. By now substituting prognostication for declaration of right, Mr. Spencer seeks to convey the false impression that the Edinburgh reviewer has been guilty of carelessness, and the writer in the *St. James's* of misrepresentation, and that he himself has never gone further than to express the guarded opinion that at some time, a great way off, men *may* substitute a common ownership of land for private ownership.

Mr. Spencer is more than unfair, too, in assuming that the charge of upholding communism, etc., is applicable to me, though not to him. For, although my book was too visionary for him to read, he had at least read the *Edinburgh's* article, and knew that the charge against me had no other ground than that against him — the denial of the moral validity of private property in land.

Even what he says about such a plain matter of fact as the withdrawal of "Social Statics" from circulation in England conveys untruth.

The grievance that Mr. Spencer here alleges is that the *Edinburgh Review* had commented on a book "published thirty-two years ago, which I have withdrawn from circulation in England, and of which I have interdicted translations." What is to be understood from this, and what Mr. Spencer evidently intended to have understood, is that he had, presumably years before, withdrawn "Social Statics" from circulation — not in the mere territory of England, as distinguished from Scotland, Ireland or the United States, but — in English. To make sure of this understanding, he adds that he has interdicted translations — which means, not in other places, but in other languages than English. Now the truth is, that at the time he thus wrote, that book was being published by his arrangement in the United States, as it had been for years before, and continued to be for years afterwards; and that up to this very time he had been importing it into England, and circulating it there. The only filament of truth in this statement, which though made incidentally is of prime importance to his purpose, is, as we now discover from his own utterance in 1892, that at this very time, or possibly a few weeks previous, *he had resolved* not again to import any more copies of "Social Statics" into England from the United

States, though still keeping the book in circulation there, to be bought by whomsoever would buy!

As for the rest of this letter, the admirers of Mr. Spencer may decide for themselves what kind of ethical views they are that will not harmonize with political economy, and what kind of political economy it is that will not harmonize with ethics, and what they think of an ethical teacher who, on a question that involves the health and happiness, nay, the very life and death of great bodies of men, shelters himself behind such phrases as, "it may be doubted," "it may be," "it seems possible," and so on, and endeavors to make them show that he regards the matter of right as one to deal with in the future and not at present.

This letter is not a withdrawal or a recantation of what Mr. Spencer had said against private property in land. It does not rise to that dignity. It is merely an attempt to avoid responsibility and to placate by subterfuge the powerful landed interests now aroused to anger. But it does indicate that a moral change had come over Mr. Spencer since he wrote "Social Statics."

In several places in that book occurs the strong, idiomatic phrase, "a straight man." This letter to the *St. James's* is not the letter of a straight man.

But as hypocrisy is the homage vice pays to virtue, so the very crookedness of this letter indicates Mr. Spencer's reluctance to flatly deny the truth to which he had borne witness. He no more wanted to deny it than Simon Peter to deny his Lord. But the times had changed since he wrote "Social Statics." From an unknown man, printing with difficulty an unsalable book, he had become a popular philosopher, to whom all gratifications of sense, as of intellect, were open.[1] He had tasted the sweets of London society, and in the United States, from which he had just returned, had been hailed as a thinker beside whom Newton and Aristotle were to be mentioned only to point his superiority. And, while the fire in the hall of the High Priest was warm and pleasant, "society" had become suddenly aroused to rage against those who questioned private property in land. So when the *St. James's* and the *Edinburgh*, both of them chosen organs of Sir John and his Grace, accused Herbert Spencer of being one of these, it was to him like the voices of the accusing damsels to Peter. Fearing, too, that he might be thrust out in the cold, he, too, sought refuge in an alibi.

---

[1] His recreations have been systematic — concerts, operas, theatres, billiards, salmon-fishing, yachting, city rambles, and country excursions; and it has been his fixed rule, when work grew burdensome, to strike his tasks abruptly and go away for pleasure and amuse himself till work itself again became attractive and enjoyable. — *Preface, by Professor E. L. Youmans, to " Herbert Spencer on the Americans and the Americans on Herbert Spencer, being a full report of his interview and of the proceedings at the Farewell Banquet of Nov. 9, 1882." New York: D. Appleton & Co.*

CHAPTER II.

"THE MAN *VERSUS* THE STATE."

MR. SPENCER'S letter to the *St. James's Gazette* seems to have produced the effect he intended, and though in the United States, D. Appleton & Co. continued to advertise and sell "Social Statics," and to send to Mr. Spencer his royalties upon it;[1] in England, Sir John and his Grace were satisfied that he had been much maligned by garbled extracts from an early work that he had since suppressed.

But Mr. Spencer himself seems to have felt that to make his position among the adherents of the House of Have quite comfortable, he must do something positive as well as negative. So we find his next work to be one which the Liberty and Property Defence League, a society formed in London for defending private property in land, have ever since been active in pushing.

In 1884 Mr. Spencer issued four magazine articles, "The New Toryism," "The Coming Slavery," "The Sins of Legislators," and "The Great Political Superstition," which were then published in a volume entitled "The Man *versus* the State," and have since

[1] The American people have returned the compliment by purchasing more than a hundred thousand of his books reprinted in this country, and upon every volume of which he has been paid as if he had been an American author. —*Professor E. L. Youmans: "Herbert Spencer on the Americans and the Americans on Herbert Spencer."*

been used (1892) to fill out the revised edition of "Social Statics."

These essays are strongly individualistic, condemning even bitterly any use of governmental powers or funds to regulate the conditions of labor or alleviate the evils of poverty. In this Mr. Spencer was continuing and accentuating a line begun in "Social Statics," and, in the view of those who think as I do, was in the main right; for governmental interferences and regulations and bonuses are in their nature restrictions on freedom, and cannot cure evils that primarily flow from denials of freedom.

But what in these essays marks a new departure, what makes their individualism as short-sighted as socialism, and brutal as well, is that they assume that nothing at all is needed, in the nature either of palliative or remedy; that they utterly ignore the primary wrong from which proceed the evils that socialism blindly protests against. In them Mr. Spencer is like one who might insist that each should swim for himself in crossing a river, ignoring the fact that some had been artificially provided with corks and others artificially loaded with lead. He is like the preachers who thundered to slaves, "Thou shalt not steal!" but had no whisper against the theft involved in their enslavement.

The burden of these essays is, "If any would not work, neither should he eat!" This is declared to be a tenet of the Christian religion, justified by science, as indeed, though much ignored by Christians and by scientists, it is.

To whom does Mr. Spencer refer as the idlers who yet eat?

"Why, of course," the reader of "Social Statics" would say, "he refers to Sir John and his Grace, and to the land-holding dukes to whom in 'Social Statics' he refers by name — to them and their class, pre-eminently. For they never work, and take pride that their fathers and grandfathers and great-grandfathers never worked. Yet they eat, whoever else goes hungry, and that of the best."

But the reader of "Social Statics" would be wrong. Mr. Spencer does not refer to them, nor allude to them, nor seem to think of them. The people on whom he would enforce the command "If any would not work, neither should he eat!" are not the fashionable idlers, whose only occupation is to kill time and "get an appetite," but the poor idlers who say they have no work. "Say, rather, that they either refuse work or quickly turn themselves out of it!" cries the indignant philosopher, regardless now of what he once insisted on — that these men are disinherited; robbed by unjust law of their birthright, of their rightful share in the element without which no man can work; dependent, therefore, on others for leave to work, and often not getting that leave.

In 1850, while condemning the socialistic palliatives for poverty, Mr. Spencer at the same time recognized the truth that prompts them. He was not content to show the futility of such attempts to assuage the evils of undeserved poverty without pointing out the giant wrong from which undeserved poverty springs. He began his enumeration of the evils of over-government, not as now, by merely denouncing what is done in kindly though misplaced efforts to help the down-trodden, but by recognizing the primary wrong. Beginning this enumeration (page 293, "Social Statics") he says:

As the first item on the list there stands that gigantic injustice inflicted on nineteen-twentieths of the community by the usurpation of the soil — by the breach of their rights to the use of the earth. For this the civil power is responsible — has itself been a party to the aggression — has made it legal, and still defends it as right.

And of the moral truth involved in theories that in "The Man *versus* the State" he unreservedly denounces, he says ("Social Statics," pp. 345–46):

Erroneous as are these poor-law and communist theories — these assertions of a man's right to a maintenance and of his right to have work provided for him — they are, nevertheless, nearly related to a truth. They are unsuccessful efforts to express the fact, that whoso is born on this planet of ours thereby obtains some interest in it — may not be summarily dismissed again — may not have his existence ignored by those in possession. In other words, they are attempts to embody that thought which finds its legitimate utterance in the law — all men have equal rights to the use of the Earth. The prevalence of these crude ideas is natural enough. A vague perception that there is something wrong about the relationship in which the great mass of mankind stand to the soil and to life, was sure eventually to grow up. After getting from under the grosser injustice of slavery men could not help beginning in course of time, to feel what a monstrous thing it was that nine people out of ten should live in the world on sufferance, not having even standing room, save by allowance of those who claimed the earth's surface. Could it be right that all these human beings should not only be without claim to the necessaries of life — should not only be denied the use of those elements from which such necessaries are obtainable — but should further be unable to exchange their labor for such necessaries, except by leave of their more fortunate fellows? Could it be that the majority had thus no better title to existence than one based upon the good-will or convenience of the minority? Could it be that these landless men had "been *mis*-sent to this earth, where all the seats were already taken"? Surely not. And if not, how ought matters to stand? To all which questions, now forced upon men's minds in more or less definite shapes, there come, amongst other answers, these theories of a right to a maintenance and a right of labor. Whilst, therefore, they must be rejected as untenable, we may still recognize in them the imperfect utterance of the moral sense in its efforts to express equity.

The wrong done to the people at large, by robbing them of their birthright — their heritage in the earth — is, indeed, thought by some a sufficient excuse for a poor law, which is regarded by such as an instrumentality for distributing compensation. There is much plausibility in this construction of the matter. But . . . why organize a diseased state? Sometime or other this morbid constitution of things, under which the greater part of the body politic is cut off from direct access to the source of life, must be changed.

Of anything like this there is in "The Man *versus* the State" no word. Mr. Spencer again takes up his parable against government interference; but he takes it up with every reference to the gigantic injustice inflicted upon nineteen-twentieths of his countrymen omitted; with everything excluded that might be offensive to the rich and powerful.

Nor does he shrink from misrepresenting those who stand for the truth he has now virtually, though not openly, abandoned. In his letter to the *St. James's Gazette* he declared that he had not read my work; but in "The Coming Slavery" occurs this:

Communistic theories, partially indorsed by one Act of Parliament after another, and tacitly if not avowedly favored by numerous public men seeking supporters, are being advocated more and more vociferously by popular leaders, and urged on by organized societies. There is the movement for land nationalization which, aiming at a system of land-tenure, equitable in the abstract, is, as all the world knows, pressed by Mr. George and his friends with avowed disregard for the just claims of existing owners, and as the basis of a scheme going more than half-way to state-socialism.

And in "The Sins of Legislators" this:

And now this doctrine [that society as a whole has an absolute right over the possessions of each member], which has been tacitly assumed, is being openly proclaimed. Mr. George and his friends, Mr. Hyndman and his supporters, are pushing the theory to its logical issue. They have been instructed by examples, yearly increasing in number, that the individual has no rights but what the community may equitably over-ride; and they are now saying — "It shall go hard, but we will better the instruction, and abolish individual rights altogether."

Charity requires the assumption that when Mr. Spencer wrote these passages he had not read anything I had written; and that up to the present time when he has again reprinted them he has not done so.

For in nothing I have ever written or spoken is there any justification for such a characterization. I am not even a land nationalizationist, as the English and German and Australian land nationalizationists well know. I have never advocated the taking of land by the state or the holding of land by the state, further than needed for public use; still less the working of land by the state. From my first word on the subject I have advocated what has come to be widely known as "the single tax;" *i.e.*, the raising of public revenues by taxation on the value of land irrespective of the improvements on it — taxation which, as fast as possible and as far as practicable, should be made to absorb economic rent and take the place of all other taxes. And among the reasons I have always urged for this has been the simplification of government and the doing away of the injustice of which governments are guilty in taking from individuals property that rightfully belongs to the individual. I have not gone so far as Mr. Spencer in limiting the functions of government, for I believe that whatever becomes a necessary monopoly becomes a function of the state; and that the sphere of government begins where the freedom of competition ends, since in no other way can equal liberty be assured. But within this line I have always opposed governmental interference. I have been an active, consistent, and absolute free-trader, and an opponent of all schemes that would limit the freedom of the individual. I have been a stauncher denier of the assumption of the right of society to the possessions of each member, and a clearer and more resolute upholder of the rights of property than has Mr. Spencer. I have opposed every proposition to help the poor at the expense of the rich. I have always insisted that no man should be taxed because of his wealth, and that no matter how many millions a man might rightfully get, society should leave to him every penny of them.

All this would have been evident to Mr. Spencer if he had read any one of my books before writing about me. But he evidently prefers the easier method which Parson Wilbur, in Lowell's "Biglow Papers," was accustomed to take with "a print called the *Liberator*, whose heresies," he said, "I take every proper opportunity of combating, and of which, I thank God, I have never read a single line."

To do him justice, I do not think Mr. Spencer had any desire to misrepresent me. He was prompted to it by the impulse that always drives men to abuse those who adhere to a cause they have betrayed, as the readiest way of assuring Sir John and his Grace that no proposal to disturb their rentals would in the future come from *him*.

Another thing, however, is to be noticed here — the admission that the movement for land nationalization is "aiming at a system of land-tenure equitable in the abstract." Mr. Spencer has not reached the point of utterly denying the truth he had seen. The abolition of private property in land he still admits is equitable in the abstract.

Now, what is meant by equitable in the abstract? Let "Social Statics," page 64, tell us:

> For what does a man really mean by saying of a thing that it is "theoretically just," or "true in principle," or "abstractedly right"? Simply that it accords with what he, in some way or other, perceives to be the established arrangements of Divine rule. When he admits that an act is "theoretically just," he admits it to be that which, in strict duty, should be done. By "true in principle," he means in harmony with the conduct decreed for us. The course which he calls "abstractedly right," he believes to be the appointed way to human happiness. There is no escape. The expressions mean this, or they mean nothing.

CHAPTER III.

LETTER TO THE TIMES.

No one can boldly utter a great truth, and then, when the times have become ripe for it, and his utterance voices what is burning in hearts and consciences, whisper it away. So despite his apology to landlords in the *St. James's Gazette*, and the pains he had taken to make his peace with them in "The Man *versus* the State," what he had said on the land question in "Social Statics" came up again to trouble Mr. Spencer.

But for a long time his position on the land question was almost as dual as that of Dr. Jekyll and Mr. Hyde. In his personal circle it was doubtless assumed that he was a staunch supporter of private property in land, and if his earlier opinions were known there it was understood that he was sorry for them. And he had become, if not an active member, at least a valued ally of the Liberty and Property Defence League. But in a wider circle what he had written against private property in land was telling with increasing force. For to this wider circle his *St. James's* apology had hardly reached, and even when known was not deemed a recantation of the opinions deliberately expressed in "Social Statics," which he still, through D. Appleton & Co., continued to publish, without any modification whatever. The steady growth of the movement that began with the publication of "Progress and Poverty" everywhere enlisted active men in the propagation of the idea of the equality of rights to land and called wide attention to what he had said on that subject. They naturally seized on the argument against the justice of private property in land in Chapter IX. of "Social Statics," and spread it broadcast, as the utterance of one now widely esteemed the greatest of philosophers. Of all else that Mr. Spencer has written, there is nothing that has had such a circulation as has thus been given to this chapter. It was printed and is still being printed by many American newspapers,[1] and was issued in tract form for free distribution in the United States, Canada and Australia; editions of hundreds of thousands being issued at a time,[2] many of which must have reached Great Britain, even if it was not reprinted there.

This wide circulation of his condemnation of private property in land did not, it is probable, much trouble Mr. Spencer, since it did not reach his London circle. But in November, 1889 — six years after his letter to the *St. James's Gazette* — some echoes of it made their way into the *Times*, the very journalistic centre of high English respectability.

The matter thus got into the *Times:* Mr. John Morley, Member of Parliament for Newcastle, being

---

[1] Even as I write I am constantly receiving, especially from the West, copies of papers which contain Chapter IX. of "Social Statics," and which in ignorance of all he has since said, continue to speak of Mr. Spencer as an advocate of equal rights to land.

[2] About the time I ran for Mayor of New York (1886) on a platform which attracted great attention to the idea of equal rights to land, one enthusiastic advocate of the idea, Mr. W. J. Atkinson, himself printed some 500,000 copies.

in that city, was interviewed by some of his constituents, representing a labor organization. Among other questions land nationalization was brought up; Mr. John Laidler, a bricklayer, speaking for it. Mr. Morley expressing dissent, Mr. Laidler cited the authority of Mr. Spencer in support of the ideas that land had been made private property by force and fraud, and should be appropriated by the community for the benefit of all. The *Times* of November 5th contained a report of this interview.

This report in the *Times* aroused Mr. Spencer at once. For although he had no objection to the circulation of his radical utterances in America, where through D. Appleton & Co. he was still publishing and advertising "Social Statics," it was evidently quite a different matter to him that they should be known in the pleasant circle wherein with Sir John and his Grace and the peers and judges of the Liberty and Property Defence League he was personally dwelling. He promptly sent this letter to the *Times*. It appeared on the 7th.

To the Editor of the Times.

SIR: During the interview between Mr. Morley and some of his constituents, reported in your issue of the 5th inst., I was referred to as having set forth certain opinions respecting land ownership. Fearing that, if I remain silent, many will suppose I have said things which I have not said, I find it needful to say something in explanation.

Already within these few years I have twice pointed out that these opinions (made to appear by those who have circulated them widely different from what they really are, by the omission of accompanying opinions) were set forth in my first work, published forty years ago; and that, for the last twelve or fifteen years, I have refrained from issuing new editions of that work and have interdicted translations, because, though I still adhere to its general principles, I dissent from some of the deductions.

The work referred to — "Social Statics" — was intended to be a system of political ethics — absolute political ethics, or that which ought to be, as distinguished from relative political ethics, or that which is at present the nearest practicable approach to it. The conclusion reached concerning land ownership was reached while seeking a valid basis for the right of property, the basis assigned by Locke appearing to me invalid. It was argued that a satisfactory ethical warrant for private ownership could arise only by contract between the community, as original owner of the inhabited area, and individual members, who became tenants, agreeing to pay certain portions of the produce, or its equivalent in money, in consideration of recognized claims to the rest. And in the course of the argument it was pointed out that such a view of land ownership is congruous with existing legal theory and practice; since in law every land-owner is held to be a tenant of the Crown — that is, of the community, and since, in practice, the supreme right of the community is asserted by every Act of Parliament which, with a view to public advantage, directly or by proxy takes possession of land after making due compensation.

All this was said in the belief that the questions raised were not likely to come to the front in our time or for many generations; but, assuming that they would sometime come to the front, it was said that, supposing the community should assert overtly the supreme right which is now tacitly asserted, the business of compensation of land-owners would be a complicated one —

> One that perhaps cannot be settled in a strictly equitable manner. . . . Most of our present land-owners are men who have, either mediately or immediately, either by their own acts or by the acts of their ancestors, given for their estates equivalents of honestly earned wealth, believing that they were investing their savings in a legitimate manner. To justly estimate and liquidate the claims of such is one of the most intricate problems society will one day have to solve.

To make the position I then took quite clear, it is needful to add that, as shown in a succeeding chapter, the insistence on this doctrine, in virtue of which "the right of property obtains a legitimate foundation," had for one of its motives the exclusion of Socialism and Communism, to which I was then as profoundly averse as I am now.

Investigations made during recent years into the various forms of social organization, while writing the "Principles of Sociology," have in part confirmed and in part changed the views published in 1850. Perhaps I may be allowed space for quoting from "Political Institutions" a paragraph showing the revised conclusions arrived at:

> At first sight it seems fairly inferable that the absolute ownership of land by private persons must be the ultimate state which industrialism brings about. But though industrialism has thus far tended to individualize possession of land while individualizing all other possession, it may be doubted whether the final stage is at present reached. Ownership established by force does not stand on the same footing as ownership established by contract; and though multiplied sales and purchases, treating the two ownerships in the same way, have tacitly assimilated them, the assimilation may eventually be denied. The analogy furnished by assumed rights of possession over human beings helps us to recognize this possibility. For, while prisoners of war, taken by force and held as property in a vague way (being at first much on a footing with other members of a household) were reduced more definitely to the form of property when the buying and selling of slaves became general; and, while it might centuries ago have been thence inferred that the ownership of man by man was an ownership in course of being permanently established, yet we see that a later stage of civilization, reversing this process, has destroyed ownership of man by man. Similarly, at a stage still more advanced, it may be that private ownership of land will disappear. As that primitive freedom of the individual which existed before war established coercive institutions and personal slavery comes to be re-established as militancy declines, so it seems possible that the primitive ownership of land by the community, which, with the development of coercive institutions, lapsed in large measure or wholly into private ownership, will be revived as industrialism further develops. The *régime* of contract, at present so far extended that the right of property in movables is recognized only as having arisen by exchange of services or products under agreements, or by gift from those who had acquired it under such agreements, may be further extended so far that the products of the soil will be recognized as property only by virtue of agreements between individuals as tenants and the community as land-owner. Even now, among ourselves, private ownership of land is not absolute. In legal theory land-owners are directly or indirectly tenants of the Crown (which in our day is

equivalent to the state, or, in other words, the community); and the community from time to time resumes possession after making due compensation. Perhaps the right of the community to the land, thus tacitly asserted, will in time to come be overtly asserted and acted upon after making full allowance for the accumulated value artificially given. . . . There is reason to suspect that, while private possession of things produced by labor will grow even more definite and sacred than at present, the inhabited area, which cannot be produced by labor, will eventually be distinguished as something which may not be privately possessed. As the individual, primitively owner of himself, partially or wholly loses ownership of himself during the militant *régime*, but gradually resumes it as the industrial *régime* develops, so possibly the communal proprietorship of land, partially or wholly merged in the ownership of dominant men during evolution of the militant type, will be resumed as the industrial type becomes fully evolved (pp. 643–646).

The use of the words "possible," "possibly," and "perhaps" in the above extracts shows that I have no positive opinion as to what may hereafter take place. The reason for this state of hesitancy is that I cannot see my way toward reconciliation of the ethical requirements with the politico-economical requirements. On the one hand, a condition of things under which the owner of, say, the Scilly Isles might make tenancy of his land conditional upon professing a certain creed or adopting prescribed habits of life, giving notice to quit to any who did not submit, is ethically indefensible. On the other hand, "nationalization of the land," effected after compensation for the artificial value given by cultivation, amounting to the greater part of its value, would entail, in the shape of interest on the required purchase-money, as great a sum as is now paid in rent, and indeed a greater, considering the respective rates of interest on landed property and other property. Add to which, there is no reason to think that the substituted form of administration would be better than the existing form of administration. The belief that land would be better managed by public officials than it is by private owners is a very wild belief.

What the remote future may bring forth there is no saying; but with a humanity anything like that we now know, the implied reorganization would be disastrous.

I am, etc., HERBERT SPENCER.

ATHENÆUM CLUB, Nov. 6.

CHAPTER IV.

THIS APOLOGY EXAMINED.

To drop into one of Mr. Spencer's favorite methods of illustration:

"I am told," said the respectable grandmother, with a big stick in her hand, "that you are the boy who broke down my fence and told all the other boys that they were at liberty to go into my orchard and take my apples."

"It is not true," replied the trembling small boy; "I didn't do it. And I didn't mean to do it. And when I did it I was only trying to mend your fence, which I found was weak. And the reason I did it was to keep bad boys out. And I have always said you ought to be paid for your apples. And I won't do it again! And I am certain your apples would give boys stomach-ache."

This letter to the *Times* repeats the same line of excuse made six years before in the *St. James's Gazette*. Emboldened by the success of that apology, for no one seems to have thought it worth while to point out its misstatements, Mr. Spencer undertakes to face down the Newcastle bricklayer in the same way, and with even bolder crookedness.

The question in issue is a question of fact—whether, as asserted by Mr. Laidler, Mr. Spencer had in "Social Statics" advocated land nationalization, and incidentally, whether he had declared that the land had been made private property by force and fraud. Without venturing specifically to deny this, Mr. Spencer denies it by implication, and gives an impression thus expressed editorially by the *Times* on the 9th of November:

> So without denying that he did once say something of the sort, he (Mr. Spencer) explains that it was forty years ago, and that for the last fifteen years he has been doing all that he can to suppress the book in which he said it, and that he never meant his words to have any bearing upon practical questions.

Put into straightforward English, what Mr. Spencer says in this letter to the *Times* is —

That he had not favored land nationalization.

That he had been made to appear to have done so by quotations from "Social Statics" divested of their qualifying context.

That for the last twelve or fifteen years he had stopped the publication of that work.

That "Social Statics" was not intended to suggest practical political action.

That what was said therein of land-ownership was said in the effort to find a valid basis for the right of property, and to exclude socialism and communism; that it involved no departure from the existing legal theory and practice; was said in the belief that the land question would not come to the front for many generations, and admitted the right of the land-owners to compensation.

That his present conclusions are, that while possibly the community may some time resume land after due compensation to land-owners, he has no positive opinion as to whether it will or not.

That as to this he cannot harmonize ethics with political economy, for while a condition may be imagined under which private land ownership might be injurious, its abolition would require the payment to land-owners of as great and indeed a greater sum than is now paid in rent; would involve the management of land by public officials, and that with humanity anything like that we now know, this would be disastrous.

All this, so far as it relates to the question in issue, is simply not true.

Mr. Spencer, in "Social Statics," *did* condemn private property in land, *did* advocate the resumption of land by the community, *did* unequivocally and unreservedly, and with all his force, declare for what is now called land-nationalization. That he did so does not rest on any forcing of words, any wresting of sentences from their context. It is the burden of all he says on the subject, and of the most vital part of the book. In the whole volume there is no word in modification of the opinions so strongly and clearly expressed in the full quotations I have made.

Nor is it true that the conclusion of "Social Statics" concerning land ownership "was reached while seeking a valid basis for the right of property." It was reached as a primary corollary of the first principle: the freedom of every man to do all that he wills provided he infringes not the equal freedom of any other man, and was deduced directly from the facts of human existence:

Given a race of beings having like claims to pursue the objects of their desires — given a world adapted to the gratification of those desires — a world into which such beings are similarly born, and it unavoidably follows that they have equal rights to the use of this world.

Mr. Spencer's questioning of Locke's derivation of the right of property, so far from being the cause of his denial of the validity of private property in land, grows, as we have seen, out of his idea that the only right to land is that of the community. What he has to say against socialism and communism, instead of being a motive for his advocacy of land nationalization, is brought in to strengthen land nationalization by showing that it does not involve either. And so, what Mr. Spencer gives the *Times* to understand as to the congruity of the view of land ownership taken in "Social Statics" with existing legal theory and practice, is so flagrantly untrue that one wonders at its audacity.

As to what Mr. Spencer says of the intent of "Social Statics," the only intelligible meaning that can be put on it is that which the editor of the *Times* put, "That he never meant his words to have any bearing upon practical questions."

The exact phraseology is —

> The work referred to — "Social Statics" — was intended to be a system of Political Ethics — absolute political etnics, or that which ought to be, as distinguished from relative political ethics, or that which is at present the nearest practical approach to it.

If this means anything, it means that "Social Statics" was written to set forth a system of political ethics that cannot be carried into conduct now, and that no one is under any obligation to try to carry into conduct.

The applications of ethics, like the applications of mechanics, or chemistry, or any other science or body of laws, must always be relative, in the sense that one principle or law is to be taken in consideration with other principles or laws: so that conduct that would have the sanction of ethics where one is beset by robbers or murderers might be very different from the conduct that ethics would sanction under normal and peaceful conditions. In the "Data of Ethics," one of the more recent of the works which set forth the Spencerian Philosophy, written long after "Social Statics," this distinction between pure ethics and applied ethics is, by one of the confusions that in that philosophy pass for definitions, converted into a distinction between absolute ethics and relative ethics. Yet, if there be any sort of ethics that has no relation to conduct here and now, the best term for it is Pickwickian ethics.

But the question here is not a question of definition. It is a question of fact.

Now, however Mr. Spencer's opinions and wishes may have changed since "Social Statics" was written, that book still shows that, *when* he wrote it, his intention in exposing the iniquity of private property in land was to arouse public opinion to demand its abolition. In "Social Statics" he denounced not only private property in land: he denounced slavery, then in the United States and other countries, a still-living thing; he denounced protection; he denounced restrictions on the right of free speech, the denial to women of equal rights, the coercive education of children, the then existing restrictions on the franchise, the cost and delays of legal proceedings, the maintenance of poor laws, the establishment of state schools, government colonization, etc. Were all these pleas for reforms, some of which Mr. Spencer has lived to see accomplished, and others of which he is still advocating, Pickwickian also?

If Mr. Spencer, in what he had to say on the land question in "Social Statics," was talking mere abstract political ethics — something totally different from practical ethics — what did he mean by declaring that "Equity does not permit property in land"? What did he mean by saying that pure equity "enjoins a protest against every existing pretension to the individual possession of the soil, and dictates the assertion that the right of mankind at large to the earth's surface is still valid — all deeds, customs, and laws notwithstanding"? What did he mean by scornfully sneering at those who "are continually trying to reconcile yes and no," and who delight "in ifs, buts, and excepts"? What did he mean by saying, "In this matter of land-tenure the verdict of morality must be either yea or nay. Either men have a right to make the soil private property or they have not. There is no medium"? What did he mean in pointing out that what is now called land nationalization "need cause no very serious revolution in existing arrangements," and that "equity sternly commands it to be done"? What did he mean by putting, "as the first item on the list" of the injuries which government at the time he wrote was doing, "that gigantic injustice inflicted on nineteen-twentieths of the community by the usurpation of the soil — by the breach of their rights to the use of the earth"? What did he mean by saying that the only plausible defence of the poor laws was "the wrong done to people at large by robbing them of their birthright — their heritage in the earth" — by asking, "Why organize a diseased state?" — by declaring, "Some time or other this morbid constitution of things, under which the greater part of the body politic is cut off from direct access to the source of life, must be changed."

Did it all relate to the sort of ethics that has no bearing on practical questions?

Whatever may be the ethical views of Mr. Spencer now that his eyes have been put out, and he has been set to grind in the house of the lords of the Philistines, the young Samson of "Social Statics" with locks as yet unshorn by the social Delilah knew nothing of any such ethics. Not merely in what I have quoted, but throughout the book, from first page to last, the burden of "Social Statics" is the necessity, the sacred duty of destroying abuses that fetter the equal liberty of men. He sees, indeed — as who does not? — that before liberty can truly reign men must be fit for liberty; and he realizes that there may be social conditions in which liberty might temporarily work ill; but he insists again and again that whereever there is any yearning for liberty, any perception of the wrong done by its denial, there the time has come for the struggle against injustice to be made, and that the way to fit men for the enjoyment of rights is to destroy wrongs. The central thought of the book, that permeates all its parts, is that of a divinely-appointed order, which men are bound to obey — a God-given law, as true in the social sphere as the laws of physics are true in the physical sphere, to which all human regulations must be made to conform; and that this law is the law of equal freedom — the law from which is deduced the condemnation of private property in land. For those who palter with expediency; for those who would dally with wrong; for those who say that a thing is right in the abstract, but that practical considerations forbid its being carried into effect — Mr. Spencer, from the first page of "Social Statics" to the last, has nothing but the utmost contempt and scorn.

Here is one extract from the close of the introduction to "Social Statics (pp. 51, 56, 60–65) which will show how widely different were the ethics taught in "Social Statics" from what the author of the Spencerian philosophy, in 1889, told the *Times* they were:

> And yet, unable as the imperfect man may be to fulfil the perfect law, there is no other law for him. One right course only is open; and he must either follow that or take the consequences. The conditions of existence will not bend before his perversity; nor relax in consideration of his weakness. Neither, when they are broken, may any exception from penalties be hoped for. "Obey or suffer," are the ever-repeated alternatives. Disobedience is sure to be convicted. And there are no reprieves. . . .
>
> Our social edifice may be constructed with all possible labor and ingenuity, and be strongly cramped together with cunningly-devised enactments, but if there be no *rectitude* in its component parts — if it is not built on *upright* principles, it will assuredly tumble to pieces. As well might we seek to light a fire with ice, feed cattle on stones, hang our hats on cobwebs, or otherwise disregard the physical laws of the world, as go contrary to its equally imperative ethical laws.
>
> Yes, but there are exceptions, say you. We cannot always be strictly guided by abstract principles. Pru-

dential considerations must have some weight. It is necessary to use a little policy.

Very specious, no doubt, are your reasons for advocating this or the other exception. But if there be any truth in the foregoing argument, no infraction of the law can be made with impunity. Those cherished schemes by which you propose to attain some desired good by a little politic disobedience, are all delusive. . . .

The reasons for thus specially insisting on implicit obedience will become apparent as the reader proceeds. Amongst the conclusions inevitably following from an admitted principle, he will most likely find several for which he is hardly prepared. Some of these will seem strange; others impracticable; and it may be one or two wholly at variance with his ideas of duty. Nevertheless, should he find them logically derived from a fundamental truth, he will have no alternative but to adopt them as rules of conduct, which ought to be followed without exception. If there be any weight in the considerations above set forth, then, no matter how seemingly inexpedient, dangerous, injurious even, may be the course which morality points out as "abstractedly right," the highest wisdom is in perfect and fearless submission.

And these are the paragraphs with which (pp. 517, 518,) "Social Statics" closes:

Not as adventitious, therefore, will the wise man regard the faith that is in him — not as something which may be slighted, and made subordinate to calculations of policy; but as the supreme authority to which all his actions should bend. The highest truth conceivable by him he will fearlessly utter; and will endeavor to get embodied in fact his purest idealisms: knowing that, let what may come of it, he is thus playing his appointed part in the world — knowing that, if he can get done the thing he aims at — well: if not — well also; though not so well.

And thus, in teaching a uniform, unquestioning obedience, does an entirely abstract philosophy become one with all true religion. Fidelity to conscience — this is the essential precept inculcated by both. No hesitation, no paltering about probable results, but an implicit submission to what is believed to be the law laid down for us. We are not to pay lip homage to principles which our conduct wilfully transgresses. We are not to follow the example of those who, taking "*Domine dirige nos*" for their motto, yet disregard the directions given, and prefer to direct themselves. We are not to be guilty of that practical atheism, which, seeing no guidance for human affairs but its own limited foresight, endeavors itself to play the god, and decide what will be good for mankind, and what bad. But, on the contrary, we are to search out with a genuine humility the rules ordained for us — are to do unfalteringly, without speculating as to consequences, whatsoever these require; and we are to do this in the belief that then, when there is perfect sincerity — when each man is true to himself — when every one strives to realize what he thinks the highest rectitude — then must all things prosper.

Could there be any sadder commentary upon the Herbert Spencer who in 1889 wrote this letter to the *Times?*

I am not objecting that Mr. Spencer has changed his opinions. Such change might be for the better or might be for the worse, but it would at least be within his right. What I point out is that in this letter to the *Times*, as in his previous letter to the *St. James's Gazette*, Mr. Spencer does what is not within his right, what a straight man could not do — misstates what he previously did say.

And while Mr. Spencer, in this letter to the *Times*, is thus untruthful in regard to what he had taught in "Social Statics," he is equally untruthful in regard to his suppression of that book. His words are —

For the last twelve or fifteen years I have refrained from issuing new editions of that work, and have interdicted translations.

The plain meaning of this is, that for twelve or fifteen years prior to 1889 Mr. Spencer had stopped the publication of "Social Statics." There is no other honest construction. And this is the way in which it was understood. The *Times*, in its editorial comment on Mr. Spencer's letter, taking it to mean that "for the last fifteen years he had been doing all he could to suppress the book;" and Mr. Frederick Greenwood, who also commented on the letter, taking it to mean that "for the last fifteen years he had not allowed it to appear in any language."

As a matter of fact, this is not true. "Social Statics" was still being printed by Mr. Spencer's authorized publishers, D. Appleton & Co. of New York. The only scintilla of truth in this denial is that, as he has since (in 1892) stated, he had seven years before this resolved that he would import no more copies into England. As for the "interdiction of translations," I suppose this means that the book bore originally the usual English formula "Rights of translation reserved"; for, judging from its going out of print in England, and its never having been pirated in the United States, it is not likely that any further interdiction was needed to prevent its translation.

That Mr. Spencer should have continued the publication of "Social Statics" for years after he had told the readers of the *St. James's* and the *Times* that he had suppressed it, I can only account for on the ground that he did not care to deprive himself of what revenue he was drawing from its sale, and had really no objection to the circulation of his attacks on landlordism, so long as his London friends did not hear of it. Certain it is, that he could have withdrawn it at any time. Appleton & Co. are not book pirates, but honorable gentlemen, who publish Mr. Spencer's works under arrangement with their author, and even in the absence of a copyright law would certainly have ceased printing "Social Statics," if he had requested. To any one who knows them this needs no proof. But as a matter of fact, in 1885, when the controversy between Mr. Spencer and Mr. Frederic Harrison appeared in the *Nineteenth Century*, the Messrs. Appleton, thinking there would be a large American sale for it in book form, made plates and printed an edition.[1] They had barely published this when they suppressed it, as was understood, on a cabled request from Mr. Spencer. Not another copy went out. The copies printed were destroyed and the plates melted, although a rival firm did publish the controversy, and sell a considerable number. Or, if he had preferred that, D. Appleton & Co. would at any time have printed in "Social Statics" any retraction or modification of its expressions on the land question he had wished. But, while the preface prefixed to the book in 1864, and the note to Chapter IV. — a reply to Professor Sidgwick, inserted in 1875 — and the additional preface added in 1877, did set forth the modifications of Mr. Spencer's opinions about various other matters, they contain nothing to show any change of his opinions on the land question; and the book has continued to be published up to 1892 without any such modification.

---

[1] "The Nature and Reality of Religion. A Controversy between Frederic Harrison and Herbert Spencer. With an Introduction, Notes, and an Appendix on the Religious Value of the Unknowable, by Count D'Alviella." New York: D. Appleton & Co., 1, 3 and 5 Bond Street. 1885.

It is, of course, not for me to object that Mr. Spencer did not withdraw "Social Statics" in the only place where it was being published, or that he did not insert a retraction or modification of its utterances on the land question — although to me the wonder is that when, on his return to England in 1882, he seems to have definitely made up his mind to take the side of landlordism if pressed to it, he did not melt every plate and buy up every copy he could. I am only comparing Mr. Spencer's statements in the *Times* with the facts, because of the evidence the comparison gives of the character of the man, and because of the light it throws on the change in his opinions on the land question.

For this letter to the *Times* not only shows Mr. Spencer's intense desire to be counted on the side of "vested interests" in the struggle over the land question that was beginning, but it also shows how he was intending to join formally the ranks of the defenders of private property in land without the humiliation of an open recantation of what he had said in "Social Statics." By aid of double-barrelled ethics and philosophic legerdemain Mr. Spencer evidently hopes to keep some reputation for consistency and yet uphold private property in land. As compared with the apology in the *St. James's Gazette*, the new matter in this apology in the *Times* consists in the conversion of what he said in "Social Statics" (Section 7, Chapter IX.) as illustrating that "after all nobody does implicitly believe in landlordism," into a conformity with "existing legal theory *and practice*"; in the assumption that the compensation of which he had spoken (Section 9) meant compensation satisfactory to landlords; and boldest of all (for this in Chapter X., Section 3, he had expressly denied), in the assumption that the recognition of equal rights to land means the administration and management of land by public officials.

I should like also to call the attention of those who put faith in Mr. Spencer's philosophic acumen to the manner in which in this letter he withdraws to the Scilly Isles, and to the conditioning of the tenancy of land upon "professing a certain creed or adopting prescribed habits of life," his condemnation of private property in land, as ethically indefensible. They have their choice between intellectual incapacity and intellectual dishonesty. What logical difference is there between a small island and a large island? between the exaction of rent in personal services and the exaction of rent in money? Is it ethically defensible to deny to men their birthright, to permit them to live on the earth only on condition that they shall give up for the privilege all that their labor can produce save the barest living, to reduce them to straits that compel their children to grow up in squalor and vice and degradation worse than any heathenism, and to pass out of life in thousands before they are fairly in it; yet ethically indefensible to compel them to profess a certain creed or adopt prescribed habits of living? Ought it not be clear even to a philosopher's apprentice that if English landlords to-day do not prescribe the creed or habits of their tenants, it is only because they do not care to, but prefer generally to exercise their power in taking money rent? If the Duke of Westminster wanted to have a thousand retainers, clad in his livery, follow him to St. James's; if the

Duke of Norfolk cared to permit no one but Catholics to live on his estates; if the Duke of Argyll chose to have a buffoon at his elbow in cap and bells, they could have any of these things as readily, in fact even more readily, than could any Earl or Duke of the olden time. And so indeed could any of our great American land-owners. Did Mr. Spencer never see in London newspapers offers of employment, conditioned on the profession of a certain creed? Did he never, in passing to and from the Athenæum Club, see coachmen and footmen dressed in fantastic liveries and "sandwich men" clad ridiculously and shamefully? Does he not know that in the British Isles in his own time men are driven off the land to give place to wild beasts or cattle? And does he not know that the power of forbidding the use of his land gives to every land-owner the same powers of prescribing the conditions under which he will permit its use as any owner of the Scilly Isles possibly could have?

The view we thus get of Mr. Spencer's mental progress and processes is interesting both philosophically and psychologically. As, however, we shall find the lines of escape thus indicated amplified in "Justice," there is no need of examining them now. But what he here says on the matter of compensation has a special interest as throwing light on what he really meant in that incongruous passage in Section 9, Chapter IX., of "Social Statics," of which I have spoken. In this letter to the *Times* the only passage from "Social Statics" that is quoted, or indeed more than vaguely alluded to, is this. That Mr. Spencer intends the *Times* and its readers to understand this as a recognition in "Social Statics" of the justice of the claim of land-owners to compensation for their land is clear, for he carefully leaves out all mention of the closely-linked sentences that immediately follow the passage he quotes:

> But with this perplexity and our extrication from it abstract morality has no concern. Men having got themselves into this dilemma by disobedience to law, must get out of it as well as they can, and with as little injury to the landed class as may be.
>
> Meanwhile we shall do well to recollect that there are others beside the landed class to be considered. In our tender regard for the vested interests of the few, let us not forget that the rights of the many are in abeyance, and must remain so as long as the earth is monopolized by individuals. Let us remember, too, that the injustice thus inflicted on the masses of mankind is an injustice of the gravest nature . . . inferior only in wickedness to the crime of taking away their lives or personal liberties.

But while it is clear that Mr. Spencer wishes the *Times* and its readers to understand that he not only is, but always was, as good a compensationist as landlords could desire, he falls later on into an expression that again shows, as does the passage in "Political Institution," that the explanation I have put upon that seemingly incongruous passage in "Social Statics" is the one really intended. In the last part of the letter he speaks of "*compensation for the artificial value given by cultivation* amounting to the *greater part* of its value." Not compensation for *land*, but compensation only for improvements. But this would never satisfy land-owners, and so, without respect for the axiom that the whole is greater than its part, he proceeds to assert that compensation for this part will equal, and indeed exceed, the value of all they now get.

Thus we see both what the question of compensation had really been in Mr. Spencer's own mind, and how he now proposes to settle it, so that he may henceforward take the side of existing landlordism.

CHAPTER V.

SECOND LETTER TO THE TIMES.

In his letter to the *Times* Mr. Spencer had surely abased himself enough to have been let alone by those whose favor he had so dearly sought. But even those who profit by apostasy often like to show their contempt for the apostate. Though the *Times* itself accepted his apology, it added some contemptuous reproof, and gave place to letters from Mr. Greenwood, Professor Huxley and Sir Louis Mallet that must have been extremely galling to a renowned philosopher.

Here is the pertinent part of what the *Times* said:

> So, without denying that he did once say something of the sort, he explains that it was forty years ago, that for the last fifteen years he has been doing all he can to suppress the book in which he said it, and that he never meant his words to have any bearing upon practical questions. He was in fact engaged in constructing a system of "absolute political ethics, or that which ought to be," and he feels distinctly aggrieved by the transfer of his opinions from that transcendental sphere to the very different one in which Mr. Laidler and his friends are accustomed to dwell. . . . What Mr. Spencer said in his youth and inexperience he has unsaid in his maturer years and with more deliberate judgment. . . .
>
> Were we asked to point a moral for philosophers, we should bid them beware of meddling with the absolute. Forty years ago Mr. Spencer set forth in search of "ab-

solute political ethics," and constructed his system to his own satisfaction. But it turns out to have been the most relative of things after all, since for the last fifteen years it has ceased to be absolute even to the mind that conceived it. . . . Mr. Spencer settled that which ought to be, as regards land ownership, but a quarter of a century later we find him endeavoring, much to the credit of his modesty and candor, to suppress his own version of the absolute. He does not seem, however, to have abandoned the original quest, for he gives us his revised conclusions as to the absolute ethics of land-tenure, which appear to us to contain some of the original identical flaws which were to be found in the older version.

The communication from Mr. Frederick Greenwood, an able high-Tory journalist, was published by the *Times* on the 9th, under the heading "A Caution to Social Philosophers." Characterizing Mr. Spencer's letter to the *Times* as "a heavy lesson to political philosophers," Mr. Greenwood points out that "no matter how sorry Mr. Spencer may be for having misled so many poor men who habitually hang on the authority of great men like himself," yet the very quotation he makes from his "Political Institutions" contains the same seeds of error in its admission that "ownership established by force does not stand on the same footing as ownership established by contract," and in its admission that "the assimilation of the two ownerships may eventually be denied."

Sir Louis Mallet's letter, published on November 12th, was to similar effect. He pointed out that Mr. Spencer still admitted an analogy between private property in land and slavery, which, of course, to Sir Louis seemed dangerous and wicked.

Professor Huxley came at the philosopher in a bull-headed way that must have seemed very unkind.

Speaking in the name of those "to whom absolute political ethics and *a priori* politics are alike stumbling-blocks," and expressing the certainty that his friend, Mr. Spencer, would be the last person willingly to abet the tendency to sanction popular acts of injustice by antiquarian or speculative arguments, he asked him for a categorical answer to the question whether according to "absolute political ethics," A. B., who has bought a piece of land in England, as he might buy a cabbage, has a moral as well as a legal right to his land or not?

And he follows with these pertinent questions:

> If he does not, how does "absolute political ethics" deduce his right to compensation?
> If he does, how does "absolute political ethics" deduce the state's right to disturb him?

By this time Mr. Spencer must have wished he had not written to the *Times*, though it is a striking evidence of the little knowledge of "Social Statics" in England (a fact on which Mr. Spencer had evidently calculated), that in none of these letters, or in those that followed, do any of the "hecklers," with the one exception of Mr. Laidler, seem to have any knowledge of what Mr. Spencer had really said in that book — a knowledge that would have roused their ire to a far higher pitch, and enabled them to ask still harder questions.

The reader may wonder why in an attempt to deny his utterances in "Social Statics," Mr. Spencer should have printed the passage from "Political Institutions," which is in reality a re-affirmation of them. The only explanation I can offer is that he felt that he must print something, and had absolutely nothing else to print. For there is no word in all his works up to this time ("Justice" being yet to come) that gives the slightest evidence of any modification of the views set forth in "Social Statics." And since he had six years before successfully referred to this passage, as though it indicated a modification of his views, he probably felt safe in so using it a second time. Thinking that it would suffice to settle Mr. Laidler, he evidently did not calculate on its provoking a "fire in the rear," from his own friends, the adherents of landlordism, when he was giving up everything real, and only striving to save a semblance of consistency.

Mr. Spencer conveniently ignored the letters of Mr. Greenwood and Sir Louis Mallet, but he did make a pretence of answering Professor Huxley, in a letter published in the *Times*, November 15th.

Here is the letter, which, although the first paragraph only is pertinent to the task I have in mind, I give in full, in order to guard against Mr. Spencer's controversial habit of saying that his utterances have been garbled:

To the Editor of The Times.

SIR: As Professor Huxley admits that his friend A. B.'s title to his plot of land is qualified by the right of the state to dispossess him if it sees well—as, by implication, he admits that all land-owners hold their land subject to the supreme ownership of the state, that is, the community—as he contends that any force or fraud by which land was taken in early days does not affect the titles of existing owners, and *a fortiori* does not affect the superior title of the community—and as, consequently, he admits that the community, as supreme owner with a still valid title, may resume possession if it thinks well, he seems to me to leave the question standing very much where it stood; and since he, as I suppose, agrees with me that any such resumption, should a misjudgment lead to it, ought to be accompanied by due compensation for all artificial value given to land, I do not see in what respect we disagree on the land question. I pass, therefore, to his comments on absolute political ethics.

"Your treatment is quite at variance with physiological principles" would probably be the criticism passed by a modern practitioner on the doings of a Sangrado, if we suppose one to have survived. "Oh, bother your physiological principles" might be the reply. "I have got to cure this disease, and my experience tells me that bleeding and frequent draughts of hot water are needed." "Well," would be the rejoinder, "if you do not kill your patient, you will at any rate greatly retard his recovery, as you would probably be aware had you read Professor Huxley's 'Lessons on Elementary Physiology,' and the more elaborate books on the subject which medical students have to master."

This imaginary conversation will sufficiently suggest that, before there can be rational treatment of a disordered state of the bodily functions, there must be a conception of what constitutes their ordered state: knowing what is abnormal implies knowing what is normal. That Professor Huxley recognizes this truth is, I suppose, proved by the inclusion of physiology in that course of medical education which he advocates. If he says that abandonment of the Sangrado treatment was due, not to the teachings of physiology, but to knowledge empirically gained, then I reply that if he expands this statement so as to cover all improvements in medical treatment he suicidally rejects the teaching of physiological principles as useless.

Without insisting upon that analogy between a society and an organism which results from the interdependence of parts performing different functions — though I believe he recognizes this — I think he will admit that conception of a social state as disordered implies conception of an ordered social state. We may fairly assume that, in these modern days at least, all legislation aims at a better; and the conception of a better is not possible without conception of a best. If there is rejoicing because certain diseases have been diminished by precautions enforced, the implied ideal is a state in which these diseases have been extinguished. If particular measures are applauded because they have decreased criminality, the implication is that the absence of all crime is a *desideratum*. Hence, however much a politician may pooh-pooh social ideals, he cannot take steps toward bettering the social state without tacitly entertaining them. And though he may regard absolute political ethics as an airy vision, he makes bit by bit reference to it in everything he does. I simply differ from him in contending for a consistent and avowed reference, instead of an inconsistent and unacknowledged reference.

Even without any such strain on the imagination as may be required to conceive a community consisting entirely of honest and honorable men — even without asking whether there is not a set of definite limits to individual actions which such men would severally insist upon and respect — even without asserting that these limits must, in the nature of things, result when men have severally to carry on their lives in proximity with one another, I should have thought it sufficiently clear that our system of justice, by interdicting murder, assault, theft, libel, etc., recognizes the existence of such limits and the necessity for maintaining them; and I should have thought it manifest enough that there must exist an elaborate system of limits or restraints on conduct, by conformity to which citizens may co-operate without dissension. Such a system, deduced as it may be from the primary conditions to be fulfilled, is what I mean by absolute political ethics. The complaint of Professor Huxley that absolute political ethics does not show us what to do in each concrete case seems to be much like the complaint of a medical practitioner who should speak slightingly of physiological generalizations, because they did not tell him the right dressing for a wound or how best to deal with varicose veins. I cannot here explain further, but any one who does not understand me may find the matter discussed at length in a chapter on "Absolute and Relative Ethics" contained in the "Data of Ethics."

It appears to me somewhat anomalous that Professor

Huxley, who is not simply a biologist but is familiar with science at large, and who must recognize the reign of law on every hand, should tacitly assume that there exists one group of lawless phenomena — social phenomena. For if they are not lawless — if there are any natural laws traceable throughout them, then our aim should be to ascertain these and conform to them, well knowing that non-conformity will inevitably bring penalties. Not taking this view, however, it would seem as though Professor Huxley agrees with the mass of "practical" politicians, who think that every legislative measure is to be decided by estimation of probabilities unguided by *a priori* conclusions. Well, had they habitually succeeded, one might not wonder that they should habitually ridicule abstract principles; but the astounding accumulation of failures might have been expected to cause less confidence in empirical methods. Of the 18,110 public Acts passed between 20 Henry III. and the end of 1872, Mr. Janson, Vice-President of the Law Society, estimates that four-fifths have been wholly or partially repealed, and that in the years 1870–72 there were repealed 3,532 Acts, of which 2,759 were totally repealed. Further, I myself found, on examining the books for 1881–83, that in those years there had been repealed 650 Acts belonging to the present reign, besides many of preceding reigns. Remembering that Acts which are repealed have been doing mischief, which means loss, trouble, pain to great numbers — remembering, thus, the enormous amount of suffering which this helter-skelter legislation has inflicted for generations and for centuries, I think it would be not amiss to ask whether better guidance may not be had, even though it should come from absolute political ethics.

I regret that neither space nor health will permit me to discuss any of the questions raised by Sir Louis Mallet. And here, indeed, I find myself compelled to desist altogether. In so far as I am concerned, the controversy must end with this letter.

I am, etc.,

HERBERT SPENCER.

ATHENÆUM CLUB, Nov. 13.

Really, this " Answer to Professor Huxley " is no answer at all. What Mr. Spencer virtually says is : "I admit all that the land-owners may want me to admit. Let us change the subject."

Yet even in thus changing the subject, he is obliged to give up the distinction he had made between absolute political ethics and relative political ethics, for his long-drawn explanation to Professor Huxley means, if it means anything at all, that absolute political ethics *do* have a bearing on practical political conduct.

CHAPTER VI.

MORE LETTERS.

WITH this Mr. Spencer endeavored to withdraw, and no wonder. But letters from Mr. Greenwood, Professor Huxley, and a number of new participants, including Auberon Herbert for the defence, continued to appear in the *Times* for some time longer, and Messrs. Greenwood and Huxley succeeded in dragging from him another brief confession.

Professor Huxley made him give up his illustration from physiological principles, and Mr. Greenwood, pressing him as to whether, as averred by Mr. Laidler, he had ever said that to right one wrong it takes another, first made him declare that he did not remember to have said it, and then, pressing him still farther, made him declare he had not said it and to repudiate it if he had.

Although this is a mere side-issue, perhaps it may be worth while, even at this late date, to vindicate Mr. Laidler and refresh Mr. Spencer's memory. In "Social Statics," Chapter XXI., "The Duty of the State," Section 8, may be found the doctrine which Mr. Laidler referred to, when, in citing Mr. Spencer against Mr. Morley's objection to land nationalization, he said, as reported by the *Times* —

> Mr. Spencer has said that the land had been taken by force and fraud. That gentleman had also said that to right one wrong it takes another.

This in effect, if not in exact words, Mr. Spencer certainly does say in Chapter XXI., Section 8, in combating the doctrine of non-resistance. He declares all coercion immoral in itself, but (using the same terms in the same sense as Mr. Laidler) justifies government when "it uses wrong to put down wrong." He adds:

> The principle of non-resistance is not ethically true, but only that of non-aggression . . . . We may not carelessly abandon our rights. We may not give away our birthright for the sake of peace. . . . We may not be passive under aggression. In due maintenance of our claim is involved the practicability of all our duties. . . . If we allow ourselves to be deprived of that without which we cannot fulfil the Divine will, we virtually negative that will.

I thus take the trouble to refresh Mr. Spencer's memory and vindicate Mr. Laidler, for, although the latter gentleman was allowed one letter in the *Times*, it was afterwards that the question was raised by Mr. Greenwood, and I do not suppose that Mr. Laidler got another chance, the *Times* speaking of him contemptuously, as a Mr. Laidler, and printing his letter in smaller type, although it was he who first brought out Mr. Spencer, and provoked the whole discussion.

Mr. Laidler's letter, of which neither party to the controversy seemed to care to take notice, was published by the *Times* on the same day as Mr. Spencer's second letter. He said —

To the Editor of the Times.

SIR: As one of the deputation of members of the Newcastle Labor Electoral Organization who recently waited upon Mr. John Morley, M. P., to ascertain his opinion on certain political and social topics, I was intrusted by my fellow-members of the deputation with the question of the nationalization of the land, and this subject I discussed with Mr. Morley. In doing so, I sought to back up my position by quoting the ninth chapter of "Social Statics," by Mr. Herbert Spencer, and I certainly thought I had a good case when I found on my side the most distinguished authority of our time. To my great surprise, I now find that in the letters which he has addressed to you, Mr. Herbert Spencer appears to be very anxious to repudiate the doctrines which he preached so eloquently in 1850. Now, although it is a common thing for the politician of to-day to repudiate principles and deductions which he formerly warmly espoused and to adopt others which he once energetically condemned, one does not expect the same vacillation on the part of a distinguished philosopher like Mr. Herbert Spencer. I find it difficult to understand his position, which seems to be this — that while adhering to his general principles he abandons certain deductions therefrom. Now, to my mind, the ninth chapter of "Social Statics," which deals with "The Right to the Use of the Earth," seems as true, as logical, and as unanswerable an argument in favor of the nationalization of the land as it doubtless appeared to Mr. Herbert Spencer on the day it was written. Let us trace the course of his argument through the ten sections of which the chapter is composed.

Giving a short abstract of these ten sections of Chapter IX. Mr. Laidler continued —

In the foregoing digest, beyond one or two connecting words, the language is that of Mr. Herbert Spencer himself. Does it not constitute an unanswerable argument in favor of the nationalization of the land? If the author would permit it to be reprinted, what an admirable tract the ninth chapter of "Social Statics" would be for the propagation of socialistic[1] principles! But he

[1] Mr. Laidler uses the term socialistic in the vague way in which it is so commonly used in England, and doubtless means land nationalization principles.

now seems to repudiate the offspring of his own genius! We have, however, a right to ask that, instead of a vague repudiation in general terms, Mr. Herbert Spencer should tell us specifically what deductions he has abandoned and why he has abandoned them. We might then endeavor to answer his answers to his own propositions.

Yours,

JOHN LAIDLER, *Bricklayer.*

How far Mr. Spencer has tried to answer his own propositions, we shall see in "Justice."

PART III.

RECANTATION.

Equity therefore does not permit property in land. . . . Not only have present land-tenures an indefensible origin, but it is impossible to discover any mode in which land *can* become private property. . . . Ethical truth is as exact and as peremptory as physical truth; and that in this matter of land-tenure the verdict of morality must be distinctly *aye* or *nay*. Either men *have* a right to make the soil private property, or they *have not*. There is no medium. We must choose one of the two positions. There can be no half-and-half opinion. In the nature of things the fact must be either one way or the other. — *Herbert Spencer, 1850.*

CHAPTER I.

THE FATE OF "SOCIAL STATICS."

WE now come to the purpose for which the preceding lengthy examination has been made: the consideration of Mr. Spencer's present opinions on the land question, as set forth with all the weight of the "Synthetic Philosophy" in its author's most recent volume, "Justice," which bears date of June, 1891, and was published somewhat later in that year.

But it will be best to break the chronological order, and record here the fate of "Social Statics." Even after Mr. Spencer had made the *Times* and Mr. Greenwood believe that he had suppressed it years before, that book still continued to be published by Mr. Spencer's authorized publishers, D. Appleton & Co., and their edition of "Justice," published in October, 1891, contains an advertisement of it in its original form. But now, at last, it has been done for. It has not been killed outright; that would be mercy compared with its present fate. It has — and I cannot but feel that "Progress and Poverty," the Edinburgh reviewer, and Mr. John Laidler of Newcastle, have been innocent causes of its fate — it has been disembowelled, stuffed, mummified, and then set up in the gardens of the Spencerian Philosophy, where it may be viewed with entire complacency by Sir John and his Grace.

Soberly, the original volume has with this year been withdrawn from publication, to give place to a new "Social Statics," dated January, 1892, and published in February. This volume, which is, of course, now to pass in the publisher's lists as "Social Statics," has for full title, "Social Statics, abridged and revised, together with 'The Man *versus* the State.'" It consists of disjointed fragments of the old "Social Statics," which, in order to make some approach to the bulk of the original, is padded out with the magazine articles before referred to. In the preface Mr. Spencer says:

> My first intention was to call this volume, or, rather, part of a volume, "Fragments from Social Statics," and afterwards, "Selections from Social Statics." Both of these titles, however, seemed to indicate a much less coherent assemblage of parts than it contains. On the other hand, to call it an abridgment is somewhat misleading, since the word fails to imply that large and constructively important parts are omitted. No title, however, appears appropriate, and I have at length decided that *Social Statics, abridged and revised,* is the least inappropriate.

If appropriateness was what Mr. Spencer sought, it does seem as if a title much less inappropriate might have been found. For the only discernible principle of revision is the chopping-out of all that might imply a God or offend vested interests, in the same fashion that Russian censors revise distasteful works, the result being a Hamlet from which not only Hamlet himself, but the Ghost, the Queen Mother, and Ophelia, have gone. The "First Principle" is left, but everything large or small relating to land is omitted. The only allusion to land is in the cavilling at Locke, which is retained, and that what was originally Section 3, Chapter X., now converted into a chapter, headed "Socialism," is left by careless editing to begin, as in the original:

> The doctrine that all men have equal rights to the use of the earth seems at first sight to countenance a species of social organization at variance with that from which the right of property has just been deduced.*

The foot-note indicated by this asterisk is:

> * Referring to an omitted part of the last chapter, the argument of which, with modifications, will now be found in Part IV. of the Principles of Ethics.

Thus revised, "Social Statics" no further concerns us. All that Mr. Spencer originally said about the relation between men and the earth having now been definitely withdrawn, we are referred for his present opinions to the book we are about to consider.*

But the advertising of the revised "Social Statics" is worth noting, as by some blunder it lays before the American reader what was originally intended for English circulation only, and brings to mind the fiction about the suppression of "Social Statics," which did duty in the *St. James's Gazette* and the London *Times*. Here is the advertisement as published at the head of D. Appleton & Co.'s announcements in May, 1892:

> **SOCIAL STATICS.** By HERBERT SPENCER. New and revised edition, including "The Man *versus* the State," a series of essays on political tendencies heretofore published separately. 12mo. 420 pages. Cloth, $2.00.

> Having been much annoyed by the persistent quotation from the old edition of "Social Statics," in the face of repeated warnings, of views which he had abandoned, and by the misquotation of others which he still holds, Mr. Spencer some ten years ago stopped

the sale of the book in England and prohibited its translation. But the rapid spread of communistic theories gave new life to these misrepresentations; hence Mr. Spencer decided to delay no longer a statement of his mature opinions on the rights of individuals and the duty of the State.

This is a queer statement to come from D. Appleton & Co., who have been publishing and advertising the old edition of "Social Statics" up to this year, without the slightest warning to purchasers that the author had changed his views otherwise than as stated in the prefaces and notes, which, as I have before said, made no reference to any change on the land question. It is strange to hear *from them*, that the annoyed Mr. Spencer ten years ago stopped the sale of his book *in England*, when it had not been in print for over twenty years, serenely leaving it to be sold in the only country where it was in print, and that he also at the same time prohibited its translation. Why is Mr. Spencer so careful of what Englishmen in the little home island and even the "foreigner" may read, yet so careless of what is read by Americans, Canadians and Australians? And why have D. Appleton & Co., for nearly ten years, been passing off on their great constituency a book that its author would not allow to be sold in his own home or in foreign countries? These are questions this advertisement suggests but does not answer.

CHAPTER II.

THE PLACE OF "JUSTICE" IN THE SYNTHETIC PHILOSOPHY.

"JUSTICE," to which we are to look for Mr. Spencer's present opinions on the land question, is esteemed by its author his most important book. This volume, the full title of which is, "The Ethics of Social Life — Justice," is also entitled "Part IV. of Ethics." It is the tenth of the ponderous volumes already published, which are advertised as "Spencer's Synthetic Philosophy." The grand divisions of this Synthetic Philosophy, as now advertised, are: "First Principles," "The Principles of Biology," "The Principles of Psychology," "Principles of Sociology," and "Principles of Morality." Of these five grand divisions, the "Principles of Morality," as it is styled in the advertisements, or "Principles of Ethics," as it is styled in the title-page of the book itself, is the grand division to which "Justice" belongs in the Spencerian scheme. The first volume of this grand division, "The Data of Ethics," has been already published. Volume II., "The Inductions of Ethics," and Volume III., "The Ethics of Individual Life," have not yet appeared,[1] Mr. Spencer, as he states in the preface to "Justice," preferring to hasten this volume, as most important. After these two deferred volumes have been com-

[1] They have been published since this was put in plate.

pleted, there are, as he also tells us, two more volumes, "The Ethics of Social Life — Negative Benevolence," and "The Ethics of Social Life — Positive Benevolence," to which he will turn his attention, thus completing his full philosophical scheme.

This scheme of "Synthetic Philosophy" is the most pretentious that ever mortal man undertook, since it embraces no less than an explanation to mankind, without recourse to the hypothesis of Originating Intelligence, of how the world and all that is in it contained, including we ourselves, our motives, feelings, powers, instincts, habits and customs, came to be. Of this large scheme, the ethical part is the most important, being, as Mr. Spencer tells us, "that to which I regard all the preceding parts as subsidiary." And of this most important part, he also tells us that this volume, "The Ethics of Social Life — Justice," is the most important.

Thus "Justice," which so far as it treats of the land question we are about to consider, is by its author deemed the very summit and cap-stone of his whole philosophy.

And that, indeed, it must be, follows from the supreme importance of its subject-matter. For it treats of right and wrong, of what should and what should not be, in those social relations of men from which spring the most fiercely debated practical questions of our time — questions that involve the happiness or misery, the physical, mental and moral development of vast populations, the advance of civilization or its retrogression. As to the principles of right and wrong in individual relations there is little if any dispute; and not merely through Christendom, but "from Paris to Pekin," mankind are substantially agreed as to what constitutes good or bad. It is when we come to the social relations of men — to those social adjustments which prescribe and control rights of ownership, which affect the production, distribution, accumulation and enjoyment of wealth, which are the main ground of legislation, and which over and above the injunctions of individual morality throw around men a perfect network of shalls and shall nots, that we reach the befogged and debatable land — the region of burning questions.

It is where the philosopher thus passes from the region of mere curious speculation into the arena where, for men living and men yet to come, the issues of want or plenty, of ignorance or enlightenment, of slavery or freedom, must be decided, that the ordinary apprehension may best apply to his teachings the tests of usefulness and sincerity. That the proof of the pudding is in the eating, and that the tree is best known by its fruit, are maxims not to be disregarded in philosophy. What matters the teaching of any philosophy as to the origin of things, compared with its teaching on matters that affect the fullness, happiness and nobleness of life? And how shall we tell whether the philosopher be an earnest man or a mere prater, so readily and so clearly as by noting whether he takes the side of wronger or of wronged, the undeservedly rich or the undeservedly poor? Thus, "Justice" is not merely the roof and crown of the Spencerian Synthetic Philosophy; it is its touchstone as well.

CHAPTER III.

THE SYNTHETIC PHILOSOPHY.

I WISH to keep close to the land question. But to fairly understand Mr. Spencer's views on the land question as expressed in "Justice," and to discover what ground there may be for the changes they show, it is necessary to get some idea of the system of which it is the crown.

"Justice" is in fact the real revision of "Social Statics" in the new light of the system of philosophy which its author has since elaborated. Both books go over the same ground, that of social economics, and the title of one might serve for that of the other. This ground it was that first attracted Mr. Spencer, and he went over it forty-two years ago in the temper of a social reformer. He now returns to these living, burning questions of the time with the reputation of a great philosopher, after assiduous years spent in what purports to be a wider and deeper survey. For of the philosophy which he has in the meantime elaborated it is claimed not only that "it is more logically complete than any other system," but that "it is more practical than any other, because it bears immediately upon common experience, takes hold of the living questions of the time, throws light upon the course of human affairs, and gives knowledge that may serve both for public and individual guidance."[1]

I speak of Herbert Spencer in "Social Statics" as a social reformer, to distinguish his attitude at that time from his present attitude. But he was not content in that book to advocate empirical remedies for the disorder, waste and wrong that he beheld about him. He saw that expediency offered no sure guide; that such was the infirmity of human powers, and such, in the complexity of social actions and reactions, was the impossibility of calculating results, that legislation based on mere policy was constantly bringing to naught the best-laid schemes, constantly entangling men in blind ways, constantly resulting in the unforeseen and unwished. The burden of "Social Statics" is that there is a better guide in social affairs than the calculations of expediency; that what men should look to is not results but principles; that the moral sense may be trusted where the intellect is certain to go astray. Its central idea is that the universe bespeaks to us its origin in an intelligence of which justice must be an attribute; that there is in human affairs a divinely appointed order to which, if it would prosper, society must conform; that there is an eternal rule of right, by which, despite all perturbations of the intellect, social institutions may be safely measured.

This rule of right, as expressed in the first principle of "Social Statics" — this "law of equal liberty," that "each has freedom to do all that he wills

[1] E. L. Youmans, M.D., "Herbert Spencer and the Doctrine of Evolution," Popular Science Library. D. Appleton & Co., New York.

provided that he infringes not the equal freedom of any other" — what is it indeed but an expression in primary essential of the Golden Rule? What Mr. Spencer declared in "Social Statics" is in fact what the National Assembly of France declared in 1789, "That ignorance, neglect or contempt of human rights are the sole causes of public misfortunes and corruptions of government." And with clearer vision than the French Assembly, he saw and did not hesitate to assert that the most important of human rights from the neglect and contempt of which society to-day suffers, is the natural and equal right to the use of the planet.

It is its protest against materialism, its assertion of the supremacy of the moral law, its declaration of God-given rights that are above all human enactments, that despite whatever it may contain of crudity and inconsistency make "Social Statics" a noble book, and in the deepest sense a religiously minded book.

In the course Mr. Spencer thus entered in his early manhood there was work enough to have engaged the greatest powers for the longest lifetime; but work that would have involved a constant and bitter contest with the strongest forces — forces that have at their disposal not only the material things that make life pleasant, but present honor as well. Mr. Spencer did not continue the struggle that in "Social Statics" he began. He turned from the field of social reform to the field of speculative philosophy, in which he has won great reputation and authority. It is the scheme of philosophy thus developed that forms the basis of "Justice," as the ideas of a living God, of a divinely appointed order, and of an eternal distinction between right and wrong, just and unjust, form the basis of "Social Statics."

In its earlier volumes this philosophy was styled "Spencer's Evolutionary Philosophy." This title has since been abandoned for the less definite but more ambitious one of "Spencer's Synthetic Philosophy." Since synthesis is the opposite of analysis, the putting together, instead of taking apart — a synthetic philosophy is a philosophy which explains the world (a term which in the philosophic sense includes all of which we can become conscious), not by the process of taking things apart and seeing of what they are composed; but by assuming an original principle or principles, and from that starting-point mentally building up the world, thus showing how it came to be. The Book of Genesis embodies probably the oldest synthetic philosophy we have record of. Mr. Spencer's is the latest.

Spencer's "Synthetic Philosophy" is in the main a fusion and extension of two hypotheses — the nebular hypothesis of the formation of celestial bodies, and what is best known as the Darwinian hypothesis of the development of species, with a bridging over of such gulfs as the passage from the inorganic to the organic, and from matter and motion to mind, and some infusion of what I take to be Kantian metaphysics. Though Mr. Spencer objects to the characterization, I can only describe this philosophy as materialistic, since it accounts for the world and all it contains, including the human ego, by the interactions of matter and motion, without reference to any such thing as intelligence, purpose or will, except as derived from them.

It does not, of course, any more than other materialistic philosophies, pretend to explain what matter and motion are, or how they came to be. That, for it, is the unknowable, while it only deals with what may be known by men. But within the region of the knowable, all things to it have come to be, or are coming to be, by the interactions of matter and motion, in a process which it terms "evolution," and which it describes as "an integration of matter, and concomitant dissipation of motion, during which the matter passes from an indefinite, incoherent homogeneity to a definite, coherent heterogeneity, and during which the retained motion undergoes a parallel transformation."

After evolution has reached its limit and all the motion is dissipated, comes a temporary equilibrium, and then dissolution sets in, by the integration of motion and the dissipation of matter, so that, according to the Synthetic Philosophy, the universe goes on, so far as we can see, to infinity, like one of those disks boys play with, which by means of a twisted string is made to spin around one way, then to come to a momentary stop, and then spin back the other way, the process continuing so long as the boy will gently extend and then gently bring together his hands. What is it that supplies the force furnished in the case of the toy by the boy's hands? And has it, like the boy's hands, conscious will behind it? This to the Spencerian Synthetic Philosophy is the unknowable.

This unknowable is not God, though Mr. Spencer presents it to the religious sentiment as something with which it may be satisfied, and some of his followers, and sometimes even he himself, speak of it in ways that suggest identity. In "Social Statics," however, Mr. Spencer frequently uses the term God, but he certainly never thought that he knew God in the sense of comprehending Him, or that it was possible for man so to know Him. And if the unknowable of his philosophy means that —

> Being above all beings! Mighty One,
> Whom none can comprehend and none explore!
> Who fill'st existence with Thyself alone —
> Embracing all, supporting, ruling o'er —
> Being whom we call God, and know no more![1]

— why should he, with the development of his philosophy have abandoned the use of the old term for that which beneath the myths and fables and creeds by which men have endeavored to formulate spiritual perceptions has been always recognized as apparent to the human soul yet transcending human knowledge?

This unknowable must be distinguished from the unknown. It is that which not only is not, but never can be known in any way; that which not merely we cannot comprehend, but of which we can know nothing at all, even of its intelligence or non-intelligence, its consciousness or non-consciousness, its nature or its attributes. It is difficult indeed to see how we may predicate even existence of it, as we may of an unknown person or unknown thing. For this requires at least some knowledge. But of the unknowable we lack the capacity of knowing anything whatever. Air is unknowable directly to our sense of sight; we cannot directly see air. But by its resistance, its weight, its chemical and other qualities, it is knowable by our

[1] Derzhavin, Bowring's translation.

other faculties; and it is indirectly knowable even to our sight, through the moving of leaves, the motion of watery surfaces, etc.; while if air were unknowable, we could not be conscious of it in any possible way. It would be precisely the same to us as no air.

By the constitution of the human mind it is impossible for us in attempting to trace back the line of causation to find any stopping place until we reach that which thinks and wills — that to which the volition is akin which to our consciousness is an originating element in the trains of sequences that we ourselves set in motion, or at least modify and divert. Thus any materialistic or mechanical philosophy must either beg the question by assuming the eternity of matter and motion, or admit something behind them which it must take for granted and leave out of its explanation, simply denying that it can be recognized as intelligence or will apart from matter and motion, *i.e.* spirit. If the unknowable in the Spencerian Philosophy means anything more than the vacuum that is thus left where a spiritual First Cause is denied, it seems to mean what by some metaphysicians is styled "the thing in itself."

This "thing in itself" is in metaphysical language the noumenon as distinguished from the phenomenon: the thing as it really is, as distinguished from the thing as it is recognized in its qualities by the percipient being. But this, if not another name for spirit, really amounts to vacancy. Such idea of "the thing in itself" as opposed to the thing as known in phenomena, seems to come from the habit, to which our use of language leads, of associating independent existence with qualities to which we give independent names. Thus no man ever saw white except as a white thing. But as things have other colors we can readily separate the idea white from the idea thing. Forgetting, since we are only dealing with words, that the abstraction of one color implies its replacement by another color, and the abstraction of all colors would render the thing non-existent so far at least as our sight is concerned, we may mentally separate the idea of color, and imagine the thing in other respects as remaining. Extending the process of abstraction to all other qualities, we may fancy that we have still remaining the idea of the thing separated from all idea of its qualities. But what we have remaining is really only a verbal simulacrum, that sounds like something, and may be written or parsed, but which on analysis consists of negations, and means really no thing or nothing. This, as well as I can understand it, is that "thing in itself," of which, in some part, or in some aspects, Mr. Spencer's unknowable seems to consist.

But if the Spencerian philosophy is thus indefinite as to what precedes or underlies matter and motion, it certainly shows no lack of definiteness from the appearance of matter and motion onward. With matter and motion begins its knowable, and from thenceforward, without pause or break, it builds up the whole universe by the integration of the one, and the dissipation of the other, in the mode described as evolution, without recourse to any other element.

In this elimination of any spiritual element lies, it seems to me, the essential characteristic of the Spencerian philosophy. It is not, as is largely supposed, *the* evolution philosophy, but *an* evolution philosophy;

that is to say, its rejection of any spiritual element in its account of the genesis of things does not follow from its acceptance of the principle of evolution; but the peculiarity of its teachings as to evolution arises from its ignoring of the spiritual element, from its assumption that, matter and motion given, their interactions will account for all that we see, feel or know.

In reality the Spencerian idea of evolution differs as widely from that held by such evolutionists as Alfred Russell Wallace, St. George Mivart, or Joseph Le Conte, as it differs from the idea of special and direct creation. It is only when this is recognized that the real point of issue raised by or perhaps rather around the doctrine of evolution is seen. We all see that the oak is evolved from the acorn, the man from the child. And that it is intended for the evolution of something is the only intelligible account that we can make for ourselves of the universe. Thus in some sense we all believe in evolution, and in some sense the vast majority of men always have. And even the evolution of man from the animal kingdom offers no real difficulty so long as this is understood as only the form or external of his genesis. To me, for instance, who, possibly from my ignorance of such branches, am unable to see the weight of the evidence of man's descent from other animals, which many specialists in natural science deem conclusive, it yet appears antecedently probable that externally such might have been his descent. For it seems better to accord with the economy manifested through nature, to think that when the soul of man first took encasement in physical body on this earth it should have taken the form nearest to its needs, rather than that inorganic matter should be built up. And while I cannot conceive how, even in illimitable time, the animal could of itself turn into the man, it is easy for me to think that if the spirit of man passed into the body of a brute the animal body would soon assume human shape.

Let me illustrate the distinction I wish to point out:

Here is a locomotive of the first class, or a great Corliss engine, capable on the pressure of a child's finger of exerting to definite ends a mighty force. How did it come to be?

"It came to be," some one might answer, "from the integrations of matter and motion. This matter existed, not to go further back than is necessary, in ores of iron and copper and zinc, and in the wood of trees. By motion acting on matter these materials were transported, separated, combined and adjusted, until integrated into this definite, coherent heterogeneity that you see."

Such answer would not satisfy me. I would indeed see that it was quite true that from the first wresting of the ores from their beds, to the last touch of file or emery paper, every step in this construction involved the action of motion on matter; but I would know that this was not all, and that what so ordered and directed the action of motion on matter as to bring this construction into being was the intelligence and volition of man. And I would reply, "You do not go deep enough: what this construction really bespeaks is something you have omitted; something to which matter is but the material, and motion the tool — the intelligence, consciousness and freedom of human will."

Or, here is a picture. Let it be a reproduction of a Madonna of Raphael's, such as are made or might be made by self-feeding presses. Shall any one explain the impression of grace and beauty and loving purity that it produces on him who contemplates it, by explaining on the undulatory theory of light how impressions of color are produced on the retina of the eye? Or shall he account for its genesis by telling me that by integrations of matter and motion certain pigments have become disposed on paper in a certain way? Should he attempt to do so I would say to him, "You are telling me merely of the medium through which in this picture soul speaks to soul; you are merely telling me of the means by which the thought of the painter found expression in outward form."

But suppose he should answer —

"You delude yourself. I have investigated the matter, and have been to the place where such pictures as this are brought forth. I saw no painter; I saw only a series of revolving cylinders, through which an endless roll of paper was drawn by steel fingers. By the automatic motion of this machinery one cylinder impressed on the paper some patches of one color, and another some patches of another color, till at last, by such successive actions of motion on matter, a picture like this came forth."

Would I be any more convinced that such a picture could have come to be without that power, essentially different from matter and motion, which we feel in ourselves and recognize in other men, which draws a deep gulf between man and all other animals; that power which plans, contrives, and by using matter and motion creates; that power in short which we call spirit? Would I not say to him, "What you tell me of the way this picture was brought forth by no means lessens my certainty that it could primarily have originated only in the mind and soul of a painter, but only shows me in the automatic working of the presses of which you speak a higher expression of the same power of using tools to body forth thought that was shown in the use of palette and brush. In this reproduction, as in each and all of the various processes and machines by which it was brought to be, I see a manifestation of the same essential thing that the original picture would show to me — originating will, adapting mind; in short, not matter and motion, but spirit, or soul.

And of what moment would be the question whether this picture came into existence by the direct action of human will upon the paper, or indirectly through its action upon automatic machinery, as compared with the question whether its existence involved human action or not?

It is on this vital point of the existence or non-existence of spirit as a prime motor that the real issue raised by theories of evolution comes. Such evolutionism as is represented by the men of whom I have spoken, sees in evolution only a mode in which the creative spirit works. Such evolutionism as is formulated in the Spencerian philosophy eliminates spirit from its hypothesis, and takes into account only matter and motion.

Here is where all materialistic or mechanical theories of the universe ultimately fail. The belief in God, that is to say, in a Spiritual Originator, has no such utterly inadequate and ridiculous genesis as that which we shall shortly see Mr. Spencer gives for it. It springs from the same primary ineradicable perception that universally leads men, whenever they see in a thing destitute of life the evidence of adaptation involving choice, to attribute it to man. No civilized man, after inspection, ever took the rudest huts raised by savages for the structures of lower animals. No savage who might at a distance have thought a ship a bird, or a steamer a marine monster, ever failed on closer view to know that it was of man's building. No wandering Bedouin ever attributed to natural forces ruins so vast that they transcended his ideas of man's ability. On the contrary, so clear is the impress and testimony of that creative power which so widely and unmistakably distinguishes man from all other animals, that rude peoples invariably attribute constructions which they deem beyond man's ability, to genii, fairies or demons — beings possessing powers of the same kind as man, but in larger degree. And they do this for the same reason that they attribute the bringing into being of the highest of adaptations, those that embody life, to a highest of spiritual beings — the Great Spirit, or God. And when our larger knowledge shows us no wavering or confusion in the line which marks conscious adaptation, so that to the specialist the chipping of a flint taken from a long buried river-drift, or the scratching on a tusk of a preglacial animal, shows the same unmistakable evidence of man's work as does the engine or the picture, how shall we otherwise interpret the evidences of design similar in kind but infinitely higher in degree which nature on every hand reveals than as indicating the work of God?

But to return again to our illustration: If when, to him who contends that the engine or the picture has come to be by the integrations of matter and motion, I say that such structures unmistakably bespeak man's work, suppose he should reply to me:

"What is man's work but the interaction of matter and motion? What is man's hand but a certain arrangement of matter? What is the force it exerts but a dissipation of motion? Did they, too, not exist in an indefinite, incoherent homogeneous shape in the primordial mass? Do they not come to man from unnumbered transmutations in the food he eats, the water he drinks, the air he breathes; to pass from him into other numberless mutations? If you think man is not included in matter and motion, shut off even for a little while his supplies of matter and motion, and where is your man?"

"Your explanation no better satisfies me than before," I would reply. "While it may be true as far as it goes, it is inadequate and false in omitting an essential factor, and that a factor which is not last but first. Matter and motion acting to all eternity could not bring forth such a structure as this. I know, from all my experience of how things come to be, that this structure had its primary genesis in thought; that in all its parts, and as a combined whole, it was thought out before it was worked out. I grant you that, at least normally, our perceptions of thought in others are dependent on our perceptions of matter and motion. But I too think. And I know from perceptions that are even closer and truer than my perceptions of matter and motion, that thought is something different from matter and motion, and from any combination of them. I think when my body is still, when my eyes are shut, even when my senses are locked from the external world by sleep. And though I can only look out, not in; though I cannot tell you what I myself am, any more than you can tell me what matter and motion are; although I can no more tell you how I came to be than you can tell me how matter and motion came to be, nor in what way this, that I feel is I, is embodied in a material frame, I do feel directly, and know from its capacities, that it is something different from and superior to the matter and motion of that frame, and that it endures while they change. And so your explanation of the genesis of things that excludes everything but matter and motion, is to me as superficial as if you were to explain a Cæsar or Shakespeare by the food he ate; an 'In Memoriam' by pen and ink; or my recognition of my friend's voice, and our communication of thought through the telephone, by the copper wire and the current of electricity.

"So clear, so certain, am I that what I can recognize, better than I can define, as spirit, is alone competent to produce things in which I see conscious, willing intelligence, that if you were to show me a brush that seemed of itself to paint pictures, a pen that seemed of itself to write intelligible words, or even an animal that seemed to show that power which is the essential characteristic of man, I could only account for it as a manifestation of spirit acting in a way unfamiliar to me — if not spirit in a human body, playing a trick upon me, then spirit in some other form. And this would be the conclusion of all men."

While less acute thinkers profess to sneer at the evidence from design, Schopenhauer, whose great ability certainly entitles him to high rank among atheistic philosophers, is only able to avoid the conclusion of an Originating Intelligence by eliminating intelligence from will, and assuming that bare will, or desire unconjoined with intelligence, directly originates, just as the will to make a bodily movement brings about that movement without knowledge or consciousness of how it is brought about.[1]

---

[1] Schopenhauer's explanation of the origin of species is in interesting contrast to that of the evolutionary hypothesis, and to my mind comes closer to the truth. According to him the numberless forms and adaptations of animated nature, instead of proceeding from slow modifications, by which various creatures have been adapted to their conditions, are the expression of the desire or collective volition of the animal. I quote from the chapter on Comparative Anatomy in "The Will in Nature," Bohn translation:

> Every animal form is a longing of the will to live which is roused by circumstances. For instance, the will is seized with a longing to live on trees, to hang on their branches, to devour their leaves, without contention with other animals and without ever touching the ground. This longing presents itself throughout endless time in the form (or Platonic idea) of the sloth. It can hardly walk at all, being only adapted for climbing; helpless on the ground it is agile on trees and looks itself like a moss-clad bough in order to escape the notice of its pursuers. . . .
>
> The universal fitness for their ends, the obviously intentional design of all the parts of the organism of the lower animals without exception, proclaim too distinctly for it ever to have been seriously questioned, that here no forces of Nature acting by chance and without plan have been at work, but a will. . . . [That] no organ interferes with another, each rather assisting the others and none remaining unemployed; also that no subordinate organ would be better suited to another mode of existence, while the life which the animal really leads is determined by the principal organs alone, but on the contrary each part of the animal not only corresponds to every other part, but also to its mode of life: its claws for instance are invariably adapted for seizing the prey which its teeth are suited to tear and break, and its intestinal canal to digest;

But within the sphere in which we can trace origination does it anywhere appear that will without intelligence can accomplish anything? So far as

---

its limbs are constructed to convey it where that prey is to be found, and no organ ever remains unemployed . . . added to the circumstance that no organ required for its mode of life is ever wanting in any animal, and that all, even the most heterogeneous, harmonize together and are as it were calculated for a quite specially determined way of life, for the element in which the prey dwells, for the pursuit, the overcoming, the crushing and digesting of that prey — all this, we say, proves that the animal's structure has been determined by the mode of life by which the animal desired to find its sustenance, and not *vice versa*. It also proves that the result is exactly the same as if a knowledge of that mode of life and of its outward conditions had preceded the structure, and as if therefore every animal had chosen its equipment before it assumed a body; just as a sportsman before starting chooses his whole equipment, gun, powder, shot, pouch, hunting-knife and dress, according to the game he intends chasing. He does not take aim at the wild boar because he happens to have a rifle; he took the rifle with him and not a fowling-piece, because he intended to hunt the wild boar. The ox does not butt because it happens to have horns; it has horns because it intends to butt.

Now to render this proof complete we have the additional circumstance that in many animals, during the time they are growing, the effort of the will to which a limb is destined to minister, manifests itself before the existence of the limb itself, its employment thus anticipating its existence. Young he-goats, rams, calves, for instance, butt with their bare polls before they have any horns; the young boar tries to gore on either side, before its tusks are fully developed which would respond to the intended effect, while on the other hand it neglects to use the smaller teeth it already has in its mouth and with which it might really bite. Thus its mode of defending itself does not adapt itself to the existing weapons, but *vice versa*.

. . . Behold the countless varieties of animal shapes. How entirely is each of them the mere image of its volition, the evident expression of the strivings of the will which constitute its character! Their difference in shape is only the portrait of their difference in character. . . . Each particular striving of the will presents itself in a particular modification of shape. The abode of the prey therefore has determined the shape of its pursuer . . . and no shape is rejected by the will to live as too grotesque to attain its ends. . . . As the will has equipped itself with every organ and every weapon, offensive as well as defensive, so has it likewise provided itself in every animal shape with an intellect, as a means of preservation for the individual and the species. . . . Beasts of prey do not hunt nor foxes thieve because they have more intelligence; on the contrary they have more intelligence, just as they have stronger teeth and claws, because they wished to live by hunting and thieving.

we can see clearly, is it not always true that where volition without commensurate intelligence seems to result in accomplishment it is because the needed intelligence has been supplied by another will. Thus an engine-driver desires his train to move forward or backward, fast or slow, and by a motion that seems directly responsive to his will, his desire takes effect through the pulling of a lever. He may know nothing of the adjustments of the machine that in response to his will thus converts heat into motion, and utterly lack the intelligence needed to construct it. But that knowledge and intelligence were none the less necessary to this moving of the train. If not conjoined with his will they were conjoined with other wills — the wills that have constructed a machine by which a train may be moved on the pulling of a lever. The little intelligence needed in use proves the great intelligence exerted in construction.

So a lady at the opera puts her glass to her eyes and turns a screw as she wishes to make what she sees appear nearer. She may not know how many lenses her glass contains; still less their nature and properties; and is utterly without the knowledge required for making such glasses. But that she may accomplish at will results requiring such knowledge is because others possess it.

So, if we look through any part of the wide field in which human advance has brought volition nearer to result and lessened the knowledge and intelligence required by the will to use, we find its reason in the greater knowledge and intelligence shown in adaptation. If the ordinary ship-master of to-day can with the aid of a quadrant, a nautical almanac and a table of logarithms learn from the heavens his position on the trackless ocean, it is because of the high intelligence and tireless studies of others. If girls who know only how to strike a key and interpret a click, or put a peg in a hole, can talk with each other hundreds of miles apart, it is because of discoverers, inventors and constructors.

If, then, in the only field in which we can see origination taking place, we find that the originator is always intelligent, conscious will, and if we find that where the will that uses an adapation does not possess the knowledge or intelligence necessary to originate it, another will or wills conjoined with deeper knowledge and wider intelligence has done so, what is the reasonable inference as to adaptations of a higher kind, the genesis of which we cannot see, and which so far transcend the knowledge and intelligence of the creatures that through them are enabled to give their own wills effect?

What are our bodies but a more perfect adjustment of parts, such as we see in machines? what are our eyes but a more perfect adjustment of lenses, such as we see in opera-glasses? If, then, my hand closes when I will to grasp, without any knowledge on my part of the correlated movements that must necessarily intervene; if when I merely will to look, the lenses of my eyes are by delicate and complex machinery directed to the position and adapted to the distance; if all through animal and even vegetable nature I may see utilizations of knowledge and adaptations of intelligence transcending, not merely the powers of their users, but the highest human knowledge and intelligence, shall I infer that these utilizations and adaptations come without knowledge and intelligence? or shall I regard them as evidences of a deeper knowledge and wider intelligence, which, since we find intelligence and knowledge invariably associated with consciousness, must pertain to a higher consciousness?

But to come back to the Book of Genesis that is offered to us in Mr. Spencer's Synthetic Philosophy.

First — if we will insist upon a first — comes the unknowable; then force; then from force, matter and motion. Matter first appears, permeated with motion, in a state of indefinite, incoherent homogeneity, from which a principle which is styled "the instability of the homogeneous" starts the "integration of matter and concomitant dissipation of motion," called evolution, "during which the matter passes from an indefinite, incoherent homogeneity to a definite, coherent heterogeneity, and during which the retained motion undergoes a parallel transformation."

This is in brief the whole story:

Matter revolving in accordance with the nebular hypothesis gives rise to nebulous aggregations; these to suns, which throw off revolving satellites, that in the course of time cool into earths, on the crust of which continuing evolution separates gases and differentiates the strata of inorganic matter. By the multiplying effects of motion acting on matter, the earth becomes fitted for life; and from the differences in the physical mobilities and chemical activities in the segregations of matter produce in colloid or jelly-like substances, such as starch, the beginnings of life, which is defined as "the definite combination of heterogeneous changes, both simultaneous and successive, in correspondence with external co-existences and sequences." And then by forces of various kinds, but all derived from motion, and being its mechanical equivalents, all the forms of life, vegetable and animal, proceed.

By this process of evolution man was finally developed from a lower animal — he himself, with all his attributes and social institutions, being like everything else an outcome of this process, which, acting through survival of the fittest, heredity and the pressure of conditions, has been and is moulding him into harmony with those conditions.

Of primitive man we have much and very definite information from Mr. Spencer. He was smaller and less powerful, especially in the lower limbs, than man is now, but had a larger abdomen and came earlier to maturity. He was wavering and inconstant; he had no surprise or curiosity or ingenuity; his imagination was reminiscent only, not constructive; he lacked abstract ideas, was without notion of definiteness and truth, or of benevolence, equity or duty; he was unable to think even of a single law, much less of law in general; had neither the habit of expressing things definitely, nor the habit of testing assertions, nor a due sense of contrast between fact and fiction; and for him to deliberately weigh evidence was impossible. He was a cannibal; was entirely promiscuous in his sexual relations; had no idea of any other life or of any supernatural existences or powers, and no care for, no sympathy with, and no idea of the goodness or badness of acts toward any of his fellows, except so far as female primitive man was concerned with her offspring during infancy.

How this sorry monster, this big-bellied, short-legged, bad lot of an ancestor of ours managed to avoid the fate of the Kilkenny cats, and keep in existence, we are not definitely informed; but it seems from the Synthetic Philosophy that he did, and went on evoluting.

Various processes of his further evolution are in the Synthetic Philosophy described. Seeing shadows cast by the sun, the primitive man took them for other selves, which, aided by his dreams, brought him to a belief in doubles, more extensive even than that which Mr. Stead has expounded in his "Real Ghost Stories" and "More Ghost Stories." This led him to believe in another life, and his fear of chiefs and efforts to propitiate them after they were dead evolved the idea of God. Some regard for others, and some crude notion of property, was also evolved by fear of reprisal from others when he injured them or took their belongings, and by the punishment inflicted by chiefs. Cannibalism declined as the practice of slavery grew, and it became more profitable to work a captive than to eat him. But primitive man was not only a cannibal, he was a trophy-taker, given to the practice of gathering human heads and jaw bones as evidences of his prowess. This led to mutilations of the living, or self-mutilations, as marks of respect or deference, and this again led to the giving of presents; and this in its turn evolved on the one side into political and ecclesiastical revenues, and on the other into a greater respect for property, and a recognition of value, and finally into barter, and then trade. In similar ways all our perceptions, feelings, instincts and habits have arisen. As for the mooted question, whether we have innate ideas or whether all our ideas are derived from experience, the solution of the Synthetic Philosophy is, that while all our ideas are originally derived from experience, they are of two kinds — those which the experience of our ancestors has registered in our inherited nervous system, and which therefore seem to us original, or innate, and those which we ourselves derive from experience.

Such, in brief, is the scheme of philosophy that in the interval between the publication of "Social Statics" and the publication of "Justice" Mr. Spencer has developed; and which it is the purpose of the last book to apply to the moral questions gone over in the first.

Of the inadequacy of such a philosophy to account for human progress or coherently to marshal the great facts of human life and human history I have already treated at some length in Book X. of "Progress and Poverty," entitled, "The Law of Human Progress." But what we are now concerned with is the question, Where in such a philosophy is a basis for moral ideas to be found?

I cannot see, nor can I find that Mr. Spencer has been able to. Though still continuing to condemn Bentham, as he did in "Social Statics," all his efforts to obtain something like a moral sanction reach no further than expediency.

And how can it be otherwise? If, in all we are and think and feel, we are but passing phases of the interactions of matter and motion? — if behind the force manifested in matter and motion is nothing but the unknowable, and before us nothing but dissipation — personal dissipation when we die, and the matter and motion of which alone we are composed seek other forms; and then a death of the race, followed by a dissipation of the globe? — why should we not eat, drink, and be merry to the limit of opportunity and digestion? If our ideas of God and of a future life come merely from the blunders of savages so stupid that they took shadows for other selves and dreams for realities? if we would still be eating each other had it not been discovered that man might use man more profitably as a laborer than as food? if what we call the promptings of conscience are merely inherited habits, the results of the fear of punishment transmitted through the nervous system? — why should I not lie whenever I may find it convenient and safe to lie? why should I avoid any omission or commission that will bring no legal or social or personal penalty or inconvenience? why should I refrain from selling my ability, whatever it may be, to any cause or interest that has power to give me what I desire, whether it be wealth or honor?

Mr. Spencer's philosophy makes no distinction between motives and results, nor does it admit of any. If it has any gospel, it is the gospel of results, and the results that it treats as to be sought are only results that make life pleasurable. Temperance, chastity, probity, industry, public spirit, generosity, love! They have in this philosophy no promise and no reward, save as they may directly or indirectly add to the pleasure of the individual. For the self-sacrifice of the hero, the devotion of the saint, the steadfastness of the martyr; for the spirit that ennobles the annals of mankind, that has led and yet leads so many to endure discomfort, want, pain, death, for the love of the true and the pure and the good; for the noble hope of doing something to break the chains of the captive, to open the eyes of the blind, to make life for those who may come after fuller, nobler, happier; for the faith that has led men to dare all things and suffer all things; it has no breath of stimulation or praise. In the cold glare that it takes for light, such men are fools. For it knows no more of human will as a factor in the advance of mankind than it does of the Divine Will. To it what conditions exist, and what conditions will exist, are determined by the irresistible grind of forces that in the last analysis are resolvable into the integration of matter and the dissipation of motion. Its fatalism eliminates free-will. Environment and heredity are everything, human volition nothing. Carry this philosophy to its legitimate conclusion, and the man is a mere automaton who thinks he is a free agent only because he does not feel the strings that move him. That I am a man is because I have been evolved from the brute, as the bowlder is rounded from the rock; as the brute, my ancestor, was evolved from colloid, and colloid from indefinite, incoherent homogeneous matter. And that I am this or that kind of a man, with such and such powers, tastes, habits, ways of thinking, feeling, perceiving, acting, is simply the result of the external influences that registered in my ancestors the nerve impressions transmitted to me, and that have continued to mould me. Social institutions, the outgrowth of a similar evolution in which free-will had no part, will continue their evolution without help or hindrance from anything which is really choice or volition of mine.

Extremes sometimes curiously meet. The philosophy of Schopenhauer, which in deriving everything from will is the antipodes of the Spencerian philosophy, and which, like the philosophies of India, of which it is a European version, holds existence an evil, and looks for relief only to the renunciation of the will to live, would, if it were generally accepted, produce among the European races the same social lethargy, the same hopelessness of reform, the same readiness to bow before any tyrant, that have so long characterized the masses of India. It seems to me that the essential fatalism of the philosophy of Mr. Spencer would have a similar result.[1]

---

[1] In "Progress and Poverty," Book X., Chapter I., I say:

The practical outcome of this theory is in a sort of hopeful fatalism, of which current literature is full. In this view, progress is the result of forces which work slowly, steadily and remorselessly, for the elevation of man. War, slavery, tyranny, superstition, famine and pestilence, the want and misery which fester in modern civilization, are the impelling causes which drive man on, by eliminating poorer types and extending the higher; and hereditary transmission is the power by which advances are fixed, and past advances made the footing for new advances. The individual is the result of changes thus impressed upon and perpetuated through a long series of past individuals, and the social organization takes its form from the individuals of which it is composed. Thus, while this theory is, as Herbert Spencer says[1] — "radical to a degree beyond anything which current radicalism conceives;" inasmuch as it looks for changes in the very nature of man; it is at the same time "conservative to a degree beyond anything conceived by current conservatism," inasmuch as it holds that no change can avail save these slow changes in men's natures. Philosophers may teach that this does not lessen the duty of endeavoring to reform abuses, just as the theologians who taught predestinarianism insisted on the duty of all to struggle for salvation; but, as generally apprehended, the result is fatalism — "do what we may, the mills of the gods grind on regardless either of our aid or our hindrance."

Some years after this was written I had a curious illustration of its truth. Talking one day with the late E. L. Youmans, the great

---

[1] "The Study of Sociology" — Conclusion.

And as the pessimistic philosophy of the one seems to flow from the abandonment of action for mere speculation, and from the satiety and *ennui* which under certain conditions accompany it, so the evolutionary philosophy of the other seems to be such as might result from the abandonment of a noble purpose — from a turning from the thorny path which an attack upon vested wrongs must open, to embrace the pleasanter ways of acquiescence in things as they are.

It is not for me to say what is cause and what is effect; but the correspondence of Mr. Spencer's philosophy, which ignores the spiritual element and knows nothing of duty, with his own attitude as shown in his letters to the *St. James's Gazette* and the *Times* and in "The Man *versus* the State," is very striking. In "Justice" we shall see more of this correspondence.

---

popularizer of Spencerianism in the United States, a man of warm and generous sympathies, whose philosophy seemed to me like an ill-fitting coat he had accidentally picked up and put on, he fell into speaking with much warmth of the political corruption of New York, of the utter carelessness and selfishness of the rich, and of their readiness to submit to it, or to promote it wherever it served their money-getting purposes to do so. He became so indignant as he went on that he raised his voice till he almost shouted.

Alluding to a conversation some time before, in which I had affirmed and he had denied the duty of taking part in politics, I said to him, "What do you propose to do about it?"

Of a sudden his manner and tone were completely changed, as remembering his Spencerianism, he threw himself back, and replied, with something like a sigh, "Nothing! You and I can do nothing at all. It's all a matter of evolution. We can only wait for evolution. Perhaps in four or five thousand years evolution may have carried men beyond this state of things. But we can do nothing."

CHAPTER IV.

THE IDEA OF JUSTICE IN THE SYNTHETIC PHILOSOPHY.

As the culminating development of his evolutionary or synthetic philosophy, Mr. Spencer now comes to treat of those social-economic questions that involve the idea of justice, in a book which he entitles "Justice."

But what is justice?

It is the rendering to each his due. It pre-supposes a moral law, and its corollaries, natural rights which are self-evident. But where in a philosophy that denies spirit, that ignores will, that derives all the qualities and attributes of man from the integration of matter and the dissipation of motion, can we find any basis for the idea of justice?

"Justice," says Montesquieu, "is a relation of congruity which really subsists between two things. This relation is always the same, whatever being considers it, whether it be God, or an angel, or lastly a man." This, too, in "Social Statics," was Mr. Spencer's conception. Justice he tells us there means equalness — that is to say, a relation of congruity or equality which is always the same, and always apprehensible by men, no matter what be their condition of development or degree of knowledge. As the basis of all his reasoning he postulates an inherent moral sense, which "none but those committed to a preconceived theory can fail to recognize" — a perception that bears to morality the same relationship that the perception of the primary laws of quantity bear to mathematics; and which enables us to recognize an "eternal law of things," a "Divine order," in which, and not in any notions of what is expedient either for the individual or for all individuals, we may find a sure guide of conduct, the apprehension of right and wrong. And this it seems to me is necessarily and universally involved in the idea of justice, so that when a man, whatever be his theories, thinks of right or wrong, just or unjust, he thinks of a relation, like that of odd and even, or more and less, which is always and everywhere to be seen by whoever will look.

But this self-evidence of natural rights the Synthetic Philosophy denies. It admits the existence of natural rights — that is to say, rights which pertain to the individual man as man, and are consequently equal; but it derives the genesis of these rights, or at least their apprehension by man, from this process of his gradual evolution, by virtue of which they evolve, or he becomes conscious of them, after a certain amount of "social discipline," and not before. If such rights exist before, it must be potentially, or in some such way as the Platonic ideas. But as this would involve an appointed order; and hence intelligent will, to which we must attribute equity; and hence God; it seems inconsistent with Mr. Spencer's present view — not necessarily with that part which derives our physical constitutions from lower animals and primarily from the integrations of matter and motion — for this is a mere matter of external form, and that our bodies come, somehow, "from the dust of the earth" as the Scriptures put it, is as clear as that ice comes from water — but with that part which gives to the *ego* the same genesis, and accounts for our mental and moral qualities by variation, survival of the fittest, the pressure of conditions, social discipline and heredity of acquired characteristics.

Mr. Spencer realizes this inconsistency, for, abandoning altogether his original derivation and explanation of justice, he proceeds in "Justice" to make another derivation and explanation in accordance with his new philosophy, devoting to this the first eight chapters, or something more than a fifth of the book. With its validity or invalidity, its coherency or incoherency, I am not here concerned; my object being merely to show how he arrives at the conception of justice and what it is, so that we may judge the teachings of "Justice" from its own avowed standpoint.

To present Mr. Spencer's argument as intelligibly as I can, I will make a synopsis of the first eight chapters of "Justice," as far as possible in his own words, but without quotation marks, employing smaller type where the exact words can be used at some length.

These chapters are —

1. — *Animal Ethics.*

During immaturity, benefits received must be inversely proportioned to capacities possessed. After maturity, benefits must vary directly as worth, measured by fitness for the conditions of existence. The ill-fitted must suffer the evils of unfitness, and the well-fitted prove their fitness.

2.— *Sub-Human Justice.*

The law of sub-human justice is that each individual shall receive the benefits and the evils of its own nature and its consequent conduct.

3.— *Human Justice.*

Each individual ought to receive the benefits and the evils of his own nature and consequent conduct, neither being prevented from having whatever good his actions normally bring him, nor allowed to shoulder off this evil on other persons.

4.— *The Sentiment of Justice.*

Our feeling that we ourselves ought to have freedom to receive the results of our own nature and consequent actions, and which prompts maintenance of the sphere for this free play, results from inheritances of modifications produced by habit, or from more numerous survivals of individuals having nervous structures which have varied in fit ways, and from the tendency of groups formed of members having this adaptation to survive and spread. Recognition of the similar freedom of others is evolved from the fear of retaliation, from the punishment of interference prompted by the interests of the chief, from fear of the dead chief's ghost, and from fear of God, when dead-chief-ghost worship grows into God worship, and, finally, by the sympathy evolved by gregariousness.

5.— *The Idea of Justice.*

It emerges and becomes definite from experiences, generation after generation, which provoke resentment and reactive pains, until finally there arises a conception of a limit to each kind of activity up to which there is freedom to act. But it is a long time before the general nature of the limit common to all cases can be conceived. On the one hand there is the positive element, implied by each man's recognition of his claims to unimpeded activities and the benefits they bring; on the other hand there is the negative element implied by the consciousness of limits which the presence of other men having like claims necessitates. Inequality is suggested by the one, for if each is to receive the benefits due his own nature and consequent conduct, then, since men differ in their powers, there must be differences in the results. Equality is suggested by the other, since bounds must be set to the doings of each to avoid quarrels, and experience shows that these bounds are on the average the same for all. Unbalanced appreciation of the one is fostered by war, and tends to social organization of the militant type, where inequality is established by authority, an inequality referring, not to the natural achievement of greater rewards by greater merits, but to the artificial apportionment of greater rewards to greater merits. Unbalanced appreciation of the other tends to such theories as Bentham's greatest happiness principle, and to communism and socialism. The true conception is to be obtained by noting that the equality concerns the mutually limited spheres of action which must be maintained if associated men are to co-operate harmoniously, while the inequality concerns the results which each may achieve by carrying on his actions within the implied limits. The two may be and must be simultaneously asserted.

6.— *The Formula of Justice.*

It must be positive in so far as it asserts for each that, since he is to receive and suffer the good and evil of his own actions, he must be allowed to act. And it must be negative in so far as, by asserting this of every one, it implies that each can be allowed to act only under the restraint imposed by the presence of others having like claims to act. Evidently, the positive element is that which expresses a prerequisite to life in general, and the negative element is that which qualifies this prerequisite in the way required, when, instead of one life carried on alone, there are many lives carried on together.

Hence, that which we have to express in a precise way is the liberty of each limited only by the like liberties of all. This we do by saying, Every man is free to do what he wills, provided he infringes not the equal freedom of any other man.

7. — *The Authority of this Formula.*

The reigning school of politics and morals has a contempt for doctrines that imply restraint on the doings of immediate expediency. But if causation be universal, it must hold throughout the actions of incorporated men. Evolution implies that a distinct conception of justice can have arisen but gradually. It has gone on more rapidly under peaceful relations, and been held back by war. Nevertheless, where the conditions have allowed, it has evolved slowly to some extent, and formed for itself approximately true expressions, as shown in the Hebrew Commandments, and without distinction between generosity and justice, in the Christian Golden Rule, and in modern forms in the rule of Kant. It is also shown on the legal side, in the maxims of lawyers as to natural law, admitted inferentially even by the despotically-minded Austin.

These, it will be objected, are *a priori* beliefs. The doctrine of evolution teaches that *a priori* beliefs entertained by men at large must have arisen, if not from the experiences of each individual, then from the experiences of the race. Fixed intuitions must have been established by that intercourse with things which throughout an enormous past has directly and indirectly determined the organization of the nervous system, and certain resulting necessities of thought. Thus had the law of equal freedom no other than *a priori* derivations, it would still be rational to regard it as an adumbration of a truth, if not still literally true. And the inductive school, including Bentham and Mill are, on analysis, driven to the basis of *a priori* cognitions.

But the principle of natural equity, expressed in the freedom of each, limited only by the like freedom of all, is not exclusively an *a priori* belief.

Examination of the facts has shown it to be a fundamental law, by conformity to which life has evolved from its lowest up to its highest forms, that each adult individual shall take the consequences of its own nature and actions: survival of the fittest being the result. And the necessary implication is an assertion of that full liberty to act which forms the positive element in the formula of justice; since, without full liberty to act, the relation between conduct and consequence cannot be maintained. Various examples have made clear the conclusion manifest in theory, that among gregarious creatures this freedom of each to act has to be restricted; since if it is unrestricted there must arise such clashing of actions as prevents the gregariousness. And the fact that, relatively unintelligent though they are, inferior gregarious creatures inflict penalties for breaches of the needful restrictions, shows how regard for them has come to be unconsciously established as a condition to persistent social life.

These two laws, holding, the one of all creatures and the other of social creatures, and the display of which is clearer in proportion as the evolution is higher, find their last and fullest sphere of manifestation in human societies. We have recently seen that along with the growth of peaceful co-operation there has been an increasing conformity to this compound law under both its positive and negative aspects; and we have also seen that there has gone on simultaneously an increase of emotional regard for it, and intellectual apprehension of it.

So that we have not only the reasons above given for concluding that this *a priori* belief has its origin in the experiences of the race, but we are enabled to affiliate it on the experiences of living creatures at large, and to perceive that it is but a conscious response to certain necessary relations in the order of nature.

No higher warrant can be imagined; and now, accepting the law of equal freedom as an ultimate ethical principle, having an authority transcending every other, we may proceed with our inquiry.

8. — *Its Corollaries.*

That the general formula of justice may serve for guidance, deductions must be drawn severally applicable to special classes of cases. The several particular freedoms deducible from the laws of equal freedom may fitly be called, as they commonly are called, *rights.* Rights truly so called are corollaries from the law of equal freedom, and what are falsely called rights are not deducible from it.

It is not worth while to examine this argument. It is sufficient for our purpose to see that in "Justice" Mr. Spencer re-asserts the same principle from which in "Social Statics" he condemned private property in land.

CHAPTER V.

MR. SPENCER'S TASK.

THE first eight chapters of "Justice," as we have seen, bring Mr. Spencer by a different route to the same "first principle" which he had laid down forty years before in "Social Statics," and from which he had deduced the equal right of all men to the use of land and the ethical invalidity of private property in land — "all deeds, customs, and laws notwithstanding."

We are not concerned now with "Social Statics." We are not concerned with any of Mr. Spencer's changes in opinion, teleological, metaphysical, or of any other kind. We have here merely the Synthetic philosopher, who from grounds based on the doctrine of evolution lays down as the fundamental formula of justice, the axiomatic principle from which all the rights of men in their relations with each other are to be deduced: that all men have freedom to do as they will, provided they infringe not the equal freedom of all others.[1] What follows, with regard to the use

[1] From Appendix A of "Justice," it seems that Mr. Spencer has hitherto supposed that his statement of this "first principle" of "Social Statics," was the first time it had been thus put. In 1883 Professor Maitland had, however, pointed out that "Kant had already enunciated in other words a similar doctrine." Mr. Spencer tells us that, "Not being able to read the German quotation given by Mr. Maitland," he was unable to test the statement until, in the

of land, from this fundamental principle of the evolutionary philosophy? Is it not, unavoidably and irresistibly what Mr. Spencer stated years before? —

> Given a race of human beings having like claims to pursue the objects of their desires — given a world adapted to the gratification of those desires — a world into which such beings are similarly born, and it unavoidably follows that they have equal rights to the use of this world. For if each of them "has freedom to do all that he wills, provided he infringes not the equal freedom of any other," then each of them is free to use the earth for the satisfaction of his wants, provided he allows all others the same liberty. And conversely, it is manifest that no one, or part of them, may use the earth in such a way as to prevent the rest from similarly using it; seeing that to do this is to assume greater freedom than the rest, and consequently to break the law.

Is there one single deduction in Chapter IX. of "Social Statics" that does not as clearly follow from this reasoning of "Justice" — one single word that requires alteration to fit it for a place in the deductions to be drawn from this formula, except the single word God? And the substitution of "The

---

preparation of "Justice," he reached Chapter VI., when he discovered in a recent English translation of Kant certain passages which he gives, that "make it clear that Kant had arrived at a conclusion, which, if not the same as my own, is closely allied to it."

I mention this as showing the importance Mr. Spencer yet attaches to the "first principle," from which he deduced the condemnation of private property in land. Otherwise the matter is of no interest. His statement of this principle or formula was a good one, and doubtless original with him. Who had stated it before made no more difference than who first stated that one and one equal two. There are some things which to the human mind are self-evident — that is to say, which may be seen by whoever chooses to look — and this is one of them.

Unknowable" or "Evolution" for "God" would in no wise alter or lessen the force of the reasoning.

How, then, shall Mr. Spencer justify private property in land, which in his letters to the *Times* he had bound himself to do? How shall he deduce the rights of land-owners to compensation for their land or in any way assert for them rights that will lessen or modify, or in any way condition, the equal right of all their fellows to the use of land?

To men like Professor Huxley there is a short and easy way of doing this. It is simply to deny the existence of natural rights; that is to say, rights having any higher or more permanent sanction than municipal regulation. To be sure this opens a most awkward dilemma, for if power, or if you please legislative enactment, be the only sanction of right, what remains for the House of Have, when the House of Want shall muster its more numerous forces, either on the field of brute strength or in legislatures already controlled by popular suffrage? But, "after us, the deluge!" and such considerations do not much trouble those who take this short and easy way. Mr. Spencer, however, is debarred from taking it; not by what he has before said on the land question, for that could be unsaid, but by his philosophy. If there is no right but might, what does that philosophy mean and what is it for? If there is no law but that of the state, why does he write books to tell us what the state ought and ought not to do? And, furthermore, he has just deduced as his formula of justice, having, he says, the highest imaginable warrant — the same first principle from which in "Social Statics" he deduced the invalidity of private property in land.

The short and easy way of justifying private property in land, because it exists, or because it is sanctioned by the state, is therefore not open to Mr. Spencer, unless he is ready to abandon the last shred and figment of philosophic claim. His is a more difficult task. What he has to do, is to prove that the disinheritance of nineteen-twentieths of his countrymen accords with his "ultimate ethical principle having an authority transcending every other" — his formula of justice, that "Every man is free to do that which he will, provided he infringes not the equal freedom of any other man." To show that the so-called rights of existing land-owners to monopolize the land on which all must live are real rights, he must, on his own statement, show that they are deducible from the law of equal freedom.

Knowing, then, from Mr. Spencer's more recent utterances that he is determined at any cost to get on the comfortable side of the land question, we may be certain in advance that "Justice" will afford a spectacle both interesting and instructive. Interesting as the effort of a man of ability to accomplish a feat of intellectual legerdemain equivalent, not to swallowing a sword, but to swallowing himself. Instructive as showing how far a man so able that many people think him the greatest philosopher that has ever yet appeared; a man who has the advantage of knowing what can be said on the other side, can, on grounds which admit the equal right of men to be in the world, succeed in justifying that existing social arrangement which gives to a few the exclusive ownership of the world, and denies to the many any right to its use, save as they purchase the privilege of these few world-owners.

A Lord Bramwell or a Professor Huxley or a Duke of Argyll would rush in boldly and proceed frankly. But Mr. Spencer knows that to accomplish his task the attention of the reader must be confused and the real issue avoided. The effort to do this is to be seen at a glance the moment we come to the vital part of "Justice."

In "Social Statics" the discussion of "The Rights of Life and Personal Liberty" occupies hardly more than a single page, being treated as "such self-evident corollaries from our first principle as hardly to need a separate statement." In "Justice" it is padded out into two chapters — "The Right to Personal Integrity" and "The Rights to Free Motion and Locomotion," which, by references to the Fijians, the Wends, the Herculeans, the Homeric Greeks, and so on, are made to occupy some twelve or thirteen times as much space. But, although Mr. Spencer also refers to the Abors, the Nagas, the Lepchas, the Jakuns, and other far-off people, he takes no notice of such infractions of the right of free motion and locomotion by land-owning dukes as in 1850 excited his indignation.

In place of the chapter on "The Right to the Use of the Earth," which stands out so clearly and so prominently in "Social Statics," we find in "Justice" a chapter on "The Rights to the Uses of Natural Media," of which only a part is devoted to the right to the use of land, though a short note, having something of the same relation to it that the traditional lady's postscript has to her letter, is inserted in the Appendix.

This treatment of land, or the surface of the earth,

as but one of the natural media is in the highest degree unphilosophic, and could only be adopted for the purpose of confusion. For so far as man is concerned all natural media are appurtenant to land; and the term land in political economy and law comprises all natural substances and powers. To treat land as one of such natural media as light and air is therefore as unphilosophic as it would be to treat it as one of such sub-divisions of itself as water, rock, gravel or sand. The clearest and only philosophic terminology is that adopted in "Social Statics" — the right to the use of the earth, or the right to the use of land. For the right to the use of all natural elements comes from and with, and is inseparably involved in and annexed to, the right to the use of land.

Mr. Spencer's reasons for thus treating land as but one of the natural media appear as we read. Not merely is the burning question thus minimized and confused, but it becomes easier by means of analogy to slide over the injustice of the present treatment of land — an injustice which, as Mr. Spencer had himself previously seen, is inferior only to murder or slavery — and to bring private property in land into the category of things with which we need not concern ourselves.

CHAPTER VI.

"THE RIGHTS TO THE USES OF NATURAL MEDIA."

HERE in full is Chapter XI. of "Justice":

CHAPTER XI. — THE RIGHTS TO THE USES OF NATURAL MEDIA.

§ 49. A man may be entirely uninjured in body by the actions of fellow-men, and he may be entirely unimpeded in his movements by them, and he may yet be prevented from carrying on the activities needful for maintenance of life, by traversing his relations to the physical environment on which his life depends. It is, indeed, alleged that certain of these natural agencies cannot be removed from the state of common possession. Thus we read:

> "Some things are by nature itself incapable of appropriation, so that they cannot be brought under the power of any one. These got the name of *res communes* by the Roman law; and were defined, things the property of which belongs to no person, but the use to all. Thus, the light, the air, running water, etc., are so adapted to the common use of mankind, that no individual can acquire a property in them, or deprive others of their use." (*An Institute of the Law of Scotland* by John Erskine (ed. Macallan), i., 190).

But though light and air cannot be monopolized, the distribution of them may be interfered with by one man to the partial deprivation of another man — may be so interfered with as to inflict serious injury upon him.

No interference of this kind is possible without a breach of the law of equal freedom. The habitual interception of light by one person in such way that another person is habitually deprived of an equal share, implies disregard of the principle that the liberty of each is limited by the like liberties of all; and the like is true if free access to air is prevented.

Under the same general head there must, however, by an unusual extension of meaning, be here included something which admits of appropriation — the surface of the Earth. This, as forming part of the physical environment, seems necessarily to be included among the media of which the use may be claimed under the law of equal freedom. The Earth's surface cannot be denied to any one absolutely, without rendering life-sustaining activities impracticable. In the absence of standing-ground he can do nothing; and hence it appears to be a corollary from the law of equal freedom, interpreted with strictness, that the Earth's surface may not be appropriated absolutely by individuals, but may be occupied by them only in such manner as recognizes ultimate ownership by other men; that is — by society at large.

Concerning the ethical and legal recognitions of these claims to the uses of media, not very much has to be said: only the last demands much attention. We will look at each of them in succession.

§ **50**. In the earliest stages, while yet urban life had not commenced, no serious obstruction of one man's light by another man could well take place. In encampments of savages, and in the villages of agricultural tribes, no one was led, in pursuit of his ends, to overshadow the habitation of his neighbor. Indeed, the structures and relative positions of habitations made such aggressions almost impracticable.

In later times, when towns had grown up, it was unlikely that much respect would forthwith be paid by men to the claims of their neighbors in respect of light. During stages of social evolution in which the rights to life and liberty were little regarded, such comparatively trivial trespasses as were committed by those who built houses close in front of others' houses, were not likely to attract much notice, considered either as moral transgressions or legal wrongs. The narrow, dark streets of ancient continental cities, in common with the courts and alleys characterizing the older parts of our own towns, imply that in the days when they were built the shutting out by one man of another man's share of sun and sky was not thought an offence. And, indeed, it may reasonably be held that recognition of such an offence was in those days impracticable; since, in walled towns, the crowding of houses became a necessity.

In modern times, however, there has arisen the perception that the natural distribution of light may not be interfered with. Though the law which forbids the building of walls, houses, or other edifices of certain heights, within prescribed distances from existing houses, does not absolutely negative the intercepting of light; yet it negatives the intercepting of it to serious degrees, and seeks to compromise the claims of adjacent owners as fairly as seems practicable.

That is to say, this corollary from the law of equal freedom, if it has not come to be overtly asserted, has come to be tacitly recognized.

§ 51. To some extent interference with the supply of light involves interference with the supply of air; and, by interdicting the one, some interdict is, by implication, placed on the other. But the claim to use of the air, though it has been recognized by English law in the case of windmills, is less definitely established: probably because only small evils have been caused by obstructions.

There has, however, risen into definite recognition the claim to unpolluted air. Though acts of one man which may diminish the supply of air to another man, have not come to be distinctly classed as wrong; yet acts which vitiate the quality of his air are in modern times regarded as offences — offences for which there are in some cases moral reprobations only, and in other cases legal penalties. In some measure all are severally obliged, by their own respiration, to vitiate the air respired by others, where they are in proximity. It needs but to walk a little distance behind one who is smoking, to perceive how widely diffused are the exhalations from each person's lungs; and to what an extent, therefore, those who are adjacent, especially indoors, are compelled to breath the air that has already been taken in and sent out time after time. But since this vitiation of air is mutual, it cannot constitute aggression. Aggression occurs only when vitiation by one, or some, has to be borne by others who do not take like shares in the vitiation; as often happens in railway-carriages, where men who think themselves gentlemen smoke in other places than those provided for smokers: perhaps getting from fellow-passengers a nominal, though not a real, consent, and careless of the permanent nuisance entailed on those who afterwards travel in compartments reeking with stale tobacco-smoke. Beyond the recognition of this by right-thinking persons as morally improper, it is forbidden as improper by railway-regulations; and, in virtue of by-laws, may bring punishment by fine.

Passing from instances of this kind to instances of a graver kind, we have to note the interdicts against various nuisances — stenches resulting from certain businesses carried on near at hand, injurious fumes such as those from chemical works, and smoke proceeding from large chimneys. Legislation which forbids the acts causing such nuisances, implies the right of each citizen to unpolluted air.

Under this same head we may conveniently include another kind of trespass to which the surrounding medium is instrumental. I refer to the production of sounds of a disturbing kind. There are small and large trespasses of this class. For one who, at a *table d'hôte,* speaks so loudly as to interfere with the conversation of others, and for those who, during the performance at a theatre or concert, persist in distracting the attention of auditors around by talking, there is reprobation, if nothing more: their acts are condemned as contrary to good manners, that is, good morals, for the one is a part of the other. And then when inflictions of this kind are public, or continuous, or both — as in the case of street-music and especially bad street-music, or as in the case of loud noises proceeding from factories, or as in the case of church-bells rung at early hours, the aggression has come to be legally recognized as such and forbidden under penalty: not as yet sufficiently recognized, however, as is shown in the case of railway-whistles at central stations, which are allowed superfluously to disturb tens of thousands of people all through the night, and often to do serious injury to invalids.

Thus in respect of the uses of the atmosphere, the liberty of each limited only by the like liberties of all, though not overtly asserted, has come to be tacitly asserted; in large measure ethically, and in a considerable degree legally.

§ 52. The state of things brought about by civilization does not hinder ready acceptance of the corollaries thus far drawn; but rather clears the way for acceptance of them. Though in the days when cannibalism was common and victims were frequently sacrificed to the gods, assertion of the right to life might have been received with demur, yet the ideas and practices of those days have left no such results as stand in the way of unbiassed judgments. Though during times when slavery and serfdom were deeply organized in the social fabric, an assertion of the right to liberty would have roused violent opposition, yet at the present time, among ourselves at least, there exists no idea, sentiment, or usage, at variance with the conclusion that each man is free to use his limbs and move about where he pleases. And similarly with respect to the environment. Such small interferences with others' supplies of light and air as have been bequeathed in the structures of old towns and such others as smoking fires entail, do not appreciably hinder acceptance of the proposition that men have equal claims to uses of the media in which all are immersed. But the proposition that men have equal claims to the use of that remaining portion of the environment — hardly to be called a medium — on which all stand and by the products of which all live, is antagonized by ideas and arrangements descending to us from the past. These ideas and arrangements arose when considerations of equity did not affect land-tenure any more than they affected the tenure of men as slaves or serfs; and they now make acceptance of the proposition difficult. If, while possessing those ethical sentiments which social discipline has now produced, men stood in possession of a territory not yet individually portioned out, they would no more hesitate to assert equality of their claims to the land than they would hesitate to assert equality of their claims to light and air. But now that long-standing appropriation, continued culture, as well as sales and purchases, have complicated matters, the *dictum* of absolute ethics, incongruous with the state of things produced, is apt to be denied altogether. Before asking how, under these circumstances, we must decide, let us glance at some past phases of land-tenure.

Partly because in early stages of agriculture, land, soon exhausted, soon ceases to be worth occupying, it has been the custom with little-civilized and semi-civilized peoples, for individuals to abandon after a time the tracts they have cleared, and to clear others. Causes aside, however, the fact is that in early stages private ownership of land is unknown: only the usufruct belongs to the cultivator, while the land itself is tacitly regarded as the property of the tribe. It is thus now with the Sumatrans and others, and it was thus with our own ancestors: the members of the Mark, while they severally owned the products of the areas they respectively cultivated, did not own the areas themselves. Though it may be said that at first they were members of the same family *gens*, or clan, and that the ownership of each tract was private ownership in so far as the tract belonged to a cluster of relations; yet since the same kind of tenure continued after the population of the Mark had come to include men who were unrelated to the rest, ownership of the tract by the community and not by individuals became an established arrangement. This primitive condition will be clearly understood after contemplating the case of the Russians, among whom it has but partially passed away.

"The village lands were held in common by all the members of the association [*mir*]; the individual only possessed his harvest, and the *dvor* or enclosure immediately surrounding his house. This primitive condition of property, existing in Russia up to the present day, was once common to all European peoples." — (*The History of Russia*, A. Rambaud, trans. by Lang, vol. i. p. 45).

With this let me join a number of extracts from Wallace's "Russia," telling us of the original state of things and of the subsequent states. After noting the fact that while the Don Cossacks were purely nomadic — "agriculture was prohibited on pain of death," apparently because it interfered with hunting and cattle-breeding, he says: —

"Each Cossack who wished to raise a crop ploughed and sowed wherever he thought fit, and retained as long as he chose the land thus appropriated; and when the soil began to show signs of exhaustion, he abandoned his plot and ploughed elsewhere. As the number of agriculturists increased, quarrels frequently arose. Still worse evils appeared when markets were created in the vicinity. In some stanitzas [Cossack villages] the richer families appropriated enormous quantities of the common land by using several teams of oxen, or by hiring peasants in the nearest villages to come and plough for them; and instead of abandoning the land after raising two or three crops they retained possession of it. Thus the whole of the arable land, or at least the best parts of it, become actually, if not legally, the private property of a few families."—(*Ib.* ii. 86).

Then he explains that as a consequence of something like a revolution:

"In accordance with their [the landless members of the community's] demands the appropriated land was confiscated by the Commune and the system of periodical distributions . . . was introduced, By this system each male adult possesses a share of the land."—(*Ib.* ii. 87).

On the Steppes "a plot of land is commonly cultivated for only three or four years in succession. It is then abandoned for at least double that period, and the cultivators remove to some other portion of the communal territory. . . . Under such circumstances the principle of private property in the land is not likely to strike root; each family insists on possessing a certain *quantity* rather than a certain *plot* of land, and contents itself with a right of usufruct, whilst the right of property remains in the hands of the Commune."—(*Ib.* ii. 91).

But in the central and more advanced districts this early practice has become modified, though without destroying the essential character of the tenure.

"According to this system [the three-field system] the cultivators do not migrate periodically from one part of the communal territory to another, but till always the same fields, and are obliged to manure the plots which they occupy. . . . Though the three-field system has been in use for many generations in the central provinces, the communal principle, with its periodical re-allotment of the land, still remains intact." — (*Ib.* ii. 92).

Such facts, and numerous other such facts, put beyond question the conclusion that before the progress of social organization changed the relations of individuals to the soil, that relation was one of joint ownership and not one of individual ownership.

How was this relation changed? How only could it be changed? Certainly not by unforced consent. It cannot be supposed that all, or some, of the members of the community willingly surrendered their respective claims. Crime now and again caused loss of an individual's share in the joint ownership; but this must have left the relations of the rest to the soil unchanged. A kindred result might have been entailed by debt, were it not that debt implies a creditor; and while it is scarcely supposable that the creditor could be the community as a whole, indebtedness to any individual of it would not empower the debtor to transfer in payment something of which he was not individually possessed, and which could not be individually received. Probably elsewhere there came into play the cause described as having operated in Russia, where some, cultivating larger areas than others, accumulated wealth and consequent power, and extra possessions; but, as is implied by the fact that in Russia this led to a revolution and re-institution of the original state, the process was evidently there, and probably elsewhere, regarded as aggressive. Obviously the chief cause must have been the exercise of direct or indirect force: sometimes internal but chiefly external. Disputes and fights within the community, leading to predominance (achieved in some cases by possession of fortified houses) prepared the way for partial usurpations. When, as among the Suanetians, we have a still-extant case in which every family in a village has its tower of defence, we may well understand how the intestine feuds in early communities commonly brought about individual supremacies, and how these ended in the establishment of special claims upon the land subordinating the general claims.

But conquest from without has everywhere been chiefly instrumental in superseding communal proprietorship by individual proprietorship. It is not to be supposed that in times when captive men were made slaves and women appropriated as spoils of war, much respect was paid to pre-existing ownership of the soil. The old English buccaneers who, in their descents on the coast, slew priests at the altars, set fire to churches, and massacred the people who had taken refuge in them, would have been very incomprehensible beings had they recognized the land-ownership of such as survived. When the pirate Danes, who in later days ascended the rivers, had burnt the homesteads they came upon, slaughtered the men, violated the women, tossed children on pikes or sold them in the market-place, they must have undergone a miraculous transformation had they thereafter inquired to whom the Marks belonged, and admitted the titles of their victims to them. And similarly when, two centuries later, after constant internal wars had already produced military rulers maintaining quasi-feudal claims over occupiers of lands, there came the invading Normans, the right of conquest once more overrode such kinds of possession as had grown up, and still further merged communal proprietorship in that kind of individual proprietorship which characterized feudalism. Victory, which gives unqualified power over the defeated and their belongings, is followed, according to the nature of the race, by the assertion of universal ownership, more or less qualified according to the dictates of policy. While in some cases, as in Dahomey, there results absolute monopoly by the king, not only of the land but of everything else, there results in other cases, as there resulted in England, supreme ownership by the king with recognized sub-ownerships and sub-sub-ownerships of nobles and their vassals holding the land one under another, on condition of military service: supreme ownership being, by implication, vested in the crown.

Both the original state and the subsequent states have left their traces in existing land-laws. There are many local rights which date from a time when "private property in land, as we now understand it, was a struggling novelty." *

> "The people who exercise rights of common exercise them by a title which, if we could only trace it all the way back, is far more ancient than the lord's. Their rights are those which belonged to the members of the village community long before manors and lords of the manor were heard of." †

And any one who observes what small tenderness for the rights of commoners is shown in the obtainment of Inclosure-Acts, even in our own day, will be credulous indeed if he thinks that in ruder times the lapse of communal right into private rights was equitably effected. The private ownership, however, was habitually incomplete; since it was subject to the claims of the over-lord, and through him, again, to those of the over-

* *The Land Laws*, by Sir Fredk. Pollock, Bart., p. 2. † *Ibid.*, p. 6.

over-lord: the implication being that the ownership was subordinate to that of the head of the community.

"No absolute ownership of land is recognized by our law-books except in the Crown. All lands are supposed to be held immediately, or mediately, of the Crown, though no rent or services may be payable, and no grant from the Crown on record." *

And that this conception of land-ownership survives, alike in theory and in practice, to the present time, is illustrated by the fact that year by year State-authority is given for appropriating land for public purposes, after making due compensation to existing holders. Though it may be replied that this claim of the State to supreme land-ownership is but a part of its claim to supreme ownership in general, since it assumes the right to take anything on giving compensation; yet the first is an habitually-enforced claim, while the other is but a nominal claim not enforced; as we see in the purchase of pictures for the nation, to effect which the State enters into competition with private buyers, and may or may not succeed.

It remains only to point out that the political changes which have slowly replaced the supreme power of the monarch by the supreme power of the people, have, by implication, replaced the monarch's supreme ownership of the land by the people's supreme ownership of the land. If the representative body has practically inherited the governmental powers which in past times vested in the king, it has at the same time inherited that ultimate proprietorship of the soil which in past times vested in him. And since the representative body is but the agent of the community, this ultimate proprietorship now vests in the community. Nor is this denied by land-owners themselves. The report issued in December, 1889, by the council of "The Liberty and Property Defence League," on which sit several Peers and two judges, yields proof. After saying that the essential principle of their organization, "based upon recorded experience," is a distrust of "officialism, imperial or municipal," the council go on to say that: —

"This principle applied to the case of land clearly points to individual ownership, qualified by State-suzerainty. . . . The land can of course be 'resumed' on payment of full compensation, and managed by the 'people', if they so will it."

* *The Land Laws*, by Sir Fredk. Pollock, Bart., p. 12.

And the badness of the required system of administration is the only reason urged for maintaining the existing system of land-holding: the supreme ownership of the community being avowedly recognized. So that whereas, in early stages, along with the freedom of each man, there went joint ownership of the soil by the body of men; and whereas, during the long periods of that militant activity by which small communities were consolidated into great ones, there simultaneously resulted loss of individual freedom and loss of participation in land-ownership; there has, with the decline of militancy and the growth of industrialism, been a re-acquirement of individual freedom and a re-acquirement of such participation in land-ownership as is implied by a share in appointing the body by which the land is now held. And the implication is that the members of the community, habitually exercising as they do, through their representatives, the power of alienating and using as they think well, any portion of the land, may equitably appropriate and use, if they think fit, all portions of the land. But since equity and daily custom alike imply that existing holders of particular portions of land, may not be dispossessed without giving them in return its fairly-estimated value, it is also implied that the wholesale resumption of the land by the community can be justly effected only by wholesale purchase of it. Were the direct exercise of ownership to be resumed by the community without purchase, the community would take, along with something which is its own, an immensely greater amount of something which is not its own. Even if we ignore those multitudinous complications which, in the course of century after century, have inextricably entangled men's claims, theoretically considered — even if we reduce the case to its simplest theoretical form; we must admit that all which can be claimed for the community is the surface of the country in its original unsubdued state. To all that value given to it by clearing, breaking-up, prolonged culture, fencing, draining, making roads, farm buildings, etc., constituting nearly all its value, the community has no claim. This value has been given either by personal labor, or by labor paid for, or by ancestral labor; or else the value given to it in such ways has been purchased by legitimately earned money. All this value artificially given vests in existing owners, and cannot without a gigantic robbery be taken from them. If, during the many transactions which have brought about existing land-ownership, there have been much violence and much fraud, these have been small compared with the violence and the fraud which the community would be guilty of did it take possession, without paying for it, of that artificial value, which the labor of nearly two thousand years has given to the land.

§ **53**. Reverting to the general topic of the chapter — the rights to the uses of natural media — it chiefly concerns us here to note the way in which these rights have gradually acquired legislative sanctions as societies have advanced to higher types.

At the beginning of the chapter we saw that in modern times there have arisen legal assertions of men's equal rights to the uses of light and air: no forms of social organization or class-interests having appreciably hindered recognition of these corollaries from the law of equal freedom. And we have just seen that by implication, if not in any overt or conscious way, there has in our days been recognized the equal rights of all electors to supreme ownership of the inhabited area — rights which, though latent, are asserted by every Act of Parliament which alienates land. Though this right to the use of the Earth, possessed by each citizen, is traversed by established arrangements to so great an extent as to be practically suspended; yet its existence as an equitable claim cannot be denied without affirming that expropriation by State-decree is inequitable. The right of an existing holder of land can be equitably superseded, only if there exists a prior right of the community at large; and this prior right of the community at large consists of the sum of the individual rights of its members.

NOTE. Various considerations touching this vexed question of land-ownership, which would occupy too much space if included here, I have included in Appendix B.

Let us take breath and gather our wits. It is like going through a St. Gothard tunnel. Here we are on the other side, sure enough! But how did we get there?

Mr. Spencer brought us in, asserting the law of equal freedom as "an ultimate ethical principle, having an authority transcending every other;" declaring that "rights truly so called are corollaries from the law of equal freedom, and what are falsely called rights are not deducible from it."

He brings us out, with a confused but unmistakable assertion that the freedom to use land belongs only to the small class of landlords; with an assertion of the strongest kind of their right to deprive all other men of freedom to use the earth until they are paid for it.

How has he got there?

Has he shown that the law of equal freedom gives freedom to the use of land only to a few men and denies it to all other men? Has he shown that the right so-called of the small class of land-owners to the exclusive use of land is a true right and not a false right, by deducing it from the law of equal freedom? Has he met one of the conditions called for by his elaborate derivation and formula of justice in the preceding chapters of this very book? Has he shown the invalidity of a single one of the deductions by which he proved in "Social Statics" that justice does not permit private property in land?

It is worth while to examine this chapter in detail. Its argument is divisible into two parts — (1) as to the right to the use of light, air, etc., and (2) as to the right to the use of land. Let us consider the one part before passing to the other.

CHAPTER VII.

"JUSTICE" ON THE RIGHT TO LIGHT AND AIR.

Mr. Spencer's carelessness of thought is shown in the very opening sentence of this chapter on "The Right to the Uses of Natural Media:"

> A man may be entirely uninjured in body by the action of fellow-men, and he may be entirely unimpeded in his movements by them, and he may yet be prevented from carrying on the activities needful for maintenance of life, by traversing his relations to the physical environment on which his life depends.

How?

To ordinary apprehension, the only way in which men can be deprived of the use of "the physical environment on which life depends" is either by such bodily injuries as killing, maiming, binding, imprisoning, or by such restrictions on movement as have the threat of bodily injury behind them, like the taboo among the South Sea Islanders, or private property in land among us. Nor have the tyrants of the world, much as they would have liked to, ever been able to find any other way.

Without condescending to explain, Mr. Spencer goes on to quote Erskine to the effect that "the light, the air, running water, etc., are so adapted to the common use of mankind that no individual can acquire a property in them or deprive others of their use."

This again shows carelessness in apprehension and statement. What Erskine really means is that the law does not, and that because it can not, give property in the substance of matter, so that the molecules or atoms of which it is composed may be identified and reclaimed through all changes in form or place; but that ownership can only attach to matter in its relation to form or place. For instance, I buy to-day a dog or a horse. I acquire in this purchase the ownership of what matter is now, or at any time in the future may be, contained in the form of this dog or horse, not the ownership of a certain amount of matter in whatever form it may hereafter assume. That no law could give me, nor could I even set up a claim to it, for it would be impossible for me to identify it. For the matter which my dog or horse embodies for the moment, like the matter of which my own frame is composed, is constantly passing from that form to other forms. The only thing tangible to me or other men is this form. And it is in this that ownership consists. If my dog eats your mutton chop, your property in the chop does not become property in the dog. If the law gives you any action it is certainly not that of replevin.

The principle of the law that Erskine refers to is thus stated by Blackstone (Chapter 2, Book II.):

> I cannot bring an action to recover possession of a pool or other piece of water either by superficial measure for twenty acres of water or by general description, as for a pond or a rivulet; but I must bring my action for what lies at the bottom and call it twenty acres of land covered with water. For water is a movable, wandering thing, and must of necessity continue common by the

law of nature, so that I can only have a temporary, transient, usufructuary property; wherefore if a body of water runs out of my pond into another man's I have no right to reclaim it. But the land which that water covers is permanent, fixed and immovable, and therefore in this I may have a certain substantial property, of which the law will take notice and not of the other.

Now the comparatively rough distinctions that are amply sufficient for the purposes of the lawyer are not always sufficient for the purposes of the philosopher. If we analyze this principle of the law, we see that no real distinction is made as to ownership between the substance of water and the substance of land — that is to say, between the more or less stable forms of matter of which the body of the universe consists. The distinction is as to tangible form. I may bring an action for ice, which is water that has assumed tangible form by the lowering of temperature, or for water in barrels or bottles, which in another way gives it form. And the real reason why in an action for the possession of a body of water I must describe it as land covered by water is that it is the land which holds the water in place and gives it form.

So, on the other hand, if a freshet or a water-burst carry the fertile soil from my field into that of my neighbor, I can no more reclaim it by action at law than I can reclaim the water that runs out of my pond. Or if a volcanic convulsion were to shift the position of a mineral deposit, it would cease to belong to one land-owner and the other would acquire legal possession. The legal resnlt would be precisely the same as the legal result of a change in a rivulet's course. In ruder times, ere the art of surveying was so well developed as now, it was customary to fix the boundaries of legal possession by natural objects deemed immovable, such as mountains, ocean shores, rivers, etc., and in places where this method has been retained changes in landmarks frequently change the ownership of considerable bodies of land, as on the shifting banks of the lower Mississippi. But our modern surveying takes for its bases latitude and longitude. And this is the essential idea of land ownership: It is the ownership, not of certain atoms of matter, be they rock, soil, water or air, or of certain forms of energy, such as heat, light or electricity, but the ownership of a certain section of space and of all that may be therein contained.

Mr. Spencer is confusing two essentially different ideas — the idea of substance and the idea of form or locality. In the one sense nothing whatever may be owned — land no more than light or electricity. In the other, all natural substances and powers may be owned — water, air, light, heat or electricity, as truly as land. And they *are* owned, though, since in our legal terminology space and its contents are known as land, they must in law be described as land. Whoever, under our laws, acquires ownership in land *may* deprive others of light, air, running water, etc., and *does* acquire a property in their use, which is frequently a tangible element, and at times the only element in the value of an estate — as where the purity of the air, the beauty of the view, the abundance of sunlight which a favorable exposure gives, the presence of mineral springs, or the access to streams, are elements in the price at which land can be sold or rented.

In the next sentence we are told that "light and air cannot be monopolized." But they *are* monopolized in the monopolization of land, and this as effectually as any monopolizer could wish. It is true that air and sunlight are not formally bought, sold and rented. But why? Not that they could not be measured off and determined by metes and bounds, but simply because they are to our physical constitutions inseparable from land, so that whoever owns the land owns also the air it is bathed in and the light that falls on it. Light and air *are* monopolized whenever land is monopolized; and the exclusive use to them *is* bought and sold whenever land is bought and sold.

It is not merely that, as the flying-machine has not yet been perfected, the owner of land holds the means of access to the air above it and the light that falls on it; it is that the owner of land *is* the owner of such light and air, not merely virtually, but formally and legally. And were the air-ship perfected, he would have the same legal right to forbid trespass on *his* light and air, and to demand payment for any use made of it or any passage through it, thousands of feet above the surface, as he now has to forbid trespass on his ground or to demand payment for any use of or any passage through what lies thousands of feet below it. In English law, land does not mean merely the surface of the earth within certain metes and bounds, but all that may be above and all that may be below that surface; and under the same legal right by which the land-owner holds as his private property any certain part of the surface of the globe he also holds the rocks and minerals below it and the air and the light above it. As Blackstone says: "The word 'land' includes not only the face of the earth, but everything under it or over it. . . . By the name of land everything terrestrial will pass." The land-owner is, in law as well as in fact, not a mere surface owner, but a universe owner. And just as in some places land-owners sell the surface right, retaining mineral rights; or sell mineral rights, retaining surface rights; or sell the right of way, retaining rights to other use: so, where there is occasion, the right to use light and air may be separated, in sales and purchases and title-deeds, from the right to the use of the ground.

An invention which would make practicable the use of light and air without possession of the surface, would at once bring out the fact that, legally, they belong to land-owners, just as subterranean mining and the projection of underground railways have brought out the fact that land-owners are legal owners of all beneath the surface. In fact, existing deeds furnish instances in which the real thing bought and sold, though properly enough styled land in the conveyances, is not land at all in the narrow meaning, but light and air, or the right to their use. To cite a case: The city of Cleveland, Ohio, some years since, desired to convert the viaduct bridge over the Cuyahoga river into a swinging bridge. To do this it was necessary that one end of the bridge should in its swing pass for a short distance through the air over a strip of land belonging to a private owner. The city of Cleveland had, therefore, to buy the right to use this air, and I have before me a copy of the deed, executed on the 28th of February, 1880, by which, in consideration of $9,994.88, Meyers, Rouse & Co. sell and convey to the city of Cleveland the right to swing such bridge over a small area thirty-five feet above the ground. Of this estate in the air the grantors describe themselves as holding a good and indefeasible title in fee simple, with the right to bargain and sell the same. Were it thirty-five hundred or thirty-five hundred thousand feet above the surface, the legal right of ownership would be the same. For the ownership which attaches to land under our laws is not to be really measured by linear feet and inches, but by parallels of latitude and meridians of longitude, starting from the centre of the earth and indefinitely extendible. And while Meyers, Rouse & Co. have sold to the city of Cleveland a slice of their air of perhaps fifteen feet in depth, they still retain the legal ownership of all the air above it, and could demand toll of or refuse passage to any flying machine that should attempt to cross it.

The same lack of analytic power continues to be shown by Mr. Spencer when he goes on to tell us that the equal rights to the use of light and air, though not recognized in primitive stages, have, in the course of social evolution, come to be completely or all but completely recognized now. So far is this from being true, that in such countries as England and the United States there is no recognition whatever of the equal right to the use of light and air. To the list of interdictions which he cites as recognitions of this equal right, he might as well have added that of shying bricks through these media at passers-by. For where the interdictions he mentions — of interceptions of light and air, of smoking in certain places, of the maintenance of stenches and fumes, of the making of disturbing noises — are not mere interdictions of certain species of assault; they are interdictions based on and involved in the ownership of land.

Mr. Spencer might have seen this for himself, where he speaks of "the law which forbids the building of walls, houses, or other edifices within prescribed distances of other houses . . . and seeks to compromise the claims of adjacent owners as fairly as seem practicable."

Owners of what? Why, owners of land. It is only as an owner of land, or as the tenant of an owner of land, that under our English law any one has a right to complain of the interception of light and air by another land-owner. The owner of land may intercept light and air, may make noises and create stenches to any extent he pleases, provided he infringes not the equal rights of other owners of land, for light and air are considered by English law as what they truly are, so far as human beings are concerned, appurtenances of land. No one in England, be he stranger or native born, has any legal right whatever to the use of English light and English air, save as the owner or grantee of an owner of English land. That even on the Queen's highways the public are deemed to have such rights as against adjacent land-holders I am not sure. Certain it is, that one may travel for miles through the public roads, amid the finest scenery in those countries, and find the view wantonly shut out by high and costly walls, erected for the express purpose of intercepting the light, and crowned on their tops with broken glass, to tear the clothes and cut the flesh of any one who dares climb them to get such a view as the unintercepted light would give.

The rights to the use of light, air and other natural media are in truth as inseparable from the right to the use of land as the bottom of that atmospheric ocean which surrounds our globe is inseparable from the globe's surface; and the pretence of treating them separately could only spring from Mr. Spencer's evident desire to confuse the subject he is pretending to treat, to cover with a fog of words his abandonment of a position incapable of refutation, and from the false assumption that the liberty of each to the use of air and light, limited only by the like liberty of all, *is* practically and legally recognized, to lead to the still more preposterously false assumption that equal rights to the use of land *are* also fully recognized.

But before examining this last assumption, there is one form of it which he incidentally makes that is worth noticing — the assumption that the equal right to personal liberty and freedom of movement is already fully recognized.

It is a pity that Mr. Spencer had not intermitted his studies of the Abors, the Bodas, the Creeks, the Dhimals, the Eghas, and other queer people, to the end of the alphabet, of whom his later books are as full as those of the pedants of the last century were of classical quotations, and made some observations in his own country. They would have saved him from the astounding statement that —

At the present time, among ourselves at least, there exists no idea, sentiment, or usage at variance with the conclusion that each man is free to use his limbs and move where he pleases.

The truth is, that instead of every one being free in England "to use his limbs and move about where he pleases," there is no part of the British Isles, even though it be wild moor, bleak deer-forest or bare mountain-top, where a man is free to move about without permission of the private owner, except it be the highroads, the public places, or other strips and spots of land deemed the property of the community.

Mr. Spencer seems to have forgotten this now, but he knew it when in "Social Statics" he denounced the system that permitted the Duke of Leeds to warn off tourists from Ben-muich-Dhui, the Duke of Atholl to close Glen Tilt, the Duke of Buccleuch to deny Free Church sites, and the Duke of Sutherland to displace Highlanders with deer.

"Verily, they have their reward." The name of Herbert Spencer now appears with those of about all the Dukes in the Kingdom as the director of an association formed for the purpose of defending private property in land that was especially active in the recent London County Council election.

CHAPTER VIII.

"JUSTICE" ON THE RIGHT TO LAND.

At last, however, as all men must, even after the flying-machine becomes practicable, Mr. Spencer is forced to come down from light and air to solid earth.

But observe how reluctantly, how tenderly, he approaches the main question, the subject he would evidently like to ignore altogether. Land — to us the one solid, natural element; our all-producing, all-supporting mother, from whose bosom our very frames are drawn, and to which they return again; our standing-place; our workshop; our granary; our reservoir and substratum and nexus of media and forces; the element from which all we can produce must be drawn; without which we cannot breathe the air or enjoy the light; the element prerequisite to all human life and action — he speaks of as "that remaining portion of the environment, hardly to be called a medium," which "*by an unusual extension of meaning*" is included in the things to which the equal liberty of all extends.

Yet, at last, and thus tenderly, after having shown to his own satisfaction that with regard to personal rights and the liberty of movement, "things as they are" in such countries as England do not differ from "things as they ought to be," except, perhaps, that there is too much smoking in railway carriages, Mr. Spencer *does* at last get to the burning question of the land. And no sooner does he get there than the power by virtue of which a truth once recognized can never be entirely forgotten or utterly ignored, forces from him this recognition:

> If, while possessing those ethical sentiments which social discipline has now produced, men stood in the possession of a territory not yet individually portioned out, they would no more hesitate to assert equality of their claims to the land than they would hesitate to assert equality of their claims to light and air.

"*If, while possessing those ethical sentiments which social discipline has now produced.*" This "if" is the assumption of the Spencerian philosophy, that our moral sentiments have been evolved by pressure of conditions, survival of the fittest and hereditary transmission, since the time when, according to it, primitive men were accustomed to eat each other. Having told us that social evolution has brought mankind in the Victorian era to the recognition of equal rights to air and light, Mr. Spencer now assumes that the idea of equal rights to the use of land is the product of a similar development instead of being a primary perception of mankind.

Now this assumption is not merely opposed to all the facts; it is inconsistent with the Spencerian philosophy.

To consider the philosophy first: It holds that man is an evolution from the animal. He comes to be man by gradual development from the monkey or from some form of life from which the monkeys have also sprung. In the course of this evolutionary process, continued since he became man, he has acquired his present instincts, habits and powers.

Now I will not ask how, since the highest animals that habitually eat their own kind are on the synthetic genealogical tree far below any of the animals, existing or extinct, from which man can have descended, the oft-repeated assumption that primitive men were habitual cannibals can be reconciled with the assumption that they derived their habits from their animal ancestors.

But I will make bold to ask how the assumption that men have only now arrived at the perception of the equality of rights to the use of the natural media, and especially land, can be reconciled with the assumption that our moral perceptions are derived from animals. Animals fight with their own kind, as men fight; or at least some of them do occasionally, though none fight so frequently and so wantonly. But is there an animal, from the monkey to the jelly-fish, that does not, with animals of its own kind, and when at peace, fail to claim for itself and accord to others the liberty to use natural media, bounded only by the equal liberty of all? If there is not, how can the assumption that it has taken man all these ages to recognize the equality of rights to the use of natural media be made to harmonize with the assumption that he primarily derives his perceptions from the animal?

I ask this question to emphasize the fact that, in his effort to smooth away the monstrous injustice of private property in land, Mr. Spencer does violence to his own theories — not alone to the theories which he held when he wrote "Social Statics," but to the theories of his Synthetic Philosophy — the theories set forth in "Justice;" that he stands ready to sacrifice to his new masters not only his moral honesty, but even what the morally depraved often cling to — the pretence of intellectual honesty. In order to ignore the gist of the land question while pretending to explain it, he is endeavoring to create the impression that the present treatment of land, if not indeed the best, is at least the highest form which the progressive development of the idea of the equality of rights to the use of natural media has assumed. But to say that the idea of equal rights to land is the product of advancing social discipline is to say that it has proceeded from the contrary idea — that of unequal rights, or private property in land. Since the animals show no trace of this idea, this assumption is inconsistent with the doctrine that primitive man came closest to the animals. And to assume, as Mr. Spencer does in this chapter, that men start with the idea of unequal rights to land, and have been working up through social discipline to the idea of equal rights, is likewise inconsistent with all the points in the elaborate derivation of the idea of justice, which occupy the first eight chapters of this very book.

The assumption that the idea of equal rights to land is the product of social discipline is at both ends contradicted by the facts. In America, Australia and New Zealand, men of English speech, possessing "those ethical sentiments which social discipline has now produced," *have* stood in possession of territory not yet individually portioned out: but, instead of asserting the equality of claims to land, they have proceeded to individually portion out this territory as fast as they could. Thus the effect upon their ethical sentiments of the social discipline to which they have been subjected has been the precise opposite of what Mr. Spencer asserts. Instead of leading them from non-perception to a perception of the equality of rights to land, social discipline, dominated by land-owners, and continued steadily and rigorously, had, within comparatively recent times, almost entirely crushed out the idea of natural rights in land among the English people, and taught them to look on private property in land as in nowise differing from property in other things.

Or, try Mr. Spencer's assumption from the other end.

Among the aboriginal races in the countries we modern English have overrun, the idea of equal rights to land, and of course to other natural media, has been so clearly perceived that they were unable to comprehend the artificial notion of private property in land — could no more see than could Mr. Spencer in 1850 *how* land could equitably become private property. To this very day, and in spite of the pressure of the national government and of the surrounding whites, the Cherokees, the Choctaws, and other civilized remnants of the aboriginal tribes of the United States, though recognizing fully the right of property in things produced by labor, and recognizing also the right of private *possession* of land, refuse to recognize land as the *property* of the individual; and no man can hold land among them except while putting it to use. The idea that land itself can become subject to such individual ownership as attaches to things that man produces by labor, is as repugnant to the human mind, undisciplined by generations of cruel repression and undistorted by persistent misteachings, as the idea that air or sunlight may be so owned.

Mr. Spencer himself, while stating that the perception of the equality of natural rights to land is the product of the social advance that has brought men of the highest civilization to their present ethical condition, goes on in the next paragraph to show at length that "in early stages private ownership of land is unknown," and that private property in land has arisen from "the exercise of direct or indirect force, sometimes internal but chiefly external." [1]

What Mr. Spencer thus admits is that private property in land has no derivation from perceptions of justice, whether these be original or acquired by evolution, but that its only genesis is force. And then comes his supreme effort. In the reference to the feudal system and the assumption that the rights

---

[1] It may be worth noting that here Mr. Spencer again confuses equal rights with joint rights. The primitive idea is not that of deeming land the property of the tribe, and the relations of individuals to the soil one of joint ownership. Although within generally vague territorial limits each tribe may claim the right to exclude other tribes, yet the idea is not that of property in the land, but of that sort of separation which took place between Lot and Abraham; and the relation of the members to the land is not that of joint ownership, but of equal right to use — such regulations as in the earlier stages become necessary, being merely those which secure this equality in use. Among no primitive people would it be thought that a member of the tribe required the consent of the whole to make use of land no one else was using. He would do that without question, as a matter of individual right.

of the monarch, as representative of the whole people, are still exercised by the people's representatives, lies the pivotal point of his whole argument.

To return to my illustration of the tunnel. This is the way he gets there:

We are told that when private property in land did arise, it was habitually incomplete, since it was subject to the claims of the over-lord, the implication being that the ownership was subordinate to that of the head of the community; and that this conception survives alike in theory and in practice to the present time, since the state now takes land for public purposes after making due compensation to existing holders. The supreme power of the monarch having been replaced by the supreme power of the people, the people are now the supreme owners of the land, and may take it, if they please, on payment of full compensation. Thus, individual freedom has been re-acquired with regard to land, and to-day, in the existing theory and practice of English law, and like their equal rights to light and air, the equal rights of all to the use of land are fully recognized.

All that has gone before is the by-play of the juggler to distract attention. In this the transmogrification is worked.

Here, with one flash of synthetic logic, the horse-chestnut becomes a chestnut horse! Here is the explanation of what was averred in Mr. Spencer's letter to the *Times* — that the view of land-ownership he has taken all along is "congruous with existing legal theory and practice." Here is his reconciliation of his formula of justice — that "each is at liberty to do all that he wills, provided that he infringes not the equal liberty of any other man"—with the views of that august body, the Land and Próperty Defence League, "on which sit several peers and two judges." Both are harmonized in the assumption that the equal rights of all to the use of land are to-day recognized in the right of Parliament to take land for public purposes on paying for it.

What, it may be asked, has become of the nineteen-twentieths of the people of England who, as "Social Statics" told us, were being robbed of their birthright—their heritage in the earth—by a gigantic injustice inferior only in wickedness to murder and enslavement? Why, having the privilege of voting for members of one branch of the Legislature, which Mr. Spencer has, in this very book, page 49, described as "a motley assemblage of nominees of caucuses, ruled by ignorant and fanatical wire-pullers," they have been transmogrified into supreme owners of the land.

What, it still may be asked, has become of that part of them that do not have even the poor privilege of voting for this motley assemblage of nominees of caucuses?

There is no answer. We may search Chapter IV. of the "Principles of Ethics — The Ethics of Social Life: Justice," in vain. They have incontinently dropped out of sight.

It may be worth while to examine that part of Mr. Spencer's logical process where it is assumed that the legal theory and practice by which the British Legislature, on the payment of compensation, now takes land for public purposes is identical with the theory and practice by which the feudal monarch, as representing the whole people, was the supreme owner of land. This is all that he ventures specifically to assert, and the question raised by it is much narrower than the real question, whether the present legal theory and practice does adequately recognize the equal rights of all to land. Yet, even here, Mr. Spencer clearly suppresses the vital fact.

The taking of land for public purposes on payment of compensation — or by process of condemnation, as it is termed — is neither an exercise nor recognition of the supreme ownership of land. In the American States where the ownership of land is by their constitutions declared allodial, the same powers of condemning land are exerted, and more freely exerted than in England. If pictures are bought for the national galleries, not condemned, it is merely because there is no need for condemnation. The same legal power exists to take pictures for public use as to take land. In case of necessity, such as war, the power of taking anything is habitually exercised, and ships, horses, railways, provisions, and even men are taken for public uses. The power to do this is a power incident to the supreme authority and at times necessary to society.

When, in 1889, Johnstown, Pennsylvania, was cut off from the rest of the world by the flood that destroyed pre-existing organization, a British subject, Arthur J. Moxham, was placed in charge by what a Quaker would call "the sense of the meeting." His first acts were to seize all food, to destroy all liquor, and to put every able-bodied man at work, leaving the matter of compensation to be determined afterwards. He voiced the will of the society, driven by crushing disaster into a supreme effort for self-preservation, and the man who had resisted his orders would, if need be, have been shot.

But the theory of English law that the crown is the only owner of English land, and that the highest estate an individual can hold is that of tenancy, though often confused with the right of eminent domain, has in reality a different origin. Now a mere fiction, it had in feudal times expression in practice. When William the Conqueror divided England, he conditioned his grants on the payment of rent in dues or services. This was the essence of the feudal principle. In a rough and partial but still substantial way, it recognized the right of the community to rent. It was a rude attempt to carry out that system of land nationalization which Mr. Spencer in "Social Statics" declares the only equitable system of land-tenure. Under it the holding of valuable land entailed payment or service. The crown lands maintained the sovereign and the civil list. From the church lands the expenses of public worship, and of education, the care of the sick and the relief of wayfarers were provided; the holders of military tenures had to maintain the army and do the fighting, and on occasions, such as the ransom of the king, the knighting of his eldest son, the marriage of his eldest daughter, etc., were called on for extra payments; while the right of all Englishmen to the use of some portion at least of English soil was recognized in the numerous public commons. This spirit of the feudal system was the origin of primogeniture, of wardships and liveries and other feudal incidents, which, where they remain on the law-books of to-day are but meaningless and useless survivals.

Mr. Spencer, in his "glance at some past phases of land-tenure," has told us of the Sumatrans, the Don Cossacks, the Russians, the Suanetians, and the Dahomeans, but he has failed to tell us how we of the English speech have lost those fragments of the equal right to the use of land that we retained long after the last conquest of England. I do not charge him with ignorance. If he does not tell us, it is not because he does not know, for "Political Institution" shows that he does know.[1] But he does not tell us, because the facts are inconsistent with the juggle by which he is trying to impose on the reader. It was in reality by a gigantic series of no-rent declarations on the part of the class that had got possession of English land on condition of paying rent for it. The crown lands were given away by profligate sovereigns without any stipulation of return in rent to the community. Henry VIII. made over the greater part of the church lands to his favorites, and the people were robbed of the services and benefits that they had received from the former holders. Finally, by act of the Long Parliament, confirmed after the restoration

---

[1] In the chapter on Political Differentiation, page 297, "Principles of Sociology," Volume II., he quotes from Hallam: —

"William the Conqueror . . . divided this kingdom into about 60,000 parcels, of nearly equal value [partly left in the hands of those who previously held it, and partly made over to his followers as either owners or suzerains], from each of which the service of a soldier was due."

And again, in the chapter on Property, page 553 of the same book, occurs the passage once before quoted: —

In our case the definite ending of these tenures took place in 1660; when for feudal obligations (a burden on land-owners) was substituted a beer-excise (a burden on the community).

by a close majority, the military dues were abolished; and, growing in power by what they fed on, the landholders, now actually land-owners, appropriated to themselves, by the simple process of inclosure, nearly all the common lands.

The essence and meaning of the supreme ownership of the land of England by the crown is thus gone. What remains is but a legal fiction, a mere survival of form, of no more validity than was in the time of George III. the form by which he styled himself King of France. Yet in this empty phrase, and in the taking of land for public use on payment of full compensation, Mr. Spencer tells his disinherited countrymen that their equal rights are actually recognized.

Thus the equal right of Englishmen to the use of English land amounts to the privilege of buying it at its full value! What, then, has the Englishman as Englishman? A Russian or a Turk, a Winans or a Carnegie, may use land in England by paying for it.

If we put the conclusion as to the right to the use of land to which Mr. Spencer thus comes in "Justice" in the same form which he uses in "Social Statics," we have this:

Given a race of beings having like claims to pursue the objects of their desires — given a world adapted to the gratification of those desires — a world into which such beings are similarly born, and it unavoidably follows that they have the right to use this world as soon as they have paid the full value of it to those of their number who call themselves its owners.

But this telling the disinherited masses that their equal rights to land *are* already acknowledged seems hardly satisfactory to Mr. Spencer himself, for he at once proceeds to re-enforce it, by the plea that for them to claim any more than the right of buying land at its full value would be ethically wrong. This is a putting of the cart before the horse. For a wrong is only the violation of a right. Rights, as Mr. Spencer has just before told us, are the particular freedoms deducible from the law of equal freedom, and to assert wrong he must show violation of that law. Let us, however, follow his reasoning.

The first proposition is that —

> Since equity and daily custom alike imply that existing holders of particular portions of land may not be dispossessed without giving them in return its fairly estimated value, it is also implied that the wholesale resumption of the land by the community can be justly effected only by the wholesale purchase of it.

Is it? By equity and custom when the state takes any part of the wealth of a particular person it compensates him. But when it takes part of the wealth of all persons, or of all persons of a special class, as it is constantly doing by taxation, does it compensate them?

The reason for compensation, when land is taken from particular owners, is that otherwise a discrimination would be made between them and other land-owners. Equity, as Mr. Spencer once told us, means equalness. It would not be equitable for the community to resume possession of the land of this or that particular land-owner without compensation, while leaving to other land-owners their land, for while this would be to leave unredressed the unequalness between land-holders and others, it would be to treat land-owners unequally as between themselves. But if all land were resumed equity would require no compensation, for while land-owners would be treated equally as between themselves, the inequality between them and other members of the community would be removed, and all would be treated with equalness. And since they, too, are members of the community, the resumption of all land by the community would place all in a condition of equalness with respect to the land.

But, continues Mr. Spencer — herein admitting that the community may in equity take the *land* —

> Were the direct exercise of ownership to be resumed by the community without purchase, the community would take, along with something which is its own, an immensely greater amount of something which is not its own.

How so? The proposition is only to take the land, not to take anything else.

Because, Mr. Spencer continues —

> Even if we ignore those multitudinous complications which, in the course of century after century, have inextricably entangled men's claims theoretically considered — even if we reduce the case to its simplest theoretical form —

Well, all classes of land resumptionists would quickly reply, we are quite willing to do so. Since, as laid down in "Social Statics," men derive their equal rights to the use of the world, from their equal presence in the world, there can be no complications that can entangle their equal claims to the use of land, either considered theoretically or in any other way.

But without heeding this, Mr. Spencer goes on to say, that *even* if we ignore what no one proposes to consider, and *even* if we reduce the case to simple theoretical form —

> We must admit that all which can be claimed for the community is the surface of the country in its original unsubdued state. To all that value given to it by clearing, breaking-up, prolonged culture, fencing, draining, making roads, farm-buildings, etc., constituting nearly all its value, the community has no claim. This value has been given either by personal labor, or by labor paid for, or by ancestral labor; or else the value given to it in such ways has been purchased by legitimately earned money. All this value artificially given vests in existing owners, and cannot without a gigantic robbery be taken from them. If, during the many transactions which have brought about existing land-ownership, there have been much violence and much fraud, these have been small compared with the violence and the fraud which the community would be guilty of did it take possession, without paying for it, of that artificial value which the labor of nearly two thousand years has given to the land.

What does Mr. Spencer mean? If he means that all that can be claimed by the community is the land itself, and that land-owners should retain the value of their improvements, and of all things else that they may possess, we admit it — not entirely as a matter of strict justice, for much of things other than the land itself, which existing land-owners now possess, they have obtained by their unjust appropriation of land. But we wish to be within our right, and to let bygones be bygones, and so all that we propose is just what Mr. Spencer in "Social Statics" proposed — the resumption of equal rights in land, leaving to existing land-owners, without question as to how it was obtained, the whole value of their improvements in or on land, and all their other property.

But what, then, does Mr. Spencer mean by talking of "the surface of the country in its original unsubdued state," as all the community can claim? What does he mean by talking of that "artificial value which the labor of nearly two thousand years has given to the land?" Vague as are his notions of value, can it be that he means that, even if their natural rights are admitted, the people of England are only entitled to what value the land had before there were any people? and that they must pay the land-owners for the value of all the labor that has been expended on that land since Cæsar landed?

What the people of England are entitled to by natural right, and what we propose by the single tax to take for their use, is the value of land *as it is*, exclusive of the value of improvements *as they are* in or on the land privately owned. What would thus be left to the land-owners would be their personal or movable property, the value of all existing improvements in or on their land, and their equal share with all other citizens in the land value resumed. This is perfectly clear, and if not perfectly fair, is only so because it would leave to the land-owners in their personal property and the value of their improvements much not due to any exertion of labor by themselves or their ancestors, but which has come to them through the unjust appropriation of the proceeds of others' labor.

The value of the land when the country was in its original unsubdued state has nothing to do with the matter; what we have to deal with is the value of the land as it is. Nor has the labor expended since Cæsar's time anything to do with it; the value of improvements to be left to land-owners is the value of existing improvements. Surely if Mr. Spencer were to try to formulate his notions it would be too preposterous even for him to contend that in resuming our rights in the land — not the rights of the ancient Britons, nor the rights of primitive man, nor the rights of the animals that existed before man was — we should credit the existing land-owners with the value which attaches to the land from our presence, and charge them only with what value the land might have if we did not exist. And surely he would not contend that the land-owners are alone entitled to the value which the existing social environment gives to land — to the sole benefit of the introduction of Christianity, the extirpation of wolves, the beating off or civilizing of the Danes, the defeat of the Spanish armada, the building of public roads and the lighting of public streets, the introduction of vegetables and fruits and the improvement of domestic animals, the utilization of steam and electricity and labor-saving appliances, the discoveries of science and the progress of the arts!

Nor yet would he formally assert the notion that in addition to the present value of their improvements the land-owners must be credited with the value of all such improvements when they were new, and with the cost of all the draining, hedging, fencing, digging, manuring, building, etc., that has gone on for two thousand years — that the owner of land in the city of London, for instance, must be credited, not only with the present value of his houses, but with the value of the houses that existed before the great fire, and from the time of the first Roman camp! This would be equally preposterous.

It is hard to say what Mr. Spencer really does mean. But he is evidently trying to get some sort of vague excuse for assuming that it would not pay the disinherited to claim their rights in land, since to compensate land-owners would take more than the land is worth. Let us, therefore, try to form some idea of what would be the present value of the land of England in its "original, unsubdued state," population and social environment, and the existing buildings, which we propose to leave to the land-owners, remaining as they are.

If, whenever a house was pulled down, or destroyed by fire, in Threadneedle street or Lombard street, in Cheapside or at Charing Cross, the ground on which it stood were to spring into its original condition, how much less would be its value to those who, in renting or buying it, seek not so much soil or rock or sand, but so many square feet of standing-place in those centres of population and trade? How much less would be the value of the land that around London and Manchester and Liverpool and Birmingham and Leeds and all the growing English towns is being turned from agricultural uses into house-sites, were it to revert to its condition in Roman times? While as for the country outside the cities and towns, would it not, could such a miracle be worked, become more rather than less valuable? Something of draining, hedging, walling, manuring and digging would be lost; but would not the accumulated richness of virgin soil, the great forests that in England now would have enormous value, the stores of coal and iron and other minerals that have now been exhausted or can only be worked at great depths, much more than make up?

If Mr. Spencer would go to the greater Englands growing up in Australia and the American West, he would cease thinking of Romans, or Saxons or Normans as having anything to do with the present value of English land; for he would see that it is not what has been done in the past, but the population and activity of the present, that give value to land. He would see from Chicago or Johnstown that London might be swept by fire or flood, and yet, if the causes that concentrate population and trade there still remained, land, instead of being less valuable, would really become more valuable, from the better improvements that the clearing would bring about. He would see that, if the population and business of London could be transported to a newly-risen island in the antipodes, land there would become as valuable as land in London now; and that, though all improvements were to be left behind, the value of land in London would disappear.

What the new countries will show us is, that as man lives in the present so he lives *by* the labor of the present and the immediate past, truly from hand to mouth; and what we get from our ancestors is little more than language, traditions, laws, habits, and the store of transmitted knowledge, including also prejudices and superstitions. And thus rich and poor, learned and ignorant, we are alike "the heirs of all the ages." While if some of us are richer than we ought to be, and more of us are poorer than we ought to be, it is not because of the wrongful appropriations of wealth that took place in a dead and gone past, but from the wrongful appropriations of wealth that are taking place now.

Barring the appendix, which is yet to be considered, we have now gone through Mr. Spencer's defence of existing landlordism — his answer, in his maturest years, to the arraignment of private property in land which he made in "Social Statics." Stripped of its padding it amounts simply to the assumption (1) that the equal rights of all to the use of land are recognized in the right of the state to take land for public purposes on paying compensation; which is backed by the assumption (2) that equity requires that existing owners shall be paid the full value of the land they hold before equal rights to land can be acknowledged.

Of the first assumption, the only attempt at support is in the last paragraph, the reasoning of which on analysis will be found to be this:

The equal right of all electors to the use of land is recognized by implication in the right asserted by Parliament to take land for public use on paying full compensation for its value; *because* —

If it is not, there is no equitable warrant for the state so taking land for public uses, since the only right by which the land-owners can be superseded is the right of the community at large: *hence* —

As the state has this right, which it can only get as the sum of the individual rights of its members; *therefore*, by its exercise, the individual rights of members of the state to the use of land are now recognized.

Of the second assumption, the only attempt at support is another obviously false assumption — that the value of land cannot be distinguished from the value of improvements.

This is the argument of the lauded Synthetic Philosophy in the most important part of the most important book of its most important sub-division.

I commend the study of such logical processes to those who on authority of Herbert Spencer's philosophy believe that man is an evoluted monkey, who got the idea of God from observing his own shadow.

As for anything deserving the name of reasoning, anything on which may be founded either a denial of the equal right of all to the use of land, or an affirmation of the exclusive right of existing land-owners, there is nothing whatever. It is not merely that the reasoning of "Social Statics" is not impugned: it is that the reasoning of "Justice" itself is utterly ignored. No connection whatever is made between the conclusions here assumed and the formula of justice, the law of equal freedom, which in preceding chapters of this very book has been declared the ultimate ethical principle.

The reader has just been told that rights are the particular freedoms deducible from the law of equal freedom; that what are truly called rights are deducible from it, and that what are falsely called rights are not deducible from it. But where does Mr. Spencer, or how can he, deduce the right which he asserts for land-owners, the right to the exclusive use of land until they are paid its full value, from the law of equal freedom? Or, if we go back through all the links of his derivation of the formula of justice can we find any connection between what he now asserts as right, and what he has just asserted as justice in any of its evolutionary stages?

Does not the ownership by some to the exclusion of others, of elements essential to all life, the legal giving of the products of labor to those who do no labor, by taking it away from those who do labor, violate what he declares to be the principle of animal ethics—that the ill-fitted must suffer the evils of unfitness, and the well-fitted prove their fitness?

Does it not violate what he declares to be the principle of sub-human justice, that each individual shall receive the benefits and evils of its own nature and consequent conduct?

Does it not violate what he declares to be the principle of human justice, that no one should be prevented from having whatever good his actions normally bring to him, nor allowed to shoulder off on other persons whatever evil they bring?

Does it not violate what he declares to be the sentiment of justice, the feeling that we ourselves ought to have freedom to receive the results of our own nature and consequent actions, and which prompts the maintenance of this sphere of free play for others?

Does it not violate what he declares to be the idea of justice, the equality as to mutually limited spheres of action, the inequality in the results which each may achieve within these mutual limits? Does it not establish inequality by authority—an inequality referring not to the natural achievement of greater rewards by greater merits, but to the artificial apportionment of rewards to no merits at all?

Does it not violate what he declares to be the formula of justice, that every man is free to do that which he wills, provided he infringes not the equal freedom of any other man?

Does it not set at defiance what he declares to be the authority of this formula, the relation between conduct and consequence, which he bases on his compound law?

Private property in land, which Herbert Spencer in "Justice" defends by the darkening of counsel and baseless assumptions! Does it not openly, notoriously, flagrantly, deny to men the equal use of natural opportunities to live their lives, develop their powers, and reap the rewards of their conduct? Does it not give to the idle, the stupid, the profligate, the vicious, through the accidents of birth or luck, or successful forestalling, the natural rewards of industry, energy, temperance and thrift? Does it not proportionately, and far more than proportionately (for it involves enormous wastes), deny these rewards to those who have really earned them? Does it not give wealth, honor, the command of everything that labor in a high civilization can produce, to idlers, idiots, gamesters, profligates? Does it not, on the other hand, condemn toil to penury, and honest labor, to contempt and grinding want? Does it not, wherever our civilization extends, make the mere opportunity to work a boon? keep men in idleness whose strongest desire is to earn a living? fill prisons and almshouses? condemn to ignorance minds that might enlighten and bless mankind? debase and embrute great masses of men and women? rob little children of the grace and sweetness and glory of life, and force them before their time out of a world in which monopoly denies them room?

Try Herbert Spencer by the ideas that he once held—the idea of a Living God, whose creatures we are, and the idea of a divine order, to which we are bound to conform. Or try him by what he now professes—the idea that we are but the evolutionary results of the integrations of matter and motion. Try him by the principles of "Social Statics," or try him by the principles of "Justice." In this chapter he proves himself alike a traitor to all that he once held and to all that he now holds—a conscious and deliberate traitor, who assumes the place of the philosopher, the office of the judge, only to darken truth and to deny justice; to sell out the right of the wronged and to prostitute his powers in the defence of the wronger.

Is it a wonder that intellectually, as morally, this chapter is beneath contempt?

CHAPTER IX.

"JUSTICE."—THE RIGHT OF PROPERTY.

IN "Justice" as in "Social Statics," the chapter on the right to land is followed by a chapter on the right of property. That in "Social Statics" I have reprinted in full, to meet Mr. Spencer's subsequent assertion that it modified the radical conclusions of the preceding chapter. But it is hardly necessary thus to treat the similar chapter of "Justice." It begins (Section 54):

> Since all material objects capable of being owned are in one way or other obtained from the earth, it results that the right of property is originally dependent on the right to the use of the earth. While there were yet no artificial products, and natural products were therefore the only things which could be appropriated, this was an obviously necessary connection. And though, in our developed form of society, there are multitudinous possessions, ranging from houses, furniture, clothes, works of art, to bank-notes, railway-shares, mortgages, government bonds, etc., the origins of which have no manifest relation to use of the earth; yet it needs but to remember that they either are, or represent, products of labor, that labor is made possible by food, and that food is obtained from the soil, to see that the connection, though remote and entangled, still continues. Whence it follows that a complete ethical justification for the right of property is involved in the same difficulties as the ethical justification for the right to the use of the earth.

Since all material things capable of being owned consist either of land or products of land, the roundabout connection between such things as are here specified and the earth, through the food consumed by laborers, is a queer one, which indicates what in some parts of "Social Statics" may be suspected, that in speaking of land Mr. Spencer, as is often the case with English writers, is really thinking only of agricultural land.

The difficulties of which he speaks are the difficulties he raises in "Social Statics," by confounding equal rights with joint rights, and he here again takes issue with Locke and assumes, as before, that for production to give title, the right of the producer to the use of material must be shown to be "greater than the pre-existing rights of *all* other men put together." The forty-one years that have elapsed have left Mr. Spencer still entangled by this self-raised difficulty. But he now goes on to say that the difficulty arising from the question whether by labor "a man has made his right to the thing greater than the pre-existing rights of all other men put together[1] . . . may be avoided however. There are three ways in which, under savage, semi-civilized, and civilized conditions, men's several rights of property may be established with due regard to the equal rights of all other men."

---

[1] Mr. Spencer speaks of such usages as that an unsuccessful hunter in passing might take a deer from a trap for food, leaving head, skin, and saddle for the owner, as implying the belief of the tribesmen that "this prey was in part theirs before it was killed." But it no more implies this than the custom by which, among the early California rancheros, any traveller might catch a fresh horse, transfer his saddle and leave the tired one implied common property in horses, or than the kindly customs of essentially the same kind that are to be found wherever the struggle for existence that has developed with our civilization has not become intense.

In the savage condition, he says there is a tacit agreement that having equal opportunities of utilizing such products, appropriation achieved by one shall be passively assented to by the others.

As to the semi-civilized condition, he says:

We meet with usages having the same general implications. . . . It is perceived that the assent of the clan to ownership of food grown on an appropriated portion by any one, is implied in the assumptions of kindred ownership similarly established by all others. . . . In this case then as in the first, the right of property arises in conformity with the law of equal freedom.

So far then Mr. Spencer derives, and properly derives, the right of property from the exertion of labor under conditions in which all are equally free to make use of land. He now comes to his third division, where he is to show how in civilized conditions the right of property "may be established with due regard to the equal rights of all other men." I will quote this in full:

Though we cannot say that ownership of property, thus arising, results from actual contract between each member of the community and the community as a whole, yet there is something like a potential contract; and such potential contract might grow into an actual contract if one part of the community devoted itself to other occupations, while the rest continued to farm: a share of the produce being in such case payable by agreement to those who had ceased to be farmers, for the use of their shares of the land.[1] We have no evidence that such a relation between occupiers and the community, with consequent

[1] Here is another instance of the habit of thinking of land as only agricultural land. The assumption here is that farmers are the only users of land, whereas the obvious truth is that there is no occupation that can be carried on without the use of land, and that many other occupations require the use of much more valuable

authorized rights of property in the produce which remained after payment of a portion equivalent to rent, has ever arisen; for, as we have seen, the original ownership by the community has habitually been usurped by internal or external aggressors, and the rent, taking the shape, if not of produce, then of labor or military service, has been habitually paid to the usurper, a state of things under which equitable rights of property, in common with equitable rights of all kinds, are submerged. But out of such usurpations there has grown up, as we have seen, ownership by the state and tenancy under it; from which there may again arise a theoretically equitable right of property. In China, where "the land is all held directly from the Crown" "on payment of an annual tax," "with composition for personal service to the government," the legitimate proprietorship of such produce as remains after payment of rent to the community, can be asserted only on the assumption that the emperor stands for the community. In India, where the government is supreme land-owner, and where, until the zemindar system was established, it was the direct receiver of rents, the derivation of a right of property by contract between the individual and the community can be still less asserted without a strained interpretation. Nor at home, where the theory that each land-owner is a tenant of the crown is little more than a theory, is there any better fulfilment of the ethical requirement. Only here and there, where state-ownership is not potential but actual, and ordinary rents are paid by occupiers to the Crown (which has now in such cases come to be identified with the community), has there been consequently established that kind of use of the earth which gives a theoretically valid basis to the right of private property.

Now what is it that Mr. Spencer here says? It is that a theoretically equitable right of property does not now exist in civilized conditions; but that it may arise if the now nominal and potential supreme own-

---

land than does farming. In the occupancy of his London apartments Mr. Spencer himself is more of a land user, value considered, than many a small farmer.

ership of land by the state is made real and actual by the taking for the use of the community, by the representatives of the community, of the rents that are (or should be) paid by occupiers of land.

Truly "Justice" is a suprising book. Here we have Mr. Spencer going back to the very principle he has just recanted.

In one sentence of this paragraph he says that we have no evidence that this equitable adjustment of the rights to land in conformity with the needs of the civilized state has ever arisen, since the original ownership of land by the community has been habitually usurped, and in another sentence he says vaguely that it has arisen only here and there. But that it may arise and ought to arise, and would give an even theoretically perfect basis to the right of property, this section states, if not as clearly, but yet on careful reading as unmistakably as does "Social Statics" itself.

The paragraph just quoted is followed by this recapitulatory paragraph, with which the section closes:

> But admitting that the establishment of an ethically complete right of property is beset with difficulties like those which beset the establishment of an ethically complete right to the use of the earth, we are nevertheless shown by a survey of the facts which existing primitive societies present, and the facts traceable in the early histories of civilized societies, that the right of property is originally deducible from the law of equal freedom; and that it ceases to be so deducible only when the other corollaries from the law of equal freedom have been disregarded.

Or to put this statement of the propositions of this section in fuller form, they are: (1) That the establishment of the right of property is beset by the difficulties of showing that the right of a man to the material element from which property is obtained is greater than the rights of all existing men put together. (2) But in primitive societies and in the early history of civilized societies, where the use of land is open to all, this equality of access to land enables us to deduce the right of property in things produced by labor from the law of equal freedom; and (3) it ceases to be so deducible where equality in the use of land is denied, as in civilized societies at present; but would again become deducible from the law of equal freedom if the rent of land were taken for the use of the society.

If Mr. Spencer had written "Justice" under coercion; if imprisoned in the chambers of an Inquisition, and under fear of the rack, he had been forced against his will, like Galileo, to recant what he still held to be true, we might well believe that this Section 54 of "Justice" contained his sign to posterity that in spite of the denials he had just been compelled to make he in his heart held to the truth.

But though, unfortunately, the conditions do not admit of such a conclusion, this section is perhaps an even stronger testimony to the power of truth. In the preceding chapter Mr. Spencer has forced back his better nature, and defended landlordism as well as the man who had written "Social Statics" could. But when after an interval of over forty years he begins to rewrite his old chapter on "The Right of Property," the truth he once held reasserts its sway, and though he cuts out all that might give open offence to his new clients, the perception of truth, as by "unconscious cerebration," causes him in the very first section to relapse, and to tell us — unmistakably, if not clearly — that in the civilized state it is only the appropriation of rent to the use of the whole community that can give to property an ethical basis.

But Mr. Spencer soon recovers himself. Having in Section 54 shown that in rude societies there is a substantial basis for the right of property, but that in highly civilized countries, such as England, the equitable right of property has been submerged by the usurpation of land-ownership, he proceeds in Section 55 to assert, as he did in the preceding chapter, that the course of modern civilization has been more fully to establish this right.

Section 55 begins:

> This deduction [*i.e.*, of the right of property from the law of equal freedom through the equal right to the use of land], early recognized in custom and afterwards formulated by legislators, has come to be elaborated and enforced more and more fully as society has developed.

Then comes something about primitive societies, the patriarchal group and the house community, in which occurs the reference to inherent value already quoted on page 51, and the section thus closes:

> To trace the development of the right of property as established by rulers and administered by their agents, setting out with the interdict on theft in the Hebrew commandments, and continuing down to modern days, in which proprietorships of all kinds have been legally formulated in multitudinous detail and with great precision, would be no less out of place than it would be superfluous. It suffices for present purposes to note that this implication of the principle of justice, perceived from the first perhaps more clearly than any other, has

gained in the course of social progress increased definiteness of recognition as well as increased extension and increased peremptoriness; so that now, breach of the right of property by unauthorized appropriation of a turnip or a few sticks, has become a punishable offence; and there is ownership of a song, of a pattern, of a trade-mark.

The principle of justice in the right of property perceived from the first, as Mr. Spencer has just explained, is equality in the use of natural opportunities. Has this principle gained by a social progress, which as exemplified in England, now denies nineteen-twentieths of the people of all right whatever in the land of their birth, punishes them if they take a handful of wild fruit or a few sticks from the abundant offerings of nature, creates private ownership in a salmon fishery, a coal mine, an advowson or a hereditary pension, and condemns millions to chronic pauperism?

This is what Mr. Spencer's examination of the right of property in "Justice" amounts to: First showing that the right of property in civilized societies has to-day no ethical basis, he goes on to make believe that it has, and from this basis of make-believe to assume the ethical validity of existing conditions. And then he virtuously turns on the communists. They are a feeble folk and have no friends.

In this he follows the order of "Social Statics," but the spirit is that of "The Man *versus* the State." He ignores what he once saw plainly, the incentive to communistic and socialistic schemes in the bitter wrong and widespread suffering of the existing order, declares their motive to be the desire to take from the worker the produce of his work, and assumes that between them and existing social conditions lies the only choice. Here is the section :

§ **56**. Supposing themselves to be justified, and indeed enjoined by moral principle, many in our days are seeking to over-ride this right. They think it wrong that each man should receive benefits proportionate to his efforts — deny that he may properly keep possession of all which his labor has produced, leaving the less capable in possession of all which their labors have produced. Expressed in its briefest form, their doctrine is — Let unlike kinds and amounts of work bring like shares of produce — let there be "equal division of unequal earnings."

That communism implies violation of justice as defined in foregoing chapters, is manifest. When we assert the liberty of each bounded only by the like liberties of all, we assert that each is free to keep for himself all those gratifications and sources of gratification which he procures without trespassing on the spheres of action of his neighbors. If, therefore, one obtains by his greater strength, greater ingenuity, or greater application, more gratifications or sources of gratification, than others, and does this without in any way trenching on the spheres of action of others, the law of equal freedom assigns him exclusive possession of all such extra gratifications and sources of gratification ; nor can others take them from him without claiming for themselves greater liberty of action than he claims, and thereby violating the law.

In past times the arrangements made were such that the few superior profited at the expense of the many inferior. It is now proposed to make arrangements such that the many inferior shall profit at the expense of the few superior. And just as the old social system was assumed by those who maintained it to be equitable, so is this new social system assumed to be equitable by those who propose it. Being, as they think, undoubtedly right, this distribution may properly be established by force; for the employment of force, if not avowedly contemplated, is contemplated by implication.

With a human nature such as has been known throughout the past and is known at present, one who, by higher power, bodily or mental, or greater endurance of work, gains more than others gain, will not voluntarily surrender the excess to such others: here and there may be found a man who would do this, but he is far from being the average man. And if the average superior man will not voluntarily surrender to others the excess of benefit gained by his superiority, the implication is that he must be obliged to do this, and that the use of force to oblige him is justifiable. That the many inferior are physically able thus to coerce the few superior is agreed on both sides, but the assumption of the communists is that the required coercion of the minority who are best by the majority who are worst would be equitable.

After what was said in the early chapter of this Part, it scarcely needs pointing out that a system established in pursuance of this doctrine would entail degeneration of citizens and decay of the community formed by them. Suspension of that natural discipline by which every kind of creature is kept fit for the activities demanded by the conditions of life, would inevitably bring about unfitness for life and either prompt or slow disappearance.

An old fable tells us that when the plague raged among the animals they concluded that among them was some great criminal, who must be sacrificed to the wrath of heaven, and agreed that to discover him all should confess their sins. The fox volunteered to act as judge. He listened with equanimity to the lion's recital of flocks devoured and men slaughtered, declaring his majesty blameless, and in the same way excused all that the tiger, the hyena, the wolf, and the bear confessed. At length came a poor ass, who told how, when his master had forgotten to give him his breakfast, he had nibbled a few leaves from his load of cabbages. "You impious rascal!" cried the fox, "it is you beyond doubt who have brought on us the anger of the gods!" and applauding the decision and following his lead, the lordly animals threw themselves on the poor ass and tore him to pieces.

As the nibbling of a cabbage leaf is to Herod's slaughter of the innocents, so is the dream of a few communists compared with what the monopoly of land is actually doing. In the highest civilization in other respects that the world has yet seen this monopoly is, even now, entailing the degradation of citizens and decay of the community, so that Mr. Spencer cannot look out of the windows of his club without seeing men turned into advertising signs; or get into a cab without having some miserable wretch officiously hasten to close the door in the hope of a penny; or travel through the three kingdoms without beholding the decay of population in the country and its congestion in the slums of towns? It is, even now, suspending "that natural discipline by which every creature is kept fit for the activities demanded by the conditions of life," so that men are being destroyed, on the one side by repletion and debauchery, and on the other side by privation and the denial of opportunities for honest work. It is, even now, taking the produce of their work from superior worker and inferior worker alike, and is giving the gratifications and sources of gratification earned by work to those who do no work — is piling up wealth in the hands of those who do nothing to produce wealth, who as land-owners are useless appropriators and worse than useless destroyers. To this giant wrong, this most monstrous of all denials of the law of equal freedom, Mr. Spencer is as complaisant as the fox was to the lion, while he vents his indignation on the poor ass of communism.

The next and final chapter shows how far Mr. Spencer really wishes to assert the right of property. It was, as he knows, by violating the right of property in putting taxes on the products of labor that the larger tenants of English land made themselves its virtual owners and that private property in land has come to be established in those wide regions to which English institutions have been extended. And it is on the line of abolishing this taxation of labor and the products of labor that, as is now evident, the struggle for the resumption of equal rights in land will in English-speaking countries be made—nay, is already beginning to be made. So in the next section Mr. Spencer brings out his double-barrelled ethics to break down the right of property and to open the door for what is essentially socialism and communism in the interests of the rich:

§ 57. While absolute ethics thus asserts the right of property, and while no such breach of it as is implied by the schemes of communists is warranted by that relative ethics which takes account of transitional needs, relative ethics dictates such limitation of it as is necessitated for defraying the costs of protection, national and individual.

The truth recognized at the outset, that the preservation of the species, or that variety of it constituting a nation, is an end which must take precedence of individual preservation, has already been cited as justifying that subordination of the right to life which is implied by exposure to possible death in defensive war, and as also justifying that subordination of the right to liberty which military service and subjection necessitate. Here it must be again cited as affording a legitimate reason for appropriating such portions of the possessions and the earnings of individuals, as may be required for adequately resisting enemies. But while there is thus a quasi-ethical justification for whatever encroachment on the right of property is necessitated for the purposes of defensive war, there is no justification for any such encroachment for the purposes of offensive war.

No less manifest is it that the right of property is legitimately subject to one further restriction. Property must be trenched upon for supporting those public administrations by which the right of property, and all other rights, are enforced. In a society wholly composed of men who duly respected one another's claims, no such partial invasion of the right of property would be called for; but in existing societies and in such societies as are likely to exist for a long time to come, the nearest approach to fulfilment of the law of equal freedom is made when the various deduced rights are sacrificed to the extent needful for preservation of the remainders. Relative ethics, therefore, warrants such equitably-distributed taxation as is required for maintaining order and safety.

Since the ethical commands, thou shalt do no murder and thou shalt not steal, mean also, thou shalt not permit thyself to be murdered or to be stolen from, the justification of defensive war needs no invention of relative ethics. Nor is this needed to justify under extraordinary circumstances what under ordinary circumstances would be violations of the right of property. Take Johnstown, when the sun rose on wreck and ruin and death in their most awful forms, and on men and women half crazed with listening all night long to the shrieks that came from the flaming mass of float-wood into which the flood was sweeping their nearest and dearest. In ordering the destruction of all liquor, the seizing of all food, and the impressment, should that be necessary, of all who could work, in a systematized effort to succor who still might be succored and to bury what remained to bury of the dead, was not Arthur Moxham acting, in the name of the reason and conscience of the community, on the same eternal principles of right and wrong that in ordinary conditions would have forbidden these things? What in form was a denial of the rights of property and person was in its essence respect for life and property.

But while changing conditions may change the application of ethical principles, it is only as the change in a ship's course turns the compass card in her binacle. The change is in the conditions not in the principles. And if there be an ethical *right* of property, then, except under conditions of imminent danger and dire stress, a community cannot be justified in taking property by force from the individual.

What Mr. Spencer does in this section, in the name of his convenient fiction of relative ethics, is to justify the habitual violations of the right of property which are committed under the name of government in all civilized countries, and thus to make his philosophy of things as they ought to be, conform the better with things as the ruling classes desire to maintain them. And he does this effectually, for he leaves the right of property without defence, save in idle platitudes, against those forms of taxation which have everywhere proved so efficient in robbing the many and enriching the few.

To be sure Mr. Spencer justifies the taking of property by taxation only for purposes of defensive war and the maintenance of order and safety. But such limitations are practically no limitations. Neither an English jingo nor an American protectionist would quarrel with them. No invading foot has trod English soil, no hostile fleet has fired a shot at an English town, since the English national debt began to form. Yet what one of all the wars for which the English masses have paid in blood and privation and of which this great debt is the reminder, has not been advocated at the time as a defensive war? Is not our monstrous American tariff declared by its advocates to be necessary to the maintenance of order and safety? What has been the assigned reason for the maintenance of every fat English sinecure but order and safety?

Granted that Mr. Spencer would abolish the more flagrant abuses of taxation; or, as in the light of his changes on the land question we may more certainly say, granted that he is in favor of abolishing them so long as Sir John and his Grace do not seriously object; yet in admitting that the right of property may justly be set aside by the state for ordinary public needs and uses, he opens the door for every abuse that the ruling power — the majority, if you please — may at any time choose to deem a use. He leaves no principle save the shifting one of expediency to guard the right of property against any interest or desire or whim that may gain control of the legislative power.

But the reign of relative ethics, like that of the old-fashioned devil, to which it bears some analogy, is not to be forever, for we are given to understand that when evolution has carried the descendants of what are now the human race to a point as far above us as it has carried us above the monkey, and brought on the agnostic millennium, relative ethics are to vanish in the unknowable pit. So Mr. Spencer tells us that "in a society composed of men who duly respected one another's claims, no such partial invasion of the rights of property would be called for." But then, he continues, it is called for "in existing societies and in such societies as are likely to exist for a long time to come." What ground does that give me to assert that I am robbed directly by the blackmail demanded in the name of duty at the American post-office every time a friend sends me a book from a foreign country, or even from Canada, and am robbed indirectly every day of my life in the purchases I make? The protectionist, if a Spencerian and disposed to argue, would simply reply, "You are talking absolute ethics, whereas, as Herbert Spencer has shown, we are now under the rule of relative ethics."

It is true, but in a sense that Mr. Spencer does not mean, that if men duly respected one another's claims, no taking of individual property in taxation by the state would be necessary. For if men duly respected one another's claims to the use of land, all necessity for invading the right of property by taxation would disappear. Either by the single tax on land values or by the crude and clumsy scheme of land nationalization proposed by Mr. Spencer himself in "Social Statics," enough revenue would accrue to the state to defray all needed expenses without taking a penny of any man's property. But if men are to continue to disregard each other's claims to the use of land, and to continue to treat that element as belonging to a few individuals — and this Mr. Spencer now insists on — then there is no possible improvement in society or in the race that could dispense with the taking of property by taxation.

Mr. Spencer evidently entertains the innocent notion that could the soldier and the policeman be done away with, there would be no further need for public revenues, and all organized government could be dispensed with. But would not civilized societies still need revenues for building and keeping roads and bridges, for paving and cleaning streets, for establishing lighthouses and supporting a fire service, and doing the many things which become increasingly necessary to the public health, safety, comfort, and convenience, as social integration goes on? Or in the millennium of the Spencerians, as in the millennium of the anarchists, is each one to pave, clean and light the street before his door, when and how he pleases? are roads, bridges and public works, as to which competition is impossible, to be left to private individuals and companies, charging what they please and rendering what service they choose? and are all other public functions to be dependent on volunteer service or voluntary subscription?

CHAPTER X.

THE RIGHT OF PROPERTY AND THE RIGHT OF TAXATION.

Of such primary and practical importance is the question just raised, that it is worth while to discuss it more fully.

Mr. Spencer, in a book he has re-issued this year, has flippantly accused "Mr. George and his friends" with asserting the absolute right of the community over the possessions of each member. Yet in nothing is the divergence between us and the common opinion more sharply shown than in this, that we utterly deny the right of the community to take the property of the individual for any purpose whatsoever, except under circumstances where all rights must yield to the supreme right of self-preservation. There may be circumstances of such sudden stress and danger as would justify an individual in taking the horse or boat of another individual, in making use of his house, his goods, or anything that is his; and so there may be similar circumstances that will justify such taking of individual property on the part of a community. But short of this, which is not a limitation but an abrogation, we hold the right of property to be absolute, and deny the proposition which Mr. Spencer in the chapter just quoted asserts, and which is commonly conceded, that the right of property is limited by the right of the state to take in taxation what it may think it needs. Thus we are to-day the defenders of the right of property as against communists, protectionists, and socialists, as well as against such moderate deniers of the right of property as the revenue tariffites of the Cobden Club class, and such half-way individualists as the Liberty and Property Defence League and Mr. Auberon Herbert's associations.

How then is it that we are called deniers of the right of property?

It is for the same reason that, when I was a boy, caused nine-tenths of the good people in the United States, north as well as south, to regard abolitionists as deniers of the right of property; the same reason that made even John Wesley look on a smuggler as a kind of robber, and on a custom-house seizer of other men's goods as a defender of law and order. Where violations of the right of property have been long sanctioned by custom and law, it is inevitable that those who really assert the right of property will at first be thought to deny it. For under such circumstances the idea of property becomes confused, and that is thought to be property which is in reality a violation of property.

That such confusion exists to-day may be seen in the way in which the great struggle for better conditions of life for the masses, that all over the civilized world has begun or is impending, is generally regarded by both sides. Except by the single-tax men, and possibly by the philosophic anarchists, it is thought of as a struggle between capital and labor — a contest between the rights of man and the rights of property. It is not merely that one side charges the other side with proposing to impair the right of property. It is, that, with the exceptions noted, those who would better secure the rights of men, do propose restrictions and denials of the right of property. So, from the thorough-going socialists who would have the state appropriate all capital and direct all industry, to those milk-and-water socialists who are willing to play at doing something, by encouraging trades unions, and by two-penny alms and restrictions, and by attempts to make the rich less rich, and consequently as they think the poor less poor, through income and succession taxes and Irish Land Acts, we find those who aim, or profess to aim at improving the conditions of the laboring masses, advocating measures which are violations of the right of property. In this confusion of thought we who hold that the right of property is an absolute right, we who say that the command "Thou shalt not steal" applies to the state as fully as to the individual, are looked upon by one side as deniers of the right of property, and by the other — even by the poor, timid university socialists — as not radical enough.

Yet to whoever will grasp first principles it must be evident:

That there can be no real conflict between labor and capital — since capital is in origin and essence but the product and tool of labor;

That there can be no real antagonism between the rights of men and the rights of property — since the right of property is but the expression of a fundamental right of man;

That the road to the improvement of the conditions of the masses cannot be the road of restricting and denying the right of property, but can only be that of securing most fully the right of property; and that all measures that impair the right of property must in the end injure the masses — since while it may be possible that a few may get a living or be aided in getting a living by robbery, it is utterly impossible that the many should.

It is not as deniers, but as asserters of the equal rights of man, that we who for want of a better name call ourselves single-tax men so strenuously uphold the right of property. It is not because we would palter with a social system that condemns the masses to hard work and low wages, to absolute want and starvation more or less disguised; but because we would bring about a social system in which it would be impossible for any one to want or to starve unless he deserved to. It is not because we are less radical, but because in the true sense we are more radical than the socialists of all degrees.

Let me ask those who think there is any conflict between the rights of men and the rights of property to name any denial of the rights of men which is not or does not involve a denial of the rights of property; or any denial of the rights of property which is not or does not involve a denial of the rights of men. Take chattel slavery. Was that an assertion of the right of property or a denial of the right of property?

Or, consider any system of tyranny or oppression by which the personal liberties of men have been denied or curtailed. Take out of it the element which infringes the right of property and is not its efficacy gone?

On the other hand, take anything which denies or impairs the right of property — robbery, brigandage, piracy, war, customs duties, excises, or taxes on wealth in any of its forms — do they not all violate personal liberty, directly and indirectly?

This is not an accidental, but a necessary connection. The right of life and liberty — that is to say, the right of the man to himself — is not really one right and the right of property another right. They are two aspects of the same perception — the right of property being but another side, a differently stated expression, of the right of man to himself. The right to life and liberty, the right of the individual to himhimself, presupposes and involves the right of property, which is the exclusive right of the individual to the things his exertion has produced.

This is the reason why we who really believe in the law of liberty, we who see in freedom the great solvent for all social evils, are the stanchest and most unflinching supporters of the rights of property, and would guard it as scrupulously in the case of the millionnaire as in the case of the day laborer.

But what is property? This we must keep clearly in mind if, in attempting to see what the right of property does and does not permit, we would avoid confusion. The question is not what the state sanctions, but what it may rightfully sanction. There are those who say that the right of property, as all other rights, are derived from the state. But they do not really think this; for they are as ready as any one else to say of any proposed state action that it is right or it is wrong, in which they assert some standard of action higher than the state.

Property — not property in the legal sense, for that may be anything which greed or perversity may have power to ordain; but property in the ethical sense — is that which carries with it the right of exclusive ownership, including the right to give, sell, bequeath or destroy.

To what sort of things does such right of ownership rightfully attach?

Clearly to things produced by labor, and to no other.

And that this rightful ownership can only attach to things produced by labor is always shown by those who try to assert such right of ownership in other things. For invariably, instead of proving a right of ownership in such other things, they devote themselves to proving the right of ownership in things produced by labor, and then assume that in some way the right thus accruing has become transferred to things of a different nature.

Mr. Spencer is an example of this, as are all without exception who have ever written on the side he has now assumed. He wishes in this book to justify property in land. But he only justifies property in the products of labor, and then insinuates what he dares not clearly state — that by some process of transfer or conjoinment the right of ownership in the products of labor has become transmuted into a right of ownership in land.

In this, however, he does as well as any one who ever attempted it. The logical processes of those who attempt to prove a *right* of exclusive ownership in land are always akin to those of the bum-boat man, who, having agreed to bring the sailor a white monkey, brought him instead a yellow dog which he insisted had eaten a white monkey. They are like a lawyer who, called on to prove his client's title to an estate, should go on to prove his client's title to the money which he gave for the estate.

The ethical right of property is so perfectly clear as to be beyond all dispute — as to be testified to by all who attempt to assert some other right of property. It springs from the right of each man to use his own powers and enjoy their results. And it is a full and absolute right. Whatever a man produces belongs to him exclusively, and the same full and exclusive right passes from him to his grantor, assignee or devisee, not to the amount of eighty or fifty or any other percentage, but in full. And as is shown by reason and as is proved by the experience of the world, the advance in civilization depends upon the recognition of this right. Therefore for the State to levy taxes on that which is truly property, that is to say, upon the possession of wealth in any of its forms, is unjust and injurious — is a denial and violation of the right of property and of the rights of man.

But it may be said: In an isolated condition it is true that a man is entitled to all that he produces, and that it is robbery to take any part of it from him against his will. But in the civilized condition it is not alone the exertion of the individual that contributes to his production. Over and above what the producer receives from other producers, and for which he recompenses them in the various ways by which the claims between man and man are settled in ordered society, he is aided, in an indefinite yet tangible way, by society as a whole. Does he not therefore owe to society as a whole some return? Is not organized society, or the state, entitled therefore to claim and to take some portion of what in an isolated condition would be rightfully his exclusive property?

We reply: There is such a debt, but the producer cannot escape paying it, even though there be left to him in full what is his by the right of property. Here is a man who gives to a painter an order for a beautiful picture. Can he alone enjoy it? Here is another man who builds a factory, or works out a beneficial invention. Do what benefits he may receive, even if he be untaxed, represent the sum total of its benefits? Does not what he has done also benefit others and benefit society at large? And if society helps the individual producer, does not the individual producer also help society? These diffused benefits, these benefits which society as a whole receives, are something separate from what the right of property accords to the producer. They become tangible in the value of land, and may be taken by society without any curtailment of the right of property. To bring one beautiful picture to a town might not perceptibly increase the value of land. But bring a number, or even one famous picture, and the value of land will perceptibly increase. Place the pictures of one of the great European galleries on a piece of American land that you might now buy for a hundred dollars and you will soon find a value of millions attaching to that land. And that the erection of a factory, or even of a dwelling-house, or the utilization of a beneficial invention, will perceptibly add to the value of land every one knows. Look at the millions on millions which the elevated roads have added to the value of New York lands.

Again, it may be said, as Mr. Spencer now says, that

it is necessary for organized society to have revenues, and that therefore the society must take some part at least of the property of individuals. The proposition we admit, but the conclusion we deny. Organized society must have revenues; but the natural and proper and adequate source of those revenues is not in what justly belongs to individuals, but in what justly belongs to society — the value which attaches to land with the growth of society. Let the state take that, and there will be no need for it to violate the right of property by taking what justly belongs to the individual.

Mr. Spencer's admission in "Justice" of the right of the state to take from innividuals their property by taxation — an admission which makes impossible any clear assertion of the right of property — is forced upon him by the radical change in his teachings that his fear of Sir John and his Grace has compelled him to make. He made no such surrender of individual rights to the state in "Social Statics." On the contrary he there emphatically — though as to details not very clearly, for in many things he only saw men as trees walking — asserts the rights of the individual as against society. But in "Justice" he is compelled to admit the right of the state to take property by taxation, because of his desire to admit the right of land-owners to appropriate the revenues which are the natural provision for the needs of the state.

For the state is natural and necessary, and the state must have revenues. Hence any one who does not see, or who chooses to deny, that the natural revenue of the state is the value which social growth gives to land, is compelled to admit that for the purpose of obtaining revenue the state may take the property of individuals, and thus to deny the right of property.

Suppose some one to have asked the Herbert Spencer who wrote "Social Statics:" "Where shall the state get its necessary revenues if it scrupulously observes the right of property and does not continue to take by force what it needs of the property of individuals?"

He would have promptly replied, for the answer is in that book, "By taking through its own agents for its own purposes the rent of land, which is now taken by the agents of Sir John and his Grace for their purposes."

But the Herbert Spencer who now writes "Justice" could find no answer to such a question, since he writes for the purpose of defending the appropriations of Sir John and his Grace. Hence he is compelled to deny the right of property — justifying its appropriation by an agency which in another place in this same book he calls "the many-headed government appointed by multitudes of ignorant people;" and which, indeed, owing to the poverty, ignorance, greed and immorality which are the results of ignoring the right of property, is not undeserving of such a contemptuous characterization.

But that he really knows better; that he really sees that the taxation of the products of labor is a violation of the right of property which differs from slavery only in degree; and that he is only advocating it in the interests of that privileged class to gain whose tolerance now seems to be his supreme ambition, is clearly shown further on in this same book, where in opposing what he deems unnecessary taxation he clearly states the principle that condemns all taxation of what belongs to individuals. I quote from Chapter XXVI. of "Justice," "The Limits of State-duties," Section 121, pp. 222–224:

If justice asserts the liberty of each limited only by the like liberties of all, then the imposing of any further limit is unjust; no matter whether the power imposing it be one man or a million of men. . . . In our time the tying of men to the lands they were born on, and the forbidding any other occupations than the prescribed ones, would be considered as intolerable aggressions on their liberties. But if these larger inroads on their rights are wrong, then also are smaller inroads. As we hold that a theft is a theft whether the amount stolen be a pound or a penny, so we must hold that an aggression is an aggression whether it be great or small. . . . We do not commonly see in a tax a diminution of freedom, and yet it clearly is one. The money taken represents so much labor gone through, and the product of that labor being taken away, either leaves the individual to go without such benefit as was achieved by it or else to go through more labor. In feudal days, when the subject classes had, under the name of *corvées*, to render services to their lords, specified in time or work, the partial slavery was manifest enough; and when the services were commuted for money, the relation remained the same in substance though changed in form. So is it now. Tax-payers are subject to a state *corvée*, which is none the less decided because, instead of giving their special kinds of work, they give equivalent sums; and if the *corvée* in the original undisguised form was a deprivation of freedom, so is it in its modern disguised form. "Thus much of your work shall be devoted, not to your own purposes, but to our purposes," say the authorities to the citizens; and to whatever extent this is carried, to that extent the citizens become slaves of the government.

"But they are slaves for their own advantage," will be the reply — "and the things to be done with the money taken from them are things which will in one way or other conduce to their welfare." Yes, that is the theory — a theory not quite in harmony with the vast mass of mischievous legislation filling the statute books. But this reply is not to the purpose. The question is a question of justice; and even supposing that the benefits to be obtained by these extra public expenditures were fairly distributed among all who furnish funds, which they are not, it would still remain true that they are at variance with the fundamental principle of an equitable social order. A man's liberties are none the less aggressed upon because those who coerce him do so in the belief that he will be benefited. In thus imposing by force their wills upon his will, they are breaking the law of equal freedom in his person; and what the motive may be matters not. Aggression which is flagitious when committed by one, is not sanctified when committed by a host.

Thus, in the same book, does Herbert Spencer answer Herbert Spencer.

CHAPTER XI.

COMPENSATION.

While not needed in reply to Mr. Spencer, for his own scornful denial that there is any way in which land can equitably become private property remains unanswered by him, the wide prevalence of the idea that justice requires the compensation of land-owners if their exclusive ownership be abolished, makes it worth consideration; the more so as the same principle is involved in other questions, which are already, or may soon become, of practical importance.

That this idea will not bear examination Mr. Spencer himself shows, even when, as now, he is more than willing to be understood as accepting it. While anxious to find some ground, any ground, for assuming that land-owners are entitled to compensation *for something* equal or more than equal to the value of their land, he nowhere ventures to assert that they are entitled to compensation *for their land*. Such a notion is too preposterous to be stated by any one who has ever realized the relation of men to land.

Yet to those who have not, it seems at first most reasonable, for it accords with accustomed ideas. If it were ever customary for primitive man to eat his grandmother, as the Synthetic Philosophy would lead us to suppose, she must have been thought a wicked old woman who without compensation to the would-be eater tried to avoid that fate. In a community such as Edmond About pictured in his "King of the Mountain," where brigandage was looked on as a most respectable business, the captive who tried to escape without ransom would be deemed a violator of his captors' rights. And many a man now living can appreciate Mark Twain's portrayal of the pangs of conscience felt by Huckleberry Finn as he thought that in not denouncing his negro companion he was helping to rob a poor widow.

The habitual confusion of thought where violations of property have long been treated by custom and law as property, requires time and effort to escape from, and while justice is yet struggling for recognition there is with many a desire to compromise between the right that ought to be and the wrong that is. Thus there are to-day, in England at least, even among those who to some extent have become conscious of the injustice of denying the equal right to the use of land, many who think that before this natural right can be equitably asserted present land-owners must be compensated for their loss of legal rights.

This idea does not apply to the land question alone. It was carried out in England in the compensation paid to West India slave-owners on the abolition of slavery; in the compensation paid to the owners of rotten Irish boroughs at the time of the Union for the loss of their power to sell legislation; in the capitalization of hereditary pensions; and in the compensation paid to their holders when profitable sinecures are abolished.

Nor are we without examples of the same idea in the United States. It is often contended that it would be wrong to abolish protective duties where capital has been invested on the expectation of their continuance; and not many years since, even in the North, good, honest people, so far awake to the crime of slavery that they deemed the original enslavement of a man wickedness so atrocious as to merit death — which indeed was the penalty denounced by our laws against engaging in the external slave trade — really believed that slave-owners must be compensated before existing slavery could be justly abolished. Even after the war had fairly begun, this idea was so strong that the nation compensated owners when, in 1862, slavery was abolished in the District of Columbia, and subsequent efforts to apply the same principle to the slave States that adhered to the Union were only defeated by the opposition to any national interference with slavery.

Let us see clearly what this question of compensation is:

It does not involve the validity of any contract or agreement or promise formally made by the state. This does not exist and is not pleaded by the advocates of compensation in the cases we are considering. If it did, the question would arise how far legislative power may bind legislative power, and one generation control the action of succeeding generations. But it is not necessary to discuss that here.

It is not a question of all right of compensation. That the state should compensate when it destroys a building to make way for a public improvement, or takes goods or provisions or horses or shipping for which it may have sudden need, or demands of some citizens services which it does not demand of others, is not in question. The right of compensation in such cases is not disputed.

That is to say it is not a question whether the state should pay for its destruction of property having moral sanction, for the assertion of moral sanction involves the right of compensation. Where the right of compensation itself becomes the issue is only where the want of moral sanction in the property in question is conceded.

Thus the belief in the rightfulness of compensation for the abolition of slavery bore no determining part in the minds of those who believed in the rightfulness of slavery. The pro-slavery men, who asserted that slavery was of God's ordinance, that it was the natural right and duty of the stronger to enslave the weaker so they might paternally care for them, who insisted not merely that slavery ought not to be abolished where it existed, but that it ought to be extended where it did not exist, were not affected by belief in the rightfulness of compensation. That slave-owners ought to be compensated if slavery was abolished followed from their assertion that slavery was right and ought not to be abolished. It was only in the minds of those who had come to think that slavery was wrong and ought to be abolished, that the idea that slave-holders must be compensated assumed importance, and became the pivotal question.

So as to land. The idea of compensation is raised and has importance only where it serves as a secondary defence of private property in land. If a man believes in private property in land it is needless to address to him any argument for the necessity of compensation on its abolition. He does not believe in its abolition, but in its continuance and extension; and as the greater includes the less, he already believes in the necessity of compensation if it be abolished. But if he has come to doubt its justice and to favor its abolition, then the raising of the question of compensation, as though it were a new and separate moral question, may serve the purpose of a second embankment or second ditch in military defence, and prevent him from advocating abolition, or at least abolition that would cause any loss to vested interests. And the intermediate character of this defence of vested wrong gives it of course great attractions for those timid and prudent souls who when moral right comes in conflict with powerful interests like to keep out of the battle.

Thus the idea of compensation with which we are concerned is the idea of compensation for the abolition of something in itself conceded to be wrong. Yet it is based on moral grounds, and raises what is purely a moral question.

Those who assert this necessity of compensation for the abolition of what in itself they concede to be wrong contend that the state has incurred a moral obligation by its previous acquiescence. They say that while it would be right for it to refuse such acquiescence in the first place — as to prohibit slavery where it does not yet exist; to refrain from making private property of new land; to refuse to grant new pensions or impose new protective duties or grant new special privileges — yet where it has already done such things the state is morally bound to those who have accepted its action; and for it to destroy the value of property already acquired under its sanction would be in the nature of a retroactive law.

But in this there is evident confusion. If it were proposed that the state should undo what has already been done under its sanction — as, for instance, that it should declare invalid titles to the proceeds of slave labor already rendered, and give the slaves legal claim for previous services; or if it should call on the beneficiaries of protective tariffs for profits they had already acquired—then this reasoning might have weight. But it is not retroactive to declare that for the future the labor of the slave shall belong to himself, nor that for the future trade shall be free. To demand compensation for action of this kind is to assert, not that the state must be bound by what it has already done, but that what it has already done it is morally bound to continue to do.

The loss for which compensation is in such cases asked is not the loss of a value in hand, but the loss of an expectation. The value of a bale of cotton is an actual existing value, based on work done. But the value of a slave is not actual, but prospective; it is not based on work done, but on the expectation that the state will continue to compel him to work for his owner. So the value of a house or other improvement represents the present value of the labor thus embodied. But the value of land itself represents merely the value of the expectation that the state will continue to permit the holder to appropriate a value belonging to all. Now, is the state called on to compensate men for the failure of their expectations as to its action, even where no moral element is involved?

If it make peace, must it compensate those who have invested on the expectation of war. If it open a shorter highway, is it morally bound to compensate those who may lose by the diversion of travel from the old one? If it promote the discovery of a cheap means of producing electricity directly from heat, is it morally bound to compensate the owners of all the steam engines thereby thrown out of use and all who are engaged in making them? If it develop the air-ship, must it compensate those whose business would be injured? Such a contention would be absurd. Yet the contention we are considering is worse. It is that the state must compensate for disappointing the expectations of those who have counted on its continuing to do wrong.

When the state abolishes slavery or hereditary pensions or protective duties or special privileges of any kind, does it really take from the individuals who thereby lose, anything they actually have? Clearly not. In the abolition of slavery it merely declines for the future to compel one man to work for another. In the abolition of hereditary pensions it merely declines for the future to take property by force from those to whom it rightfully belongs and hand it over to others. In the abolition of protective duties it merely declines for the future forcibly to interfere with the natural rights of all in order that a few may get an unnatural profit. In the abolition of special privileges it merely declines for the future to use its power to give some an advantage over others.

See, then, for what in such cases compensation is really asked. It is not for any attempt to right past wrongs; it is for refusing to do wrong in future. It is not for the unequal treatment of individuals; it is for refusal to continue unequal treatment. That there may be a loss of salable value to individuals in this refusal is true. But it is not a loss of anything they now have; it is a loss of what they expected to get. It is not a loss for which these individuals can justly demand compensation or the state can justly make compensation. It is a loss of the kind that the silversmiths of Ephesus sustained from Paul's preaching; a loss of the kind that comes to liquor-sellers from the spread of a temperance movement; a loss of the kind that falls on some individuals with every beneficial invention and every public improvement. Such demand for compensation is a denial of any right of reform. It involves the idea that the state, having once done wrong, is morally bound to continue it — not merely that it must continue to do wrong or *else* compensate; but that it must continue to do wrong anyhow.

For compensation implies equivalence. To compensate for the discontinuance of a wrong is to give those who profit by the wrong the pecuniary equivalent of its continuance. Now the state has nothing that does not belong to the individuals who compose it. What it gives to some it must take from others. Abolition with compensation is therefore not really abolition, but continuance under a different form — on one side of unjust deprivation, and on the other side of unjust appropriation. When on the abolition of a hereditary pension the holder is compensated, he receives in money or bonds a sum calculated to yield him in interest the same power of annually commanding the labor of others that the pension gave. So compensation for the selling value of a slave, which disappears on the refusal of the community longer to force him to work for the master, means the giving to the master of what the power to take the property of the slave may be worth. What slave-owners lose is the power of taking the property of the slaves and their descendants; and what they get is an agreement that the government will take for their benefit and turn over to them an equivalent part of the property of all. The robbery is continued under another form. What it loses in intention it gains in extension. If some before enslaved are partially freed, others before free are partially enslaved.

That confusion alone gives plausibility to the idea of compensation for refusal to continue wrong, is seen in the fact that such claims are never put forward in behalf of the original beneficiaries of the wrong, but always in behalf of purchasers. Sometimes the confusion is that of direct substitution. Thus it is sometimes said, "Here is a man who, presuming on the continued consent of the state, invests his earnings in property depending on that consent. If the state withdraws its consent, does it not, unless it compensates him, destroy the products of his hard labor?"

The answer is clear: It does not. Let the property be, for instance, a slave. What the state destroys in abolishing slavery is not what may have been given for the slave, but the value of the slave. That the purchaser got by honest work what he exchanged for the slave is not in point. He is not injured as laborer, but as slave-owner. If he had not exchanged his earnings for the slave the abolition of slavery would have caused him no loss. When a man exchanges property of one kind for property of another kind he gives up the one with all its incidents and takes in its stead the other with its incidents. He cannot sell bricks and buy hay, and then complain because the hay burned when the bricks would not. The greater liability of the hay to burn is one of the incidents he accepted in buying it. Nor can he exchange property having moral sanction for property having only legal sanction, and claim that the moral sanction of the thing he sold attaches now to the thing he bought. That has gone with the thing to the other party in the exchange. Exchange transfers, it cannot create. Each party gives up what right he had and takes what right the other party had. The last holder obtains no moral right that the first holder did not have.

"But," it may be said, "the purchaser of what has been long treated as property stands in a different position from the original holder. In our administration of justice between man and man, this difference between the wrongful appropriator and the innocent purchaser is recognized, and long possession is held to cure defects of original title. This principle ought to be recognized by the state in dealing with individuals, and hence when, even by omission, it deprives innocent purchasers of what has long been held as property it ought to compensate them."

Innocent purchasers of what involves wrong to others! Is not the phrase absurd? If in our legal tribunals, "ignorance of the law excuseth no man," how much less can it do so in the tribunal of morals —and it is this to which compensationists appeal.

And innocence can only shield from the punishment due to conscious wrong; it cannot give right. If you innocently stand on my toes, you may fairly ask me not to be angry; but you gain no right to continue to stand on them. Now in merely abolishing property that involves wrong, the state imposes no penalty, it does not even demand recompense to those who have been wronged. In this it is more lenient than the principles on which we administer justice between man and man. For they would require the innocent purchaser of what belonged to another to make restitution, not only of the thing itself, but of all that had been received from it. Nor does the principle of market overt, which gives to the purchaser of certain things openly sold in certain places, possession even against the rightful owner unless he proves fraud; nor the principle of statutes of limitation, which refuses to question ownership after a certain lapse of time, deny this general principle.

The principle of "market overt" is, not that passage from hand to hand gives ownership, but that there are certain things so constantly passing from hand to hand by simple transfer that the interests of commerce and the general convenience are best served by assuming possession to be conclusive of ownership where wrongful intent cannot be proved. The principle of statutes of limitation is not that mere length of possession gives ownership, but that past a certain point it becomes impossible certainly to adjudicate disputes between man and man. This is one of the cases in which human law must admit its inadequacy to more than roughly enforce the dictates of the moral law. No scheme of religion and no theory of morals would hold him blameless who relied on a statute of limitations to keep what he knew belonged morally to another. But legal machinery cannot search into the conscience, it can only inquire into the evidence; and the evidence of things past is to human perceptions quickly dimmed and soon obliterated by the passage of time. So that as to things whose ownership must depend on what was done in the past, it is necessary, to avoid interminable disputes, that the state should set some limit beyond which it will not inquire, but will take possession as proof of ownership.

In our ordinary use of words everything subject to ownership and its incidental rights is accounted property. But there are two species of property, which, though often ignorantly or wantonly confounded, are essentially different and diametrically opposed. Both may be alike in having a selling value and being subject to transfer. But things of the one kind are true property, having the sanction of natural right and moral law independently of the action of the state, while things of the other kind are only spurious property, their maintenance as property requiring the continuous exertion of state power, the continuous exercise or threat of its force, and involving a continuous violation of natural right and moral law. To things of the one kind the reasonable principle of statutes of limitation properly applies; for, being in their nature property, any question of their ownership is not a question of general right, but only a question of transactions between man and man in the past. But to things of the other kind, and as between the individual and the state, this principle does not and cannot apply, for holding their character as property only from the action of the state, that character is gone the moment the state withdraws its support. The question whether this support shall or shall not be withdrawn is not a question of what was done in the past, but of what shall be done in the future — a question of general rights, not a question between individuals. Things which are brought into existence by the exertion of labor, and to which the character of property attaches from their origin as an extension of the right of the man to himself, are property of the first kind. Special privileges by which the state empowers and assists one man in taking the proceeds of another's labor, are property of the second kind.

A question of the ownership of a coat, a tool, a house, a bale of goods, is a question of the ownership of the concrete results of past labor. We know from the nature of the thing that it must be owned by somebody, but after lapse of time we cannot from the weakness of human powers undertake in case of dispute to determine who that may be; and hence, refusing to inquire so far back, we assume the right to be in the possessor, of which we have at least presumptive evidence. But a question of the maintenance or abolition of slavery or private property in land, of the continuance or non-continuance of a trade monopoly, a hereditary pension, or a protective duty, is a question whether the state shall or shall not in the future lend its power for the wrongful appropriation of the results of labor yet to be performed. There is in this no place for the principle of statutes of limitations. No indistinctness as to the past can affect the decision. It is not a question of what has been done in the past, but of what shall be done in the future. And so far from the presumption being that the possessor of this species of property is entitled to it, the moral certainty is the other way.

Again it is said, "Here is a man who invests in a slave and another who invests in a building, both being alike recognized as property by the state. The state by refusing longer to give its former sanction destroys the value of one investment while the other continues profitable. Have not these two men been treated with inequality, which in justice should be remedied by compensation? If there was a wrong involved in the one species of property, was it not a wrong of which by state sanction all were guilty? Is it just therefore that those who have happened to invest in it should bear the whole loss?"

To other confusions there is here added confusion as to the relation between the state and its members. If the maintenance by the state of a species of property that involves wrong is to be considered as the action of all its members, even of those who suffer by it, so must the resolve of the state to do so no longer be considered as the resolve of all, even of those who relatively lose by it. If the one cannot demand recompense, how can the others demand compensation?

Passing this, the moral law appealed to in the demand for compensation must be the moral law that binds individuals. Now the moral law cannot sanction immorality. It must hold as void even a specific contract to do wrong. But in the cases we are considering there is no contract. The claim is merely that the state by its wrongful action having given rise to the expectation that it would continue such wrongful action, is morally bound, should it decline to do so, to compensate those who have invested in this expectation. Would such a claim hold as between individuals? If, for instance, I have been accustomed to spend my earnings in a gambling-house or rum-shop till the proprietor has come to count on me as a source of regular profit, am I morally bound to compensate him if I stop? Or if an innocent purchaser has bought the business on the expectation that I would continue, does that bind me to compensate him?

Consider further: If a moral right of property is created by the acquiescence of the state in a wrong, then it must be morally binding on all. If the state would violate the moral law in abolishing slavery without compensation, so would the slave violate the moral law in attempting to escape without first compensating his master, and so would every one who aided him, even with a cup of cold water. This was actually held and taught and enacted into law in the United States previous to the war, and with reference to the white slaves of Great Britain is held and taught by the foremost men and journals of that country, who declare that for the masses even by strictly legal forms to resume their natural rights in the land of their birth, without compensation to present legal owners, would be a violation of the Ten Commandments!

That the state is not an individual, but is composed of individual members all of whom must be affected by its action, is the reason why its legitimate sphere is that of securing to those members equal rights. This is the equality which it is bound to secure, not equality in the results of individual actions; and whoever chooses to invest on the presumption of its denial of equal rights does so at his own risk. He cannot ask that, to secure equality of profits between him and investors who did not take this risk, the state should continue to deny equality of rights. It is the duty of the state to secure equality of rights, not to secure equality of profits.

Of the investments of all kinds constantly being made under the equal sanction of the state some result in loss and some in gain. Supposing it to be asked, "Why should not the state secure equality by compensating those who lose?"

The answer would be quick and clear. It is not the business of the state to secure investors from loss, and it would be grossly unjust for it to attempt to do so. For this would be to compel those who had made good investments to make up the losses of those who had made bad ones. It would be to take from prudence and care their natural reward and make them bear the losses of recklessness and waste; to punish forethought, to put a premium on ignorance and extravagance, and quickly to impoverish the richest community.

But would it not be even more unjust and unwise for the state to compensate those who up to the last moment had held and bought property involving wrong, thus compelling those who had refrained from holding and buying it to make up their losses? Is it true that the acquiescence of the state in a wrong of this kind proves it equally the wrong of all? Did that part of the community-consisting of slaves ever acquiesce in slavery? Did the men who were robbed of their natural rights in land ever really acquiesce?

Are not such wrongs always instituted in the first place by those who by force or cunning gain control of the state? Are they not maintained by stifling liberty, by corrupting morals and confusing thought and buying or gagging the teachers of religion and of ethics? Is not any movement for the abolition of such wrongs always and of necessity preceded by a long agitation in which their injustice is so fully declared that whoever does not wilfully shut his eyes may see it?

"*Caveat emptor*" is the maxim of the law — "Let the buyer beware!" If a man buys a structure in which the law of gravity is disregarded or mechanical laws ignored he takes the risk of those laws asserting their sway. And so he takes the risk in buying property which contravenes the moral law. When he ignores the moral sense, when he gambles on the continuance of a wrong, and when at last the general conscience rises to the point of refusing to continue that wrong, can he then claim that those who have refrained from taking part in it, those who have suffered from it, those who have borne the burden and heat and contumely of first moving against it, shall share in his losses on the ground that as members of the same state they are equally responsible for it? And must not the acceptance of this impudent plea tend to prevent that gradual weakening and dying out of the wrong which would otherwise occur as the rise of the moral sense against it lessened the prospect of its continuance; and by promise of insurance to investors tend to maintain it in strength and energy till the last minute?

Take slavery. The confidence of American slaveholders, strengthened by the example of Great Britain, that abolition would not come without compensation, kept up to the highest point the market value of slaves, even after the guns that were to free them had begun to sound, whereas if there had been no paltering with the idea of compensation the growth of the sentiment against slavery would by reducing the selling value of slaves have gradually lessened the pecuniary interests concerned in supporting it.

Take private property in land. Where the expectation of future growth and improvement is in every advancing community a most important element in selling value, the effect of the idea of compensation will be to keep up speculation, and thus to prevent that lessening in the selling value of land, that gradual accommodation of individuals to the coming change, which is the natural effect of the growth of the demand for the recognition of equal rights to land.

The question we are discussing is necessarily a moral question. Those who contend that the state is the source of all rights may indeed object to any proposed state action that it would be inexpedient, but they cannot object that it would be wrong. Nevertheless, just as we find the materialistic evolutionists constantly dropping into expressions which imply purpose in nature, so do we find deniers of any higher law than that of the state vociferous in their declarations that it would be wrong, or unjust, or wicked, for the state to abolish property of this spurious kind without compensation. The only way we can meet them with any regard for their professions is to assume that they do not quite understand the language, and that by such expressions they mean that it would be inexpedient. Their argument, I take it, may be most fairly put in this way: Experience has shown respect for property rights to be greatly conducive to the progress and well-being of mankind, and all rights of property resting (as they assert) on the same basis, the recognition of the state, the destruction of a recognized right of property by action of the state would give a shock to and cast a doubt over all rights of property, and thus work injury.

But even if we ignore any moral basis, and assume that all rights of property are derived from the state, it is still clear that while some forms of property do conduce to the general wealth and prosperity, others may be recognized by the state that lessen the general wealth and impair the general prosperity. The right of piracy, which at times and places has been recognized by the state, does not stand on the same basis of expediency with the right of peaceful commerce. The right of hereditary jurisdiction, or "the right of pit and gallows" as it was called in Scotland, where it was actually bought out by the state as a piece of valuable property; the right, long having a salable value in France, of administering justice; the right, at times recognized by the state as belonging to every petty lordling, of making private war, of collecting local dues and tolls and customs, and compelling services; the right of trampling down the fields of the husbandman in the pursuit of game; the monopolies which made valuable privileges of permissions to manufacture, to trade and to import, were certainly not promotive of the general prosperity. On the contrary the general wealth and prosperity have been greatly enhanced by their abolition.

Even if we grant that all rights of property have the same basis and sanction and eliminate all moral distinction, reason and experience still show that there is but one right of property that conduces to the prosperity of the whole community, and that this is the right which secures to the laborer the product of his labor. This promotes prosperity by stimulating production, and giving such security to accumulation as permits the use of capital and affords leisure for the development of the intellectual powers. It is respect for this, not respect for those forms of property which the perversion or folly of legislative power may at times sanction, and which consist in the power of appropriating the results of others' labor, that universal experience shows to be essential to the peace, prosperity and happiness of mankind.

So far from the destruction of those spurious and injurious rights of property which have wound around the useful rights of property, like choking weeds around a fruitful vine, being calculated to injure that respect for property on which wealth and prosperity and civilization depend, the reverse is the case. They are not merely directly destructive of what it promotes, but to class them with it and to insist that the respect due to it is also due to them is to give rise to the belief that all rights of property are injurious to the masses. The history of mankind shows that the respect for property which is essential to social well-being has never been threatened, save by the growth of these noxious parasites. And this to-day is the only thing that threatens it. Why are the socialists of to-day so hostile to capital? It is for no other reason than that they confuse with what is really capital legalized wrongs which enable the few to rob the many, by appropriating the products of labor and demanding a blackmail for the use of the opportunity to labor. To teach that the good and the bad in legal recognitions are indistinguishable, that all that the state may choose to regard as property is property, is virtually to teach that property is robbery!

And what is this state, to whose control by selfishness or ignorance or dishonesty or corruption these deniers of moral distinctions would give the power of binding men in the most vitally important matter for all future time? Caligula was the state. Nero was the state. Louis XIV. truly said, "The state, it is I." And according to Herbert Spencer the state in England consists of "a motley assemblage of nominees of caucuses, ruled by ignorant and fanatical wire-pullers." Practically, the state is always what man, what combination, what interest, may control its machinery. Hence the expediency of strictly limiting its power; and, if indeed there be no moral principle, no higher law, that will give us clear guidance as to what the state may or may not do, then it becomes all the more expedient that we carry the principle of state omnipotence over rights to its logical conclusion, and assert the power of the state in any present or any future time utterly to annul any stipulation, contract, regulation or institution of the state at any past time. If there be no moral right, no higher law, to check the action of the state, then is it all the more needful that it should be subject at least to the prospective check of sharp and complete reversal. For the more permanent and therefore the more valuable are the special privileges which the state has power to grant, the greater is the inducement to selfish interests to gain control of it. Nothing better calculated to corrupt government and to strengthen a most dangerous tendency of our time can well be imagined than the doctrine that state grants which enable one man to take the labor and property of others can never be abolished without compensation to those who may hold them.

Of different nature is the plea sometimes made, that compensation, by disarming opposition, is the easiest and quickest way of abolishing a vested wrong. As to this, not only is compensation not abolition, not only does its advocacy tend to keep in full strength the pecuniary interests which are the greatest obstacles to the reform, but it renders it impossible to arouse that moral force which can alone overcome an intrenched wrong. For to say that men must be compensated if they are prevented from doing a thing is to say that they have a right to do that thing. And this those who intelligently advocate compensation know. Their purpose in advocating compensation is to prevent abolition.

It is sometimes said that it would have been cheaper for us to pay for the Southern slaves, as Great Britain did in the West Indies, than incur the civil war. But the assumption that American slavery might thus have been got rid of and the war avoided, is far from being true. An aristocratic government, such as that of Great Britain in 1832, may abolish slavery in a few small dependencies by imposing the burden on its own people, but in a popular government and on a great scale this cannot be done. Great Britain saved no war by paying compensation, for the West Indian planters could not have fought emancipation, and if the West Indian slaves were freed more quickly with compensation than they could have been without, it was solely because the class concerned in the maintenance of vested wrongs was overpoweringly strong in the British Parliament. With even such representation as the masses now have it would have been easier to abolish slavery in the West Indies without compensation than with it. In the United States abolition with compensation was never a practical question, nor could it have become a practical question until the sentiment against slavery had reached even a stronger pitch than that which led to war. The war came before more than a small minority had seriously thought of abolishing slavery, let alone of paying for it; before either section really dreamed of war. It came from the unstable equilibrium which legalized wrong begets, from the incidental issues and passions which it always arouses when the moral sense begins to revolt against it, even before the main question is reached. It came, not from a demand for compensation on one side and a refusal to give it on the other, but from the timidity with which the moral question had been treated by those who really saw the essential injustice of slavery, and which by concessions and compromises had so strengthened and emboldened the slavery interest that in revolt at measures far less threatening to it than the discussion of abolition with compensation could have been, it flung the nation into war.

And even if the alternative of compensation or war had been fairly presented to the American people, who shall say that it would have been really wiser and cheaper for them to surrender to such a demand? Could the Nemesis that follows national wrong have thus been placated? Might not the carrying out of such a measure as the compensation for three million slaves have given rise to political struggles involving an even more disastrous war? And would the precedent established in the conscious violation of the moral sense ultimately have cost nothing? The cost of the war, in blood, in wealth, in the bitterness aroused and the corruptions of government engendered, cannot well be estimated; yet who cannot but feel that the moral atmosphere is clearer and that the great problems which still beset the republic are easier of solution than if with the alternative of compensation or war, like a pistol at its head, the nation had consciously and cravenly surrendered to wrong?

What this plea for compensation amounts to is, that it is cheaper to submit to wrong than to stand for right. Universal experience shows that whenever a nation accepts such a doctrine of submission it loses independence and liberty without even gaining peace. The peace it will secure is the peace that declining Rome bought of the barbarians, the peace of fellaheen and Bengalees.

Even in personal matters it is difficult to say what will be the result of action based on mere expediency; in the larger and more intricate scale of national affairs it is impossible. This is why, as contended by Mr. Spencer in "Social Statics" the course of true wisdom in social affairs is to follow the dictate of principle — to ask, not what *seems* to be expedient, but what *is* right. If a law or institution is wrong, if its continuance involves the continuance of injustice, there is but one wise thing to do, as there is but one right thing, and that is to abolish it.

To come back to the main question:

All pleas for compensation on the abolition of unequal rights to land are excuses for avoiding right and continuing wrong; they all, as fully as the original wrong, deny that equalness which is the essential of justice. Where they have seemed plausible to any honestly-minded man, he will, if he really examines his thought, see that this has been so because he has, though perhaps unconsciously, entertained a sympathy for those who seem to profit by injustice which he has refused to those who have been injured by it. He has been thinking of the few whose incomes would be cut off by the restoration of equal right. He has forgotten the many, who are being impoverished, degraded, and driven out of life by its denial. If he once breaks through the tyranny of accustomed ideas and truly realizes that all men are equally entitled to the use of the natural opportunities for the living of their lives and the development of their powers, he will see the injustice, the wickedness, of demanding compensation for the abolition of the monopoly of land. He will see that if any one is to be compensated on the abolition of a wrong, it is those who have suffered by the wrong, not those who have profited by it.

Private property in land — the subjecting of land to that exclusive ownership which rightfully attaches to the products of labor — is a denial of the true right of property, which gives to each the equal right to exert his labor and the exclusive right to its results. It differs from slavery only in its form, which is that of making property of the indispensable natural factor of production, while slavery makes property of the human factor; and it has the same purpose and effect, that of compelling some men to work for others. Its abolition therefore does not mean the destruction of any right but the cessation of a wrong — that for the future the municipal law shall conform to the moral law, and that each shall have his own.

I have gone over this question of compensation — this "last ditch" of the advocates of landlordism — because it is so persistently raised, not that it arises in anything I have advocated. We who propose that natural and therefore easy method of restoring their equal rights to men, which for the purpose of clearly differentiating it from all schemes of land nationalization we call the single tax, do not propose to take from land-owners anything they now have. We propose to leave to land-owners whatever they actually have, even though it be in their hands the fruits of injustice; we propose not even to change the forms of land tenure, and greatly to simplify instead of enlarging the machinery and functions of the state. We propose, in short, only so to change present methods of raising public revenues that they shall conform to the requirements of the right of property, taking for the use of the state that which rightfully belongs to the state, leaving to individuals that which rightfully belongs to the individual.

But that clumsy mode of abolishing private property in land which is properly called land nationalization requires the taking of rightful property in the improvements that have been annexed to land. In this it calls for compensation in a way that confusion of thought may carry to the ownership of land itself. And even the taking of land it proposes would be in form a taking of property. The land would have to be formally appropriated by the state and then rented out. Now we are accustomed to the compensation of owners when particular portions of land are taken for the use of the state, and this indeed as I have before pointed out is rightful, so that it is easy for the superficial to think that when the state shall take all the land for the purpose of renting it out again it should compensate all owners. Thus the scheme of land nationalization gives to the idea of compensation a plausibility that does not properly belong to it.

This is the reason why in England, where there has been a good deal of talk of land nationalization, the notion of compensation is strong among certain classes, while in America, where the movement for the recognition of equal rights to the use of land has gone from the beginning on the lines of the single tax, there is almost nothing of it, except as a reflection of English thought. And this is the reason why, although even in England the advocates of land nationalization are few and weak as compared with the great body that is advancing on the unjust privileges of landlords by the way of taxation, the English advocates of landlordism always endeavor to discuss the land question as though the actual taking of land by the state were the only thing proposed. It will be observed for instance that Mr. Spencer, in "Justice," never so much as alludes to the proposition to secure equal rights in land by taking land values, not land. Yet he cannot be so ignorant of what is going on about him as not to know that this is the line which the advance against landlordism is taking and must take. He ignores it because there is on that line no place for proposing or even suggesting compensation. Compensation to the ultimate payers of a tax is something unheard of and absurd.

The primary error of the advocates of land nationalization is in their confusion of equal rights with joint rights, and in their consequent failure to realize the nature and meaning of economic rent — errors which I have pointed out in commenting on Mr. Spencer's declarations in "Social Statics." In truth the right to the use of land is not a joint or common right, but an equal right; the joint or common right is to rent, in the economic sense of the term. Therefore it is not necessary for the state to take land, it is only necessary for it to take rent. This taking by the commonalty of what is of common right, would of itself secure equality in what is of equal right — for since the holding of land could be profitable only to the user, there would be no inducement for any one to hold land that he could not adequately use, and monopolization being ended no one who wanted to use land would have any difficulty in finding it. And it would at the same time secure the individual right, for in taking what is of common right for its revenues the state could abolish all those taxes which now take from the individual what is of individual right.

The truth is that customs-taxes, and improvement taxes, and income taxes, and taxes on business and occupations and on legacies and successions, are morally and economically no better than highway robbery or burglary, all the more disastrous and demoralizing because practised by the state. There is no necessity for them. The seeming necessity arises only from the failure of the state to take its own natural and adequate source of revenue — a failure which entails a long train of evils of another kind by stimulating a forestalling and monopolization of land which creates an artificial scarcity of the primary element of life and labor, so that in the midst of illimitable natural resources the opportunity to work has come to be looked on as a boon, and in spite of the most enormous increase in the powers of production the great mass find life a hard struggle to maintain life, and millions die before their time, of over-strain and under-nurture.

When the matter is looked on in this way, the idea of compensation — the idea that justice demands that those who have engrossed the natural revenue of the state must be paid the capitalized value of all future engrossment before the state can resume those revenues — is too preposterous for serious statement.

And while in the nature of things any change from wrong-doing to right-doing must entail loss upon those who profit by the wrong-doing, and this can no more be prevented than can parallel lines be made to meet; yet it must also be remembered that in the nature of things the loss is merely relative, the gain absolute. Whoever will examine the subject will see that in the abandonment of the present unnatural and unjust method of raising public revenues and the adoption of the natural and just method even those who relatively lose will be enormous gainers.

CHAPTER XII.

"JUSTICE" — "THE LAND QUESTION."

WHILE "Justice" shows no decadence of intellectual power, and those who have seen the utterances of a great thinker in preceding volumes of the Synthetic Philosophy will doubtless have as high an opinion of this, there is in it everywhere, as compared with "Social Statics," the evidence of moral decadence, and of that perplexity which is the penalty of deliberate sacrifice of intellectual honesty. But it were wearying, and for our purpose needless, to review the subsequent chapters of "Justice," and to show the contradictions and confusions into which Mr. Spencer falls at every turn,[1] and the manner in which he recants his previously expressed opinions on such subjects as the political rights of women, and even the equal political rights of men. To complete the examination of that cross-section of his teachings which in the beginning I proposed, let us proceed to the

---

[1] One of these may be worth quoting as particularly interesting in view of what has gone before and what is yet to come. In Chapter XVI., "The Right of Gift and Bequest," pp. 122–124, Mr. Spencer says:

> Few will deny that the earth's surface and the things on it should be owned in full by the generation at any time existing. Hence the right of property may not equitably be so interpreted as to allow any generation to tell subsequent generations for what purpose or under what conditions they are to use the earth's surface or the things on it. . . . One who holds land subject to that supreme ownership of the community which both ethics and law assert, cannot rightly have such power of willing the application of it as involves permanent alienation from the community.

consideration of his very last word on the land question, the note to which he refers the reader at the close of the chapter on "The Rights to the Uses of Natural Media."

This note is to be found among the appendices to "Justice," which consist of Appendix A, "The Kantian Idea of Rights," before referred to (page 173); Appendix B, "The Land Question;" Appendix C, "The Moral Motive," a reply to a criticism by the Rev. J. Llewelyn Davis; and Appendix D, "Conscience in Animals," which is a collection of dog stories.

The idea that for the genesis of all there is in man, even his moral perceptions, we must look down, not up, permeates the Synthetic Philosophy, seeking to obliterate the gulf between man and other animals by greedily swallowing every traveller's tale that tends to degrade man and every wonder-monger's story that ascribes human faculties to brutes. Thus "Justice" begins with "Animal Ethics" and ends with dog stories, the appendix devoted to them being twice as large as that devoted to "The Land Question" and illustrated with diagrams.[1]

---

[1] The dog stories which close this crowning book of the Synthetic Philosophy are sent to Mr. Spencer by Mr. T. Mann Jones, of Devon, with this introduction:

DEAR SIR: The following careful observations on animals other than man, may be of interest to you as supporting your idea that the idea of "duty" or "ought" (owe it) may be of non "supernatural" origin. "Supernatural" is used in the usual sense, without committing the writer to any opinion.

These "careful observations" are indorsed by Mr. Spencer as highly remarkable and instructive, and as supporting his own conclusion, and he tells us, apparently on the faith of them, that Mr. Jones is a careful, critical and trustworthy observer. To give a

These dog stories are, however, fit companions to the savage stories with which, by the assistance of a corps of readers, the volumes of the Synthetic Philosophy are profusely embellished. The wooden literalness with which, to suit himself, Mr. Spencer interprets the imagery and metaphor of which the language of all peoples who come close to nature is full, is perhaps the most comical thing in this unconsciously comic collection. I hesitate to give an instance, such is the embarrassment of riches; but here, to quote at random, is one. It is from the chapter on "The Religious Idea" in "Principles of Sociology." Mr. Spencer has been showing to his own satisfaction, and doubtless to that of the gentlemen who regard him as greater than Aristotle, how from the adoption of such family names as Wolf, and the habit of speaking of a strong man as "a bear," the less civilized peoples, whom he generically lumps as "savages," have come to believe that their ancestors passed into animals. He goes on to show "how naturally the identification of stars with persons may occur." Recalling first, what he declares to be "the belief of some North Americans that the brighter stars in the Milky Way are camp-fires made by the dead on their way to the other world," this is the fashion in which he does it:

---

sample, here is one of the observations, which as it has no diagrams, I may quote as printed:

The "ought" may be established as an obligation to a higher mind in opposition to the promptings of the strongest feelings of the animal; e.g. —

A bitch I had many years ago showed great pleasure at the attentions of male dogs, when in season. I checked her repeatedly, by *voice only*. This set up the "ought" so thoroughly, that though never tied up at such times, she died a virgin at thirteen and a half years old.

When a sportsman, hearing a shot in the adjacent wood, exclaims, "That's Jones!" he is not supposed to mean that Jones is the sound; he is known to mean that Jones made the sound. But when a savage, pointing to a particular star originally thought of as the camp-fire of such or such a departed man, says, "There he is," the children he is instructing naturally suppose him to mean that the star itself is the departed man; especially when receiving the statement through an undeveloped language. —*Principles of Sociology*, Vol. II., page 685.

"Lo, the poor Indian!"

What would happen to the beliefs of savage children if their undeveloped language enabled them to receive such information as is often conveyed through our developed language—such, for instance, as "She's a daisy!" or "He's a brick!" or "You would have to use a pick-axe to get a joke through his head"?

But I am keeping the reader from "The Land Question." This is, for our purpose at least, the most important utterance of what its author deems the most important book of the great Synthetic Evolutionary Philosophy—a book that begins with "Animal Ethics," and ends with dog stories. I quote this appendix in full:

APPENDIX B.—THE LAND QUESTION.

The course of Nature, "red in tooth and claw," has been, on a higher plane, the course of civilization. Through "blood and iron" small clusters of men have been consolidated into larger ones, and these again into still larger ones, until nations have been formed. This process, carried on everywhere and always by brute force, has resulted in a history of wrongs upon wrongs: savage tribes have been slowly welded together by savage means. We could not, if we tried, trace back the acts of unscrupulous violence committed during these thousands of years; and could we trace them back we could not rectify their evil results.

Land-ownership was established during this process; and if the genesis of land-ownership was full of iniquities, they were iniquities committed not by the ancestors of any one class of existing men but by the ancestors of all existing men. The remote forefathers of living Englishmen were robbers, who stole the lands of men who were themselves robbers, who behaved in like manner to the robbers who preceded them. The usurpation by the Normans, here complete and there partial, was of lands which, centuries before, had been seized, some by piratical Danes and Norsemen, and some at an earlier time by hordes of invading Frisians or old English. And then the Celtic owners, expelled or enslaved by these, had in bygone ages themselves expropriated the people who lived in the underground houses here and there still traceable. What would happen if we tried to restore lands inequitably taken — if Normans had to give them back to Danes and Norse and Frisians, and these again to Celts, and these again to the men who lived in caves and used flint implements? The only imaginable form of the transaction would be a restoration of Great Britain bodily to the Welsh and the Highlanders; and if the Welsh and the Highlanders did not make a kindred restoration, it could only be on the ground that, having not only taken the land of the aborigines but killed them, they had thus justified their ownership!

The wish now expressed by many that land-ownership should be conformed to the requirements of pure equity, is in itself commendable; and is in some men prompted by conscientious feeling. One would, however, like to hear from such the demand that not only here but in the various regions we are peopling, the requirements of pure equity should be conformed to. As it is, the indignation against wrongful appropriations of land, made in the past at home, is not accompanied by any indignation against the more wrongful appropriations made at present abroad. Alike as holders of the predominant political power and as furnishing the rank and file of our armies, the masses of the people are responsible for those nefarious doings all over the world which end in the seizing of new territories and expropriation of their inhabitants. The filibustering expeditions of the old English are repeated, on a vastly larger scale, in the filibustering expeditions of the new English. Yet those who execrate ancient usurpations utter no word of protest against these far greater modern usurpations — nay, are aiders and abetters in them. Remaining as they do passive and silent while there is going on this universal land-grabbing which their votes could stop; and supplying as they do the soldiers who effect it; they are responsible for it. By deputy they are committing in this matter grosser and more numerous injustices than were committed against their forefathers.

That the masses of landless men should regard private land-ownership as having been wrongfully established, is natural; and, as we have seen, they are not without warrant. But if we entertain the thought of rectification, there arises in the first place the question — which are the wronged and which are the wrongers? Passing over the primary fact that the ancestors of existing Englishmen, landed and landless, were, as a body, men who took the land by violence from previous owners; and thinking only of the force and fraud by which certain of these ancestors obtained possession of the land while others of them lost possession; the preliminary question is — Which are the descendants of the one and of the other? It is tacitly assumed that those who now own lands are the posterity of the usurpers, and that those who now have no lands are the posterity of those whose lands were usurped. But this is far from being the case. The fact that among the nobility there are very few whose titles go back to the days when the last usurpations took place, and none to the days when there took place the original usurpations; joined with the fact that among existing land-owners there are many whose names imply artisan-ancestors; show that we have not now to deal with descendants of those who unjustly appropriated the land. While, conversely, the numbers of the landless whose names prove that their forefathers belonged to the higher ranks (numbers which must be doubled to take account of inter-marriages with female descendants) show that among those who are now without land, many inherit the blood of the land-usurpers. Hence, that bitter feeling towards the landed which contemplation of the past generates in many of the landless, is in great measure misplaced. They are themselves to a considerable extent descendants of the sinners; while those they scowl at are to a considerable extent descendants of the sinned-against.

But granting all that is said about past iniquities, and leaving aside all other obstacles in the way of an equitable re-arrangement, there is an obstacle which seems to have been overlooked. Even supposing that the English as a race gained possession of the land equitably, which they did not; and even supposing that existing land-owners are the posterity of those who spoiled their fellows, which in large part they are not; and even supposing that the existing landless are the posterity of the despoiled, which in large part they are not; there would still have to be recognized a transaction that goes far to prevent rectification of injustices. If we are to go back upon the past at all, we must go back upon the past wholly, and take account not only of that which the people at large have lost by private appropriation of land, but also that which they have received in the form of a share of the returns — we must take account, that is, of Poor-Law relief. Mr. T. Mackay, author of *The English Poor*, has kindly furnished me with the following memoranda, showing something like the total amount of this since the 43d Elizabeth (1601) in England and Wales.

Sir G. Nicholls (History of Poor Law, appendix to Vol. II.) ventures no estimate till 1688. At that date he puts the poor rate at nearly £700,000 a year. Till the beginning of this century the amounts are based more or less on estimate.

1601–1630.	say	3	millions.
1631–1700.	(1688 Nicholls puts at 700,000.)	30	"
1701–1720.	(1701 Nicholls puts at 900,000.)	20	"
1721–1760.	(1760 Nicholls says 1 1-4 millions.)	40	"
1761–1775.	(1775 put at 1 1-2 million.)	22	"
1776–1800.	(1784 2 millions.)	50	"
1801–1812.	(1803 4 millions; 1813 6 millions.)	65	"
1813–1840.	(based on exact figures given by Sir G. Nicholls.)	170	"
1841–1890.	(based on Mulhall's Dict. of Statistics and Statistical Abstract.)	334	"
		734	millions.

The above represents the amount *expended* in relief of the poor. Under the general term "poor-rate," moneys have always been collected for other purposes — county, borough, police rates, etc. The following table shows the annual amounts of these in connection with the annual amounts expended on the poor:

		Total levied.	Expended on poor.	Other purposes *balance.*
Sir G. Nicholls.	In 1803.	5,348,000	4,077,000	1,271,000 ?
	" 1813.	8,646,841	6,656,106	1,990,735 ?
	" 1853.	6,522,412	4,939,064	1,583,341 ?
		Total spent.		Sum spent.
Statistical abstract.	" 1875.	12,694.208	7,488,481	5,205,727
	" 1889.	15,970,126	8,366,477	7,603,649

In addition, therefore, to sums set out in the first table, there is a further sum, rising during the century from 1¼ to 7½ millions per annum "for other purposes."

Mulhall, on whom I relied for figures between 1853 and 1875, does not give "other expenditure."

Of course of the £734,000,000 given to the poorer members of the landless class during three centuries, a part has arisen from rates on houses; only such portion of which as is chargeable against ground rents, being rightly included in the sum the land has contributed. From a land-owner, who is at the same time a Queen's Counsel, frequently employed professionally to arbitrate in questions of local taxation, I have received the opinion that if, out of the total sum received by the poor, £500,000,000 is credited to the land, this will be an under-estimate. Thus even if we ignore the fact that this amount, gradually contributed, would, if otherwise gradually invested, have yielded in returns of one or other kind a far larger sum, it is manifest that against the claim of the landless may be set off a large claim of the landed — perhaps a larger claim.

For now observe that the landless have not an equitable claim to the land in its present state — cleared, drained, fenced, fertilized, and furnished with farm-buildings, etc. — but only to the land in its primitive state, here stony and there marshy, covered with forest, gorse, heather, etc.; this only, it is, which belongs to the community. Hence, therefore, the question arises — What is the relation between the original "prairie value" of the land, and the amount which the poorer among the landless have received during these three centuries? Probably the land-owners would contend that for the land in its primitive, unsubdued state, furnishing nothing but wild animals and wild fruits, £500,000,000 would be a high price.

When, in *Social Statics*, published in 1850, I drew from the law of equal freedom the corollary that the land could not equitably be alienated from the community, and argued that, after compensating its existing holders, it should be re-appropriated by the community, I overlooked the foregoing considerations. Moreover, I did not clearly see what would be implied by the giving of compensation for all that value which the labor of ages has given to the land. While, as shown in Chapter XI., I adhere to the inference originally drawn, that the aggregate of men forming the community are the supreme owners of the land — an inference harmonizing with legal doctrine and daily acted upon in legislation — a fuller consideration of the matter has led me to the conclusion that individual ownership, subject to state-suzerainty, should be maintained.

Even were it possible to rectify the inequitable doings which have gone on during past thousands of years, and by some balancing of claims and counter-claims, past and present, to make a re-arrangement equitable in the abstract, the resulting state of things would be a less desirable one than the present. Setting aside all financial objections to nationalization (which of themselves negative the transaction, since, if equitably effected, it would be a losing one), it suffices to remember the inferiority of public administration to private administration, to see that ownership by the state would work ill. Under the existing system of ownership, those who manage the land, experience a direct connection between effort and benefit; while, were it under state-ownership, those who managed it would experience no such direct connection. The vices of officialism would inevitably entail immense evils.

Was ever philosopher so perplexed before?

Mr. Spencer started out in 1850 to tell us what are our rights to land. And, excepting that he fell into some confusion by carelessly transforming equal rights into joint rights, he clearly did so. But now, in 1892, and in the climax of the Spencerian Synthetic Philosophy, he has got himself into a maze, in which the living and the dead — Normans, Danes, Norsemen, Frisians, Celts, Saxons, Welsh, and Highlanders; old English and new English; plebeians, with aristocratic names, and aristocrats with plebeian names, and female descendants who have changed their names; ancient filibusters and modern filibusters — are all so whirling round that, in sheer despair, he springs for guidance to "a land-owner who is at the same time a Queen's counsel," and is led by him plump into the English poor law and a long array of figures.

Yet, in the mad whirl he still pretends to consistency. "I adhere," he says, "to the inference originally drawn, that the aggregate of men forming the community are the supreme owners of the land."

Here is that inference in his own words — the inference originally drawn in "Social Statics:"

> Given a race of beings having like claims to pursue the objects of their desires, given a world adapted to the gratification of those desires — a world into which such beings are similarly born, and it unavoidably follows that they have equal rights to the use of this world. . . . Equity therefore does not permit private property in land. . . . The right of mankind at large to the earth's surface is still valid; all deeds, customs, and laws notwithstanding.

What is it that Mr. Spencer here asserts? Not that men derive their rights to the use of the earth by gift, bequest or inheritance, from their ancestors, or from any previous men, but that they derive them from the fact of their own existence. Who lived on the earth before them, or what such predecessors did, has nothing whatever to do with the matter. The equal right to the use of land belongs to each man as man. It begins with his birth; it continues till his death. It can be destroyed or superseded by no human action whatever.

And this is the ground on which, without exception, stand all who demand the resumption of equal rights to land. Where there has been any reference on their part to the wrongfulness of past appropriations of land, it has merely been — as in the case of Mr. Spencer himself in "Social Statics" — by way of illustrating the origin of private property in land, not by way of basing the demand for the rights of living men on the proof of wrongs done to dead men.[1] Neither Mr. Spencer in his "straight" days, nor any one else who has stood for equal rights in land, ever dreamed of such a stultifying proposition as that the right to the use of land must be drawn from some

---

[1] I, for instance, have uniformly asserted that it made no difference whatever whether land has been made private property by force or by consent; that the equal right to its use is a natural and inalienable right of the living, and that this is the ground, and the only ground, on which the resumption of those rights should be demanded. Thus in "The Irish Land Question," in 1881, I said:

> The indictment which really lies against the Irish landlords is not that their ancestors or the ancestors of their grantors robbed the ancestors of the Irish people. That makes no difference. "Let the dead bury their dead." The indictment that truly lies is, that here and now, *they* rob the Irish people. . . . The greatest enemy of the people's cause is he who appeals to national passions and excites old hatreds. He is its best friend who does his utmost to bury them out of sight.

dispossessed generation, for this would be to assert what he so ridiculed, that "God has given one charter of privilege to one generation and another to the next."

Yet, now, this same Herbert Spencer actually assumes that the only question of moral right as to land is, who robbed whom, in days whereof the very memory has perished, and when, according to him, everybody was engaged in robbing everybody else. He not only eats his own words, denies his own perceptions, and endeavors to confuse the truth he once bore witness to, but he assumes that the whole great movement for the recognition of equal rights to land, that is beginning to show its force wherever the English tongue is spoken, has for its object only rectification of past injustices — the ridiculous search, in which he pretends to engage, as to what ancestor robbed what ancestor — and that until that is discovered, those who now hold as their private property the inalienable heritage of all may hold it still. And in the course of this "argument," this advocate of the rich against the poor, of the strong against the weak, declares that the toiling masses of England, made ignorant and brutal and powerless by their disinheritance, have lost their natural rights by serving as food for powder and payers of taxes in foreign wars waged by the ruling classes.

This is bad enough; but more follows. Mr. Spencer discovers a new meaning in the English poor laws.

In "Social Statics," be it remembered, he declared that the equal right to the use of land is the natural, direct, inalienable right of all men, having its derivation in the fact of their existence, and of which they can in no possible way be equitably deprived. He declared that equity does not permit private property in land, and that it is impossible to discover any mode by which land can become private property. He scouted the idea that force can give right, or that sale or bequest or prescription can make invalid claims valid; saying that, "though nothing be multiplied forever, it will not produce one"; asking, "How long does it take for what was originally wrong to grow into a right? and at what rate per annum do invalid claims become valid?" He declared that neither use nor improvement, nor even the free consent of all existing men, could give private ownership in land, or bar the equal right of the next child born. And he, moreover, proved that land nationalization, which he then proposed as the only equitable treatment of land, did not involve state administration.

Not one of the arguments of "Social Statics" is answered in "Justice" — not even the showing that land nationalization merely involves a change in the receivers of rent, and not the governmental occupation and use of land. There are two things, and two things only, that Mr. Spencer admits that he overlooked — the relation of the poor law to the claims of land-owners, and the amount of compensation which the landless must give to the landed "for all that value which the labor of ages has given to the land."

Mr. Spencer has discussed the poor law before. One of the longest of the chapters of "Social Statics," from which I have already quoted,[1] is devoted to it; and in recent writings he has again

[1] pp. 89–90.

referred to it. In "Social Statics" he declares that the excuse made for a poor law—that it is a compensation to the disinherited for the deprivation of their birthright—has much plausibility; but he objects, not only that the true remedy is to restore equal rights to land, but that the poor law does *not* give compensation, insisting that poor rates are in the main paid by non-landowners, and that it is only here and there that one of those kept out of their inheritance gets any part of them.

In 1884, in "The Coming Slavery," he repeats the assertion that non-landowners get no benefit from the poor law, saying—

> The amount which under the old poor law the half-pauperized laborer received from the parish to eke out his weekly income was not really, as it appeared, a bonus, for it was accompanied by a substantially equivalent decrease of his wages, as was quickly proved when the system was abolished and the wages rose.

In "The Sins of Legislators," he repeats that instead of being paid by land-owners, the poor rates really fall on non-land owners, saying—

> As, under the old poor law, the diligent and provident laborer had to pay that the good-for-nothings might not suffer, until frequently, under this extra burden, he broke down and himself took refuge in the workhouse—as, at present, it is admitted that the total rates levied in large towns for all public purposes, have now reached such a height that they "cannot be exceeded without inflicting great hardship on the small shopkeepers and artisans, who already find it difficult enough to keep themselves free from pauper taint."

But in Appendix B Mr. Spencer ignores all this. He assumes that land-owners have been the real payers and the disinherited the real receivers of the poor rates; and, adding together all that the land-owners have paid in poor rates since the time of Queen Elizabeth, he puts the whole sum to their credit in a ledger account between existing landlords and existing landless.

He begins this account at 1601. He credits the landlords and charges the landless with all that has been collected from land for poor rates between 1601 and 1890. Now, if this is done, what is to be put on the other side of the ledger? We must take the same date, the ordinary book-keeper would say, and charge the landlords and credit the landless with all the ground rents the land-owners have received from 1601 to 1890. To this we must add all that the land-owners have received from the produce of general taxes between 1601 and 1890, by virtue of their political power as landlords.[1] And to this we must again add the selling value in 1890 of the land of England, exclusive of improvements. The difference will show what, if we are to go back to 1601, and no farther, existing landlords now owe to existing landless.

This would be the way of ordinary, every-day book-keeping if it were undertaken to make up such a debtor and creditor account from 1601 to 1890. But this is not the way of Spencerian synthetic book-keeping. What Mr. Spencer does, after crediting

---

[1] The *Financial Reform Almanac* has given some idea of what enormous sums the British land-owners have received from the offices, pensions and sinecures they have secured for themselves, and from their habit of providing for younger sons and poorer relatives in the army, navy, church, and civil administration.

landlords and charging the landless with the amount collected from land for poor rates between 1601 and 1890, is, omitting all reference to mesne profits, to credit the landless and charge the landlords with the value of the land of England, not as it is, but "in its primitive, unsubdued state, furnishing nothing but wild animals and wild fruits"—that is, before there were any men. This—though by what sort of synthetic calculus he gets at it he does not tell us—Mr. Spencer estimates at £500,000,000, a sum that will about square the account, with some little balance on the side of the landlords!

Generous to the poor landless is Mr. Accountant Spencer!—so generous that he ought to make a note of it in writing Part VI. of his "Principles of Ethics"—"The Ethics of Social Life: Positive Beneficence." For is it not positive beneficence to those who are to be credited with it to say that £500,000,000 would be a high estimate of the value of England when there was nothing there but wild animals and wild fruit? To one of less wide magnificence two and threepence would seem to be rather more than a high estimate of the value of the land of England before man came.

CHAPTER XIII.

PRINCIPAL BROWN.

REALLY, this final close of the most important discussion of the most important book of the most important grand division of the great Spencerian Synthetic Philosophy can only be fitly treated by calling on the imagination for an illustration:

Mr. J. D. Brown, for some time before our civil war a prominent citizen of Vicksburg, Mississippi, was a native of Connecticut, of Puritan stock and thrifty habits. Beginning life as a clock-maker, he emigrated when a young man to that part of Ohio, settled from New England, which is still in those regions known as the Western Reserve. There he went to school-teaching, joined a local literary society, and made some speeches which were highly applauded, and in which he did not hesitate to denounce slavery as the sum of all villanies, and to declare for immediate, unconditional emancipation. Somewhat later on, he went South and settled at Vicksburg, where he became professor of moral philosophy in a young ladies' seminary, and, finally, its principal. Being prudent in speaking of the peculiar institution, and gaining a reputation for profundity, he became popular in the best society, a favorite guest in the lavish hospitalities of the wealthier planters, and, in the Southern manner, was always spoken of to visitors with pride as "Principal Brown, one of our most distinguished men, sir! — a great educator, and a great authority on moral philosophy, sir!"

The slavery question was in the mean time growing hotter and hotter. There were no abolitionists in Vicksburg or in the country about, for any one suspected of abolitionism was promptly lynched, or sent North in a coat of tar and feathers. But slaves were occasionally disappearing, among them some of especial value as mechanics; and even a very valuable yellow girl, whose beauty and accomplishments were such that her owner had refused $5,000 for her, had been spirited off by the underground railroad. And "society" in Vicksburg was becoming more and more excited. Though no one yet dreamed that it was destined ere long to redden the Mississippi, and light the skies of Vicksburg with bursting bombs, the cloud on the northern horizon was visibly swelling and darkening, and in "bleeding Kansas" a guerrilla war had already crimsoned the grass.

Still, the lines of Principal Brown were cast in pleasant places, and he received the honors due to a great philosopher, deemed all the greater by those who in their secret hearts did not find his moral philosophy quite intelligible; for he not only made a practice of using the longest words and of interlarding his discourses with references to people of whom his auditors had never heard, and of whom he could say anything he pleased, but he had taken Balzac's hint, and every now and again he strung together a series of words that sounded as though they might mean something, but really had no meaning at all.

He had thus gained a reputation for great profundity with those who vainly puzzled over them, and who attributed their difficulty to an ignorance they were ashamed to admit.

But one woful day there came to Vicksburg some echo of one of his debating-club speeches in the Western Reserve, and some of the leading citizens deemed fit to interrogate him. He had to lie a little, but succeeded in quieting them; and as not much was said about the matter, his standing in Vicksburg society was, in general, unchanged.

Following this, however, something worse happened. The Rev. Dr. Sorely, one of the most eloquent divines of the Methodist Church South, made a trip to Ohio, and in the Western Reserve delivered a lecture on the biblical and patriarchal system of labor as practised by our Southern brethren. Among the auditors was a man who remembered and quoted some of the eloquent utterances, on the other side, of the reverend doctor's friend, Principal Brown. The matter might have passed unheeded, but that the Vicksburg *Thunderbolt*, anticipating much glory to the South from the Northern visit of its eloquent defender, had sent a special correspondent with him; and a report of the lecture, including the reference to Principal Brown, duly appeared in its columns.

This was indeed a serious matter, and the Principal wrote immediately to the *Thunderbolt* with feeling and vehemence. He said that he feared that if he remained silent many would think he had said things he had not said; intimated that he had never been in Ohio, and what he had said when he was there he had said for the purpose of finding a secure basis for slavery; that he had only been talking of transcendental ethics, and not of sublunary ethics at all; that he had always insisted that the slave-owners of the South should be paid in full for their slaves; that he had never supposed that the question would come up for millions of years yet; and that the most he had said was that, "It may be doubted, if it does not possibly seem inferable, that perhaps there may be reason to suspect that at some future time the slaves may be liberated, after paying to their owners more than they are worth; but I have no positive opinion as to what may hereafter take place, and am only sure that, if emancipation ever does take place, the negroes must pay to their owners far more in interest on their purchase money than they now pay in work."

To most of the citizens of Vicksburg this seemed entirely satisfactory, but there were some dissentients. Colonel F. E. Green strongly urged patriotic citizens not to think of such a thing as treating the Principal to a coat of tar and feathers, and Professor Bullhead, of the leading young men's seminary, wrote to the *Thunderbolt*, requesting his respected colleague to give a categorical answer to the question "whether, when A B went to the slave pen and bought a negro, the negro was or was not his property, morally as well as legally." If yes, then Professor Bullhead wanted to know what his learned and respected friend meant by admitting the possibility of emancipation even some millions of years hence; and if no, then Professor Bullhead wanted Principal Brown to tell him why the slaves, before regaining their freedom, must pay their owners more than they were worth. And Professor Bullhead closed with some sarcastic references to transcendental ethics.

Principal Brown did not answer this plain question of his friend Professor Bullhead, but got rid of him as quickly as he could, telling him that there was no dispute between them, since they both insisted on the right of any citizen to work and whip his own negro, and then luring him off into a long discussion of transcendental ethics *vs.* sublunary ethics. But it was evident that something more had to be done, and the papers soon contained an announcement that Principal Brown proposed to forego for a time the publication of Volumes XXIV. and XXV. of his great work on Moral Philosophy, and immediately to bring out Volume XXVI., containing a chapter on the slavery question, which he proposed to read to the citizens of Vicksburg at a public meeting.

The lecture drew a large audience of the first citizens of Vicksburg. There was also a sprinkling of rougher citizens, some of whom before entering the hall deposited in a rear lot a long rail that they had brought with them, and some pails that smelled like tar, with a number of large but evidently light sacks. However, the lecture was a great success, and at the close, Principal Brown's hand was nearly shaken off, and he was escorted to his home by an enthusiastic and cheering crowd, who vowed that nothing like such a "demolisher to the nigger-lovers" had ever been heard in Vicksburg before.

But although the stately periods of the Principal are occasionally marred by what is evidently a reportorial tendency to the slang of the time, let me quote from the papers of the next day, which contained long reports of the speech, accompanied with glowing encomiums: —

[From the Vicksburg *Thunderbolt*, June 19, 1859.]

The wealth and beauty and fashion of Vicksburg turned out in full force last evening to listen to a lecture on the slavery question by our distinguished townsman, Principal J. D. Brown, the widely honored writer on moral philosophy. In the audience our reporter counted thirty-seven colonels, two majors, and thirty-two judges, besides the pastors of all the leading churches. It is a great pity, as many of the enthusiastic hearers said, while congratulating Principal Brown and each other at the conclusion, that William Lloyd Garrison and Wendell Phillips themselves could not have been there; for if their miserable nigger-loving hides could be penetrated by the solid blocks of learning, the unanswerable logic, and the mathematical demonstrations which Principal Brown poured into his audience, they would have sung exceedingly small; even if they had not seen the full wickedness of their efforts to rob the widow and the orphan by interfering with our beneficent domestic institution.

Much of Principal Brown's lecture it will be impossible to give to our readers this morning, for our reporter, not being well versed in Moral Philosophy, finds himself unable from his notes to make sense of some of the more profound passages, and is uncertain as to how some of the authorities cited spell their names. There was some confusion, too, in the hall when Principal Brown touched on the subject of transcendental ethics, and said that he had always held, and always would hold, that, in transcendental ethics all men were pretty much alike. But Colonel Johnson rose in his place and stilled the disturbance, asking the audience to keep their coats on till the

Principal got through; and when Principal Brown explained that transcendental ethics related to the other side of the moon, while sublunary ethics related to this side of the moon, there was silence again. It was in the wind-up, however, that the professor got in his best work, and roused his audience to the highest pitch of delight and enthusiasm. He said: —

There are people who contend that these negro slaves of the South, after they have paid their owners in full the compensation due them, ought to be put back in their native land. But how are we to find who brought them here? Some were brought in Spanish vessels, some in Portuguese vessels, some in Dutch, some in English, and some in American vessels; and these vessels are all by this time sunk or destroyed, and their owners and crews are dead, and their descendants have got mixed. Besides, they only got the negroes from the barracoons on the African coast. Who is to tell where the ancestor of each one was taken from and who took him to the coast? Many of these slaves bear such names as Brown, Smith, Jones, and Simpson, names borne by the very men who brought their progenitors here. Then they have such given names as Cæsar, Hannibal, Dick, Tom, Harry, Ephraim, Alexander, and Nebuchadnezzar, so that no one can tell from their names whether they originally came from Africa or England, Italy, Jerusalem, Greece, or Assyria. And what have these negroes ever done for freedom? Did any one ever hear of them expressing any sympathy for the independence of Greece, or protesting against the Russian invasion of Hungary, or even contributing for the conversion of the Jews, or for sending missionaries to the South Sea Islands, where only man is vile? Contrariwise, when British tyranny invaded our shores did not these negroes work just as readily for the hirelings of King George as they did for their own patriotic masters who were fighting the battles of liberty? And to-day when a nigger runs away, where does he head for? Does he not make a straight streak for Canada, a country groaning under the government of an effete monarchy, and with a full-fledged aristocrat for governor-general? One would like to know that these negro slaves, whom it is proposed to send back to their native land when they have compensated their owners, have some real love for free institutions, before thrusting freedom upon them.

To think that slavery was wrongly established is natural, and not without warrant in transcendental ethics. But if we entertain the thought of rectification, there arises in the first place the question — who enslaved them? Their owners did not. They only bought them. These negroes were enslaved by negroes like themselves, — likely enough by their own mothers, cousins, and aunts. Now which are the descendants of the one and which of the other? and where are they to be found? But supposing that they could be found, there would still have to be recognized a transaction which goes far to prevent rectification. If we are to go back upon the past at all, we must go back upon the past wholly, and take account of what it has cost to feed and clothe and keep these negroes since they have been here.

I have consulted one of our most eminent negro traders, a gentleman who has probably bought and sold more negroes than any one in the Southwest, and after a close calculation, he informs me that taking men, women, and children together, and considering the loss of their labor which their owners have to suffer in the rearing of children, sickness, and old age, and the cost of overseers, drivers, patrols, and an occasional pack of bloodhounds, the average negro costs the average owner a fraction over $267.57 per annum. But as I wish to be generous to the negro I have thrown off the 57 cents and a fraction, and will put their cost to their masters at only $267 a year.

Now, the first cargo of negro slaves was landed in Jamestown, Virginia, in the year 1620, and the external slave trade was abolished in 1808. We may therefore assume the average time during which each negro has been in this country as one hundred and fifty years. Saying nothing whatever about interest, it is thus clear that each living negro owes to his owner, as the cost of keeping him, $267 a year for one hundred and fifty years, which, excluding interest, amounts at the present time to just $40,050. (Great applause.)

Here a man in a back seat rose, and in a decidedly Yankee accent asked Principal Brown if he included negro babies? The Principal replying in the affirmative, the intruder began: "How can a negro baby just born owe any one forty thou" — The rest of the sentence was lost by the sudden exit of the intruder from the hall, over the heads of the audience. There was quite an excitement for a few moments, but Colonel Johnson again rose and restored order by asking the young men in the rear not to escort the interrupter further than the vacant lot adjoining until the close of the proceedings, as the audience were intent on enjoying the remainder of the logical feast which their distinguished townsman was laying before them. All being quiet again, Principal Brown resumed:

Observe that the negroes have not an equitable claim to themselves in their present condition — washed, clothed and fed, civilized, Christianized and taught how to work — but only to themselves in their primitive wild and uncivilized condition. Now, what is the relation between the original "wild nigger" value of each slave and what each one of them has received from his owner during one hundred and fifty years? We know that they were bought at the barracoons, delivered on board ship at prices ranging from a half-pound of beads to a bottle of rum or a Manchester musket, the owners being at the cost of transporting them to America, including the heavy insurance caused by the necessarily great mortality, items which as you will observe I have not charged against the existing slaves. My friend the slave merchant estimates that on an average 15s. 9d. English money would be a high rate. Let us call it, however, $4 American money. Thus we see that an equitable rectification would require that each negro in the South should pay his owner a balance of $40,046! (Loud and long-continued applause.)

Now, when in the Western Reserve many years ago, I drew from transcendental ethics the corollary that the ownership of a man could not be equitably alienated from the man himself, and argued that after the slaves had compensated their owners they should be freed, I had overlooked the foregoing considerations. Moreover, I did not clearly see what would be implied by the giving of compensation for all that during these one hundred and fifty years it has cost the owner to keep the slave. While, therefore, I adhere to the inference originally drawn — that is to say, as far as transcendental ethics is concerned — a fuller consideration of the matter has led me to the conclusion that slavery, subject to the right of the slave to buy himself on payment to his owner of what he has cost, say $40,046, should be maintained. But it may be readily seen that such a transaction would be a losing one to the slaves themselves, for at the present market price of negroes, they are not worth, big and little, more than $1,000 each. And, whereas I have also said that I really did not know but that in the course of some millions of years it might possibly be that the slaves could be allowed their freedom on paying to their owners full compensation, I now see, since what is due from them to their masters is constantly increasing, that with humanity as it now is, the implied reorganization would become more and more unprofitable. (Still louder and longer applause, led by Professor Bullhead, who called for three times three cheers, which were given with a will, the audience rising and the ladies waving their handkerchiefs.)

I also wish to point out that all this talk about giving their freedom to the slaves is as foolish as it is wicked. Since under our laws the slave himself is the property of the master, the slaves already have their freedom in the freedom of the master. Thus the equal freedom of each to do all that he wills, provided that he interferes not with the equal freedom of all others, as taught by transcendental ethics, is already recognized by the laws of the South, and nothing more remains for us to do, except to keep abolitionist theories from spreading in this "land of the free and home of the brave!"

The uproarious enthusiasm of the audience could no longer be restrained, and, led by Professor Bullhead, who rushed on the stage and embraced Principal Brown, our best citizens crowded round him. During this time the wretch who had interrupted the Principal was tarred and feathered in an adjoining lot, and ridden on a rail to the levee. Unfortunately all efforts of the police to discover the perpetrators of this reprehensible proceeding have failed. It is generally supposed to have been the work of some negroes who were listening through the open windows and whose feelings were hurt by the slighting insinuation of the stranger as to the value of colored infants.

While thus calling attention to the similarity between Mr. Spencer's philosophic methods and those of Principal Brown, I do not wish to make any personal comparison between the two philosophers. Since he was under fear of tar and feathers, that would be unjust to Principal Brown.

CONCLUSION.

THE MORAL OF THIS EXAMINATION.

I had rather believe all the fables in the legend, and the Talmud, and the Alcoran, than that this universal frame is without a mind. . . . It is true that a little philosophy inclineth man's mind to atheism, but depth in philosophy bringeth men's minds about to religion; for while the mind of man looketh upon second causes scattered it may sometimes rest in them and go no further; but when it beholdeth the chain of them confederate and linked together, it must needs fly to Providence and Deity. — *Bacon.*

CONCLUSION.

THE MORAL OF THIS EXAMINATION.

I HAVE laid before the reader enough to show what weight is due to Mr. Spencer's recantation of his earlier declarations on the land question.

But even his high reputation and great influence would not have led me to make so elaborate an examination, did it relate only to him. My purpose has been more than this.

In abandoning his earlier opinions Mr. Spencer has adopted those which have the stamp of the recognized authorities of our time. In seeking for excuses to justify his change he has taken the best he could find; and the confusions and fallacies and subterfuges to which he resorts are such as pass for argument with the many men of reputation and ability, who have undertaken to defend the existing system. Examination will show that no better defence of that system has been made or can be made.

Taking Mr. Spencer as the foremost representative of those who deny the justice and expediency of recognizing the equal right to land — a pre-eminence given him by his great reputation, his accorded ability, and the fact that he once avowed the opinions he now seeks to discredit — I have set forth his utterances on the land question, from his first book to his last, printing them in full in order to do him the amplest justice, and subjecting them to an examination which any one of ordinary ability and information is competent to test. I have thus given the best example to be found in the writings of one man, of what may be said for and what may be said against the equal right to land.

It is not the example of intellectual prostitution thus disclosed that I would dwell upon. It is the lesson that prompts to intellectual self-reliance. It is not merely the authority of Mr. Spencer as a teacher on social subjects that I would discredit; but the blind reliance upon authority. For on such subjects the masses of men cannot safely trust authority. Given a wrong which affects the distribution of wealth and differentiates society into the rich and the poor, and the recognized organs of opinion and education, since they are dominated by the wealthy class, must necessarily represent the views and wishes of those who profit or imagine they profit by the wrong.

That thought on social questions is so confused and perplexed, that the aspirations of great bodies of men, deeply though vaguely conscious of injustice, are in all civilized countries being diverted to futile and dangerous remedies, is largely due to the fact that those who assume and are credited with superior knowledge of social and economic laws have devoted their powers, not to showing where the injustice lies but to hiding it; not to clearing common thought but to confusing it.

It is idle to quarrel with this fact, for it is of the nature of things, and is shown in the history of every great movement against social wrong, from that which startled the House of Have in the Roman world by its proclamation of the equal fatherhood of God and the equal brotherhood of men, to that which in our own time broke the shackles of the chattel slave. But it is well to recognize it, that those who would know the truth on social and economic subjects may not blindly accept what at the time passes for authority, but may think for themselves.

It is not, however, in regard to social problems only that I trust this examination may do something to enforce the need of intellectual self-reliance. It is in regard to those larger and deeper problems of man's nature and destiny which are, it seems to me, closely related to social questions.

Stepping out of their proper sphere and arrogating to themselves an authority to which they have no claim, professed teachers of spiritual truths long presumed to deny the truths of the natural sciences. But now professed teachers of the natural sciences, stepping in turn out of *their* proper sphere and arrogating to themselves an authority to which *they* have no claim, presume to deny spiritual truths. And there are many, who having discarded an authority often perverted by the influence of dominant wrong, have in its place accepted another authority which in its blank materialism affords as efficient a means for stilling conscience and defending selfish greed as any perversion of religious truth.

Mr. Spencer is the foremost representative of this authority. Widely regarded as *the* scientific philosopher; eulogized by his admirers as the greatest of all philosophers — as the man who has cleared and illuminated the field of philosophy by bringing into it the exact methods of science — he carries to the common mind the weight of the marvellous scientific achievements of our time as applied to the most momentous of problems. The effect is to impress it with a vague belief that modern science has proved the idea of God to be an ignorant superstition and the hope of a future life a vain delusion.

Now, the great respect which in our day has attached to professed scientific teachers, and which has in large degree given to them the same influence that once attached to the teachers of religion, arises from the belief in the truthfulness of science — from the belief that in the pure, clear atmosphere in which its votaries are supposed to dwell they are exempt from temptations to pervert and distort. And this has been largely attributed to them where they have passed the boundaries of what is properly the domain of the natural sciences and assumed the teaching of politics and religion. It is his reputation as an honest, fearless thinker, bent only on discovering and proclaiming the truth, a reputation which he derives from his reputation as a scientific philosopher, that gives to Mr. Spencer the powerful influence which, having been exerted to deny all hope of a world to come, is now exerted to deny the right of the masses to the essentials of life in this world — to maintain the wrong, wider than that of chattel slavery, which condemns so many not merely to physical, but to mental and moral privation and want, to undeveloped and distorted lives and to untimely death.

While the examination we have made has only

incidentally touched the larger phases of Mr. Spencer's philosophy, it has afforded an opportunity to judge of the very things on which his popular reputation is based — his intellectual honesty and his capacity for careful, logical reasoning. It has, so to speak, brought the alleged philosopher out of what to the ordinary man is a jungle of sounding phrases and big words, and placed him on open ground where he may be easily understood and measured. In his first book, written when he believed in God, in a divine order, in a moral sense, and which he has now emasculated, he does appear as an honest and fearless, though somewhat too careless a thinker. But that part of our examination which crosses what is now his distinctive philosophy shows him to be, as a philosopher ridiculous, as a man contemptible — a fawning Vicar of Bray, clothing in pompous phraseology and arrogant assumption logical confusions so absurd as to be comical.

If the result be to shatter an idol, I trust it may also be to promote freedom of thought.

As there are many to whom the beauty and harmony of economic laws are hidden, and to whom the inspiring thought of a social order in which there should be work for all, leisure for all, and abundance for all — in which all might be at least as true, as generous and as manful as they wish to be — is shut out by the deference paid to economic authorities who have as it were given bonds not to find that for which they profess to seek, so there are many to-day to whom any belief in the spiritual element, in the existence of God and in a future life, is darkened or destroyed, not so much by difficulties they themselves find, but by what they take to be the teachings of science. Conscious of their own ignorance, distrustful of their own powers, stumbling over scientific technicalities and awed by metaphysical terminology, they are disposed to accept on faith the teachings of such a man as Mr. Spencer, as those of one who on all things knows more and sees further than they can, and to accord to what they take to be intellectual pre-eminence the moral pre-eminence that they feel ought to accompany it. I know the feeling of such men, for I remember the years when it was my own.

To these it is my hope that this examination may be useful, by putting them on inquiry. In its course we have tested, in matters where ordinary intelligence and knowledge are competent to judge, the logical methods and intellectual honesty of the foremost of those who in the name of science eliminate God and degrade man, taking from human life its highest dignity and deepest hope. Now, if in simple matters we find such confusion, such credulity, such violation of every canon of sound reasoning as we have found here, shall we blindly trust in deeper matters—in those matters which always have and always must perplex the intellect of man?

Let us rather, as I said in the beginning, not too much underrate our own powers in what is concerned with common facts and general relations. While we may not be scientists or philosophers we too are men. And as to things which the telescope cannot resolve, nor the microscope reveal, nor the spectrum analysis throw light nor the tests of the chemist discover, it is as irrational to blindly accept the dictum of those who say, "Thus saith science!" as it is in things that are the proper field of the natural sciences to bow before the dictum of those who say, "Thus saith religion!"

I care nothing for creeds. I am not concerned with any one's religious belief. But I would have men think for themselves. If we do not, we can only abandon one superstition to take up another, and it may be a worse one. It is as bad for a man to think that he can know nothing as to think he knows all. There are things which it is given to all possessing reason to know, if they will but use that reason. And some things it may be there are, that — as was said by one whom the learning of the time sneered at, and the high priests persecuted, and polite society, speaking through the voice of those who knew not what they did, crucified — are hidden from the wise and prudent and revealed unto babes.

New York, October 12, 1892.

Popular New Books

FROM THE LIST OF

CHARLES L. WEBSTER & CO.

Fiction.

The American Claimant.—By MARK TWAIN. The most widely known character in American fiction, Col. Mulberry Sellers, is again introduced to readers in an original and delightful romance, replete with Mark Twain's whimsical humor. Fully illustrated by Dan Beard. Cloth, 8vo, $1.50.

Don Finimondone: Calabrian Sketches.—By ELISABETH CAVAZZA. Though a native and resident of Portland, Me., and belonging to an old New England family, Mrs. Cavazza early became interested in Italian matters. Few American authors have so completely captured the Italian spirit as she has done in these pictures of Italian life among the lowly. ("Fiction, Fact, and Fancy Series.") Frontispiece by Dan Beard. Cloth, 12mo, 75 cents.

"Racy of the Calabrian soil."—*Cleveland Plaindealer.*

"This little book is something new and rare."—*Atlanta Constitution.*

"Each one of these sketches shows the sure touch and the constructive instinct of a born artist in letters."—*The Literary World* (Boston).

"The whole book has a pungent originality, very grateful to the jaded reader of commonplace romance."—*Christian Union.*

"Mrs. Cavazza has made a great beginning in these stories, which will bear more than one reading, and which, as the work of a New England woman, are very remarkable. They are delightful, and they are mature."—*Richard Henry Stoddard in Mail and Express.*

In Beaver Cove and Elsewhere.—By MATT CRIM, author of "Adventures of a Fair Rebel." This volume contains all of Miss Crim's most famous short stories. These stories have received the highest praise from eminent critics, and have given Miss Crim a position among the leading lady writers of America. Illustrated by E. W. Kemble. Cloth, 8vo, $1.00. Paper, 50 cents.

"Her stories bear the stamp of genius."—*St. Paul Globe.*

"A writer who has quickly won recognition by short stories of exceptional power."—*The Independent.*

"Miss Crim is a writer of rare dramatic power, and her relations of events in the old and new South are full of fire, picturesque description, and dramatic situations."—*Cincinnati Commercial-Gazette.*

"The true Crackers are of Northern Georgia, and Matt Crim is as much their delineator as is Miss Murfree the chronicler of the mountaineers of Tennessee."—*New York Times.*

Adventures of a Fair Rebel.—By MATT CRIM. This novel is the record of a deeply passionate nature, the interest in whose story is enhanced by her devotion to a lover, also a Southerner, compelled by his convictions to take service in the Northern army. Striking descriptions of the campaign in Georgia and the siege of Atlanta are given. With a frontispiece by Dan Beard. Cloth, 8vo, $1.00. Paper, 50 cents.

"It is a love-story of unusual sweetness, pathos, and candor." —*Christian Union.*

"We advise all who love a good, pure novel to read 'The Adventures of a Fair Rebel.'"—*Atlanta Herald.*

"The incidents are varied, and the interest is never allowed to flag from opening to close of this enjoyable novel."—*Philadelphia Ledger.*

"The style is simple and straightforward, with fine touches here and there. . . . The showing forth of the best aspects on both sides of the dreadful struggle is skilfully done, avoiding false sentiment, and maintaining an almost judicial tone, which does not, however, lessen the interest of the story."—*The Nation.*

The Master of Silence. A Romance.—By IRVING BACHELLER. Readers of Mr. Bacheller's stories and poems in the magazines will look with interest for his first extended effort in fiction. ("Fiction, Fact, and Fancy Series.") Cloth, 12mo, 75 cents.

"'The Master of Silence' is the first novel of Mr. Irving Bacheller, of the newspaper syndicate, and deals in a striking way with the faculty of mind-reading."—*New York World.*

"A well-named story is already on the road to success. . . . Altogether the story is a strange character study, full of suggestion, earnest in moral purpose, and worthy of attention."—*Cincinnati Enquirer.*

"There is no let up in the intrigue of 'The Master of Silence,' and there is plot and action enough in it to construct a bookcase full of novels by Howells & James."—*Cambridge Tribune.*

Mr. Billy Downs and His Likes.—By RICHARD MALCOLM JOHNSTON, author of "Dukesborough Tales." Colonel Johnston has selected a number of his most characteristic and entertaining stories, now first published in book form, for a volume of the new "Fiction, Fact, and Fancy Series." Colonel Johnston is easily the dean of Southern men of letters, and the announcement of a new volume from his pen calls for no further comment. Cloth, 12mo, 75 cents.

Moonblight and Six Feet of Romance.—By DAN BEARD. In "Moonblight" the artist-author has brought into play all those resources of humor, imagination, and sarcasm for which he is so well known, to teach under the guise of a romance the lesson of the wrongs inflicted by capital on labor. In the light of recent events at the Homestead mills, this book seems to have been prophetic. Illustrated by the author. Cloth, 8vo, $1.00.

"A strange but powerful book."—*Philadelphia Bulletin.*

"He does not construct a Utopia like Bellamy; the reforms he proposes are sensible and would be profitable, if greedy capital could be induced to consider and try them."—*Springfield Republican.*

"It is a witty, gay, poetical book, full of bright things and true things, the seer donning a jester's garb to preach in; and one may be sure, under the shrug and the smile, of the keen dart aimed at pride, prejudice, self-seeking, injustice, and the praise for whatsoever is beautiful and good." — *Hartford Courant.*

The Prince and the Pauper. A Tale for Young People of all Ages.—By MARK TWAIN. New popular edition of this "classic" of American fiction. It is a charming romance of the life and times of Edward VI., the boy king of England, and is considered by many to be Mark Twain's best work. Pronounced by high authorities one of the best child's stories ever written. Uniform with the cheap edition of "Huckleberry Finn." Illustrated. Cloth, 12mo, $1.00.

Adventures of Huckleberry Finn. (Tom Sawyer's Comrade.)—By MARK TWAIN. New cheap edition of the laughable adventures of Huck Finn and a runaway slave in a raft journey along the Mississippi. Contains the famous description of a Southern feud. Illustrated by E. W. Kemble. Cloth, 12mo, $1.00.

Ivan the Fool, and Other Stories.—By LEO TOLSTOI. Translated direct from the Russian by Count Norraikow, with illustrations by the celebrated Russian artist, Gribayédoff. Cloth, 12mo, $1.00.

"The stories in this volume are wonderfully simple and pure."—*Detroit Free Press.*

"As creations of fancy they take high rank."—*Boston Transcript.*

"'Ivan the Fool' is one of the most interesting and suggestive of Tolstoi's fables, and the work of translation is admirably performed."—*Chicago Standard.*

Life IS Worth Living, and Other Stories.—By LEO TOLSTOI. Translated direct from the Russian by Count Norraikow. This work, unlike some of his later writings, shows the great writer at his best. The stories, while entertaining in themselves, are written for a purpose, and contain abundant food for reflection. Illustrated. Cloth, 12mo, $1.00.

Merry Tales.—By MARK TWAIN. The opening volume of the new "Fiction, Fact, and Fancy Series." Contains some of the author's favorite sketches, including his personal reminiscences of the war as given in "The Private History of a Campaign that Failed." Cloth, 12mo, 75 cents.

"Very readable and amusing tales they are."—*New York Sun.*

"Thousands will welcome in permanent form these delicious bits of humor."—*Boston Traveller.*

"These tales are now brought together in an attractive and convenient volume which all those who enjoy the author's inimitable humor will appreciate."—*Public Opinion.*

"Some of these stories are deep with pathos; others bubble over with humor. All of them are intensely interesting and readable from the opening sentence to the closing line."—*New Orleans States.*

Poetry.

Selected Poems by Walt Whitman.—Chosen and edited by Arthur Stedman. Shortly before Mr. Whitman's death, the old poet for the first time consented to the publication of a selection from "Leaves of Grass," embracing his most popular short poems and representative passages from his longer lyrical efforts. Arranged for home and school use. With a portrait of the author. ("Fiction, Fact, and Fancy Series.") Cloth, 12mo, 75 cents.

"Mr. Stedman's choice is skilfully made."—*The Nation.*

"The volume represents all that is best in Walt Whitman." —*San Francisco Chronicle.*

"That in Walt Whitman which is virile and bardic, lyrically fresh and sweet, or epically grand and elemental, will be preserved to the edification of young men and maidens, as well as of maturer folk."—*Hartford Courant.*

"The intention of the editor has been to offer those of Whitman's poems which are most truly representative of his genius. The selections have been well made, and those who have yet to make acquaintance with this most original of American poets will have reason to thank the publishers for this little volume."—*Boston Transcript.*

Flower o' the Vine: Romantic Ballads and Sospiri di Roma.—By William Sharp, author of "A Fellowe and His Wife" (with Miss Howard), "Life and Letters of Joseph Severn," etc. With an introduction by Thomas A. Janvier, and a portrait of the author. As one of the most popular of the younger English poets, equal success is anticipated for this first American edition of Mr. Sharp's poems. Its welcome in the American press has been most hearty. Tastefully bound, with appropriate decorative design. Cloth, 8vo, $1.50.

"This volume of verse, by Mr. William Sharp, has a music like that of the meeting of two winds, one blown down from the Northern seas, keen and salty, the other carrying on its wings the warm fragrance of Southern fields."—*The Literary World.*

"These old ballads, whether in Scottish dialect or not, are transfused with the wild, uncanny, shivering character of all the old myths of the North, a strange pungent chill, so to speak, as if the breath that gave them voice were blown across leagues of iceberg and glacier."—*Chicago Times.*

"When Mr. Sharp leaves the North with its wild stories of love and fighting and death, and carries us away with him in the 'Sospiri di Roma' to the warmth and the splendor of the South, he equally shows the creative faculty. He is a true lover of Earth with her soothing touch and soft caress; he lies in her arms, he hears her whispered secret, and through the real discovers the spiritual."—*Philadelphia Record.*

"The poems combine a gracefulness of rhythm and a subtle sweetness."—*Baltimore American.*

Travel, Biography, and Essays.

The German Emperor and His Eastern Neighbors.—By POULTNEY BIGELOW. Cable despatches state that Mr. Bigelow has been expelled from Russia for writing this volume. Interesting personal notes of his old playmate's boyhood and education are given, together with a description of the Emperor's army, his course and policy since accession, and the condition of affairs on the Russian and Roumanian frontiers. With fine portrait of William II. ("Fiction, Fact, and Fancy Series.") Cloth, 12mo, 75 cents.

"A book to attract immediate and close attention."—*Chicago Times.*

"An interesting contribution to evidence concerning Russia." —*Springfield Republican.*

"A much-needed correction to the avalanche of abuse heaped upon the German Emperor."—*Philadelphia Inquirer.*

"The book should have a place in the library of every student of politics."—*Boston Pilot.*

Paddles and Politics Down the Danube. — By POULTNEY BIGELOW. Companion volume to "The German Emperor." A highly interesting journal of a canoe-voyage down "the Mississippi of Europe" from its source to the Black Sea, with descriptions of the resident nations, and casual discussions of the political situation. Illustrated with numerous offhand sketches made on the spot by Mr. Bigelow. ("Fiction, Fact, and Fancy Series.") Cloth, 12mo, 75 cents.

Writings of Christopher Columbus.—Edited, with an introduction, by PAUL LEICESTER FORD. Mr. Ford has for the first time collected in one handy volume translations of those letters, etc., of Columbus which describe his experiences in the discovery and occupation of the New World. With frontispiece Portrait. ("Fiction, Fact, and Fancy Series.") Cloth, 12mo, 75 cents.

Under Summer Skies.—By CLINTON SCOLLARD. A poet's itinerary. Professor Scollard relates, in his charming literary style, the episodes of a rambling tour through Egypt, Palestine, Italy, and the Alps. The text is interspersed with poetical interludes, suggested by passing events and scenes. Coming nearer home, visits to Arizona and the Bermudas are described in separate chapters. The volume is attractively illustrated by Margaret Landers Randolph, and is most suitable as a traveling companion or as a picture of lands beyond the reach of the reader. Cloth, 8vo, $1.00. (In Preparation.)

Autobiographia.—By WALT WHITMAN. Edited by Arthur Stedman. The story of Whitman's life, told in his own words. These selected passages from Whitman's prose works, chosen with his approbation, are so arranged as to give a consecutive account of the old poet's career in his own picturesque language. Uniform with the new edition of Walt Whitman's "Selected Poems." ("Fiction, Fact, and Fancy Series.") Cloth, 12mo, 75 cents.

Life of Jane Welsh Carlyle.—By MRS. ALEXANDER IRELAND. A remarkable biography of a wonderful woman, written and compiled by one in thorough sympathy with her subject, from material made public for the first time. The powerful side-light it throws upon the life and character of Thomas Carlyle will make the volume indispensable to all who venerate the genius, or are interested in the personality, of the Sage of Chelsea. Vellum, cloth (half bound), 8vo, $1.75.

Essays in Miniature.—By AGNES REPPLIER, author of "Points of View," etc. A new volume of this brilliant essayist's writings, in which she discourses wittily and wisely on a number of pertinent topics. No new essayist of recent years has been received with such hearty commendation in this country or England. ("Fiction, Fact, and Fancy Series.") Cloth, 12mo, 75 cents. (In Press.)

Miscellaneous.

Tariff Reform: The Paramount Issue.—Speeches and writings on the questions involved in the presidential contest of 1892. By WILLIAM M. SPRINGER, Chairman of the Committee on Ways and Means of the House of Representatives, Fifty-second Congress. With portraits of the author and others. This book is endorsed by Hon. Adlai E. Stevenson, Hon. Calvin S. Brice, and Hon. John G. Carlisle. Unquestionably the paramount issue of the Campaign is the Tariff. Cloth, library style, $1.50; Paper, $1.00.

Physical Beauty: How to Obtain and How to Preserve It.—By ANNIE JENNESS MILLER. A practical, sensible, helpful book that every woman should read; including chapters on Hygiene, Foods, Sleep, Bodily Expression, the Skin, the Eyes, the Teeth, the Hair, Dress, the Cultivation of Individuality, etc., etc. Fully illustrated, octavo, 300 pages. White Vellum, Gold and Silver Stamps, in Box, $2.00; Blue Vellum, $2.00.

"Every woman will be a more perfect woman for reading it; more perfect in soul and body."—*Philadelphia Inquirer.*

"Her arguments are sane, philosophical, and practical."—*New York World.*

"Parents may well place it in the hands of their young daughters."—*Cincinnati Commercial-Gazette.*

"Earnestly and gracefully written."—*New York Sun.*

"The illustrations are pretty and suggestive."—*The Critic.*

The Speech of Monkeys.—By R. L. GARNER. Mr. Garner's articles, published in the leading periodicals and journals touching upon this subject, have been widely read and favorably commented upon by scientific men both here and abroad. "The Speech of Monkeys" embodies his researches up to the present time. It is divided into two parts, the first being a record of experiments with monkeys and other animals, and the second part a treatise on the theory of speech. The work is written so as to bring the subject within reach of the casual reader without impairing its scientific value. Small 8vo, with Frontispiece, Cloth, $1.00.

www.ingramcontent.com/pod-product-compliance
Lightning Source LLC
Chambersburg PA
CBHW021121270326
41929CB00009B/980

* 9 7 8 3 3 3 7 2 3 3 2 7 3 *